Volleyball

by Gabrielle Reece

Former Pro Beach Volleyball Player,
Best-Selling Author, Entrepreneur

Travis Mewhirter

Professional Beach Volleyball Player,
Best-Selling Author, Volleyball Coach

for dummies®
A Wiley Brand

Volleyball For Dummies®

Published by: **John Wiley & Sons, Inc.**, 111 River Street, Hoboken, NJ 07030-5774, www.wiley.com

For general information on our other products and services, please contact our Customer Care Department within the U.S. at 877-762-2974, outside the U.S. at 317-572-3993, or fax 317-572-4002. For technical support, please visit https://hub.wiley.com/community/support/dummies.

Wiley publishes in a variety of print and electronic formats and by print-on-demand. Some material included with standard print versions of this book may not be included in e-books or in print-on-demand. If this book refers to media that is not included in the version you purchased, you may download this material at http://booksupport.wiley.com. For more information about Wiley products, visit www.wiley.com.

Library of Congress Control Number is available from the publisher.

ISBN 978-1-394-41862-6 (pbk); ISBN 978-1-394-41863-3 (ebk); ISBN 978-1-394-41864-0 (ebk)

Printed and bound by CPI Group (UK) Ltd, Croydon, CR0 4YY

C9781394382828_060726

Table of Contents

Introduction

Volleyball, long seen as a second-tier sport, has grown into a highly popular phenomenon. At the time of writing, NCAA indoor, in particular, is exploding, with TV viewership climbing from 786,000 in 2022 to 1.7 million in 2025. For a decade, indoor volleyball has been the most-played sport for high school girls in the United States. Also, while we write, the United States has three professional indoor volleyball leagues at the same time after decades of having none. Although all three leagues likely won't last, the point is the sentiment: Volleyball has a market. And it's exploding.

Meanwhile, its sandy sibling, beach volleyball, is having a moment of its own. More than 100 National Collegiate Athletic Association (NCAA) Division I schools sponsor a beach volleyball program. Landlocked states have created hundreds of beach volleyball facilities in places you'd least expect — from Cincinnati, Ohio to Louisville, Kentucky; Nashville, Tennessee to Denver, Colorado; Omaha, Nebraska to Dallas, Texas; and everywhere in between. One of the best beach volleyball players in the world, Taryn Brasher, hails from Sioux Falls, South Dakota.

Every four years, the most difficult ticket to get at the Olympic Games is none other than beach volleyball, which sold out every single match during the Paris Olympic Games in 2024 — 12,000 seats under the Eiffel Tower.

In short: To paraphrase the lovable character Augustus Waters in *The Fault in Our Stars,* by John Green (Penguin Books), the sport is on a roller coaster that's only going up.

This popularity probably made you decide to pick up this book. You — the parent, player, coach, or fan — want to know about the skills and how to develop them, the rules and how to adhere to them, the places to play and follow this wonderful game, no matter the surface. You've come to the right place. Along with that information, we sprinkle in some stories from our years of playing, some how-to info and narratives, some fun instruction with inspiration, and much more.

About This Book

Volleyball For Dummies is a handy guide that lays the groundwork for your knowledge of all things volleyball, both indoor and beach. Indoor and beach volleyball may share the same name — and they do have some similarities — but the two are different in some significant ways. Although they're completely different, they're similar enough to pair together in one book.

In these pages, you can find the information that you need to either play with confidence or discuss the game with other parents on the sand or in gym bleachers so that you don't have to simply stand off to the side and nod, pretending that you know what's happening.

Here's just a preview of what the book covers:

- Basic principles that you can apply to both indoor and beach volleyball
- What equipment you need for both indoor and beach volleyball
- Where you can play both indoor and beach volleyball (even if you live in a landlocked state that has no beaches)
- How you can play the game, no matter your playing level
- Where you can watch volleyball as a super fan
- What skills — ranging from hitting, setting, serving, blocking, passing, and playing defense — you need for beach and indoor volleyball
- The great players in the game, past and current
- Whether you can (and should) play both sports

Foolish Assumptions

When writing this book, we made a handful of assumptions about you. Writers must do it: We imagine an audience, and we write to that audience.

Here's what we assumed about you. You want to

- Know more about the game of volleyball because you're a parent or friend of a child, teenager, or even young woman or man who's into the sport.

» Know the basics because you're getting into volleyball yourself. You want to improve, perhaps to make your high school team, perhaps to win your local tournament. You want a road map to get you there. This book can steer you in the right direction.
» Be competitive and knowledgeable at your local league or weekend tournaments as an adult volleyball player.
» Understand what equipment you might need to play and how to use it, whether you're playing indoor or beach.
» Get acquainted with the history of the game.
» Follow this sport, which has exploded into the national and global consciousness in the past decade.

Apologies if we made incorrect assumptions and you don't fall into any of these categories. Perhaps the safest assumption we made was this: You like volleyball, or want to like volleyball, and you're looking to find out more about it.

Icons Used in This Book

Throughout these pages, you'll notice occasional icons — a small picture next to text that points out information for specific reasons. Here's what each one means:

TIP

For gems of accumulated wisdom — quite often the kind learned by painful or disappointing experience — follow this icon.

REMEMBER

This book contains a lot of information. This icon highlights the most important aspects of a certain chapter or section. Think of it like a highlighter: If you can remember only one thing, make it whatever we label with the Remember icon.

TECHNICAL STUFF

This icon highlights the jargon and concepts that you may find interesting but aren't exactly essential.

WARNING

The Warning icon points out things to avoid if you want to play and enjoy volleyball for years to come.

Beyond This Book

This book is loaded with details, tips, and pieces of helpful advice to get you started on your volleyball journey or launch you further into it. We also provide a Cheat Sheet — a quick reference guide — at www.dummies.com where you may snag a few more useful tidbits. Just search for "Volleyball For Dummies Cheat Sheet" in the main site's search text box.

The volleyball world is small, and the beach volleyball one even smaller. Do you want to grow your game beyond this book? We can't urge you enough to play, and play, and play some more. Play pickup. Play in leagues. Play in tournaments and showcases. Play for fun. Play in your backyard and at the local gym. And watch. Watch every volleyball match that you can. Watch in person. Watch online. Watch on the rare occasion this wonderful sport is on television.

The authors, Gabby and Travis, consider themselves open books, too (pardon the pun). Have a question? Reach out! We're here and accessible on social media. Instagram is the easiest place to find us (Gabby: @gabbyreece and Travis: @trammew). We wrote this book because we love this sport and the people in it. We're glad you're here for the ride.

Where to Go from Here

Dummies books are modular, which means you can read each chapter independently and in any order. We suggest you flip through the Table of Contents or the Index and find a topic that piques your interest. Flip to that chapter and start reading.

If you're not sure where to begin, start with Chapter 1 to get an overview of the book, a lay of the land. Think of this book more as a guide than a narrative that you must read from start to finish. A murder mystery, this is not. If you struggle with your defensive game, go to Part 3. Do you have offensive questions? Head to Part 2. Want to show off to the other parents sitting on the bleachers at an indoor volleyball tournament? Then flip to Chapter 5.

The best part of it all? This book will be waiting for you, on your shelf, desk, or kitchen table — wherever you keep your books — so that you can use it as a reference when you don't know all the ins and outs of a volleyball-related topic or you forget a few things.

1 Getting Started with Volleyball

IN THIS PART . . .

Discover the similarities and differences between indoor and beach volleyball.

Understand the history of the two sports and when they diverged into two truly different games.

Explore how to dress yourself for success, both indoors and out.

Figure out where you can play volleyball, no matter your skill level.

Follow the game at all levels and be an avid fan.

IN THIS CHAPTER

» Meeting the two volleyballs, indoor and beach

» Getting into offense

» Defending to win matches

» Making sure you enjoy yourself

Chapter 1
The Lowdown on Volleyball, Just the Basics

Volleyball is the sleeping giant of American sports. Indoor or outdoor, hardwood or beach — it doesn't matter.

For more than a decade, high school girls have played volleyball more than any other sport. Since 2016, National Collegiate Athletic Association (NCAA) beach volleyball has been the fastest-growing sport in the history of the NCAA, an institution that's been around for more than 120 years. At the time we're writing this book, television viewership is exploding at astonishing rates. Professional leagues are popping up quicker than you can say "side out."

The sport has come a long way from a dusty gym in Springfield, Massachusetts — where indoor volleyball was invented, right alongside basketball.

This chapter serves as your roadmap to the world of volleyball. Here, we share some of the basics and help you launch into this exciting world.

Comparing Indoor and Beach Volleyball

The foundations of both indoor and beach volleyball are the same:

- Each rally starts with a *serve*, when a player hits the ball from behind the end line over the net into the opponent's court.
- The receiving team follows with a *pass*, using their forearms to control the ball with a bump, *set* (placing the ball to their teammate for the third contact), and *hit*, where a player strikes the ball toward the opponent's court to try to score a point.
- Both sports use the same terminology.
- Most of the skills share the same principles.

REMEMBER

But indoor and beach volleyball are quite different, as well — as different from one another as a beach is from a gym.

The following sections preview indoor and beach volleyball, showing you how they're similar and different, with a focus on rules, court, and equipment. Chapter 2 explores the similarities and differences in much more detail.

Progress of play

The progress of play is basically the same between indoor and beach volleyball (Chapter 2 discusses a few exceptions). Here's what happens:

1. **A rally begins with a member of one team serving the ball.**
2. **A player on the opposing team passes the serve with either their forearms or hands.**
3. **The setter on the same team then sets that pass.**
4. **An offensive player hits the set back to the serving team's side of the net.**
5. **The serving team attempts to either block or dig the hit.**

   Blocking is when the opposing team attempts to stop the attack before it crosses the net, and *digging* is when the opposing team passes the attack before it can hit the floor for a point.

6. **That team has up to three contacts of their own to counterattack.**
7. **When the ball hits the floor, the rally is over.**

   The team on the opposite side of the net from where the ball hits the floor *inbounds* (within the court's boundaries) gets the point. If the ball lands *out of bounds* (outside the court's boundaries), then the team on defense wins the point.

8. **The team that won the point serves the ball to start the next rally.**

   The teams repeat Steps 1 through 8 until one team scores enough points to win the set.

Indoor

These sections look at the rules and specifications for indoor volleyball.

Indoor rules of play

Here are the basic rules of indoor volleyball:

- **Number of players:** Each team has six players on the court.
- **Number of sets:** Matches are decided in a best-of-five format, with the first four sets going to 25 points, in which you must win by 2 points. If you have to go to a decisive fifth set, that set goes to 15 (but you also need to win by 2).

Indoor court specifications

An indoor volleyball court measures 59 feet (18 meters [m]) long by 30 feet (9m) wide, divided into two halves, which are separated by the net (see Figure 1-1).

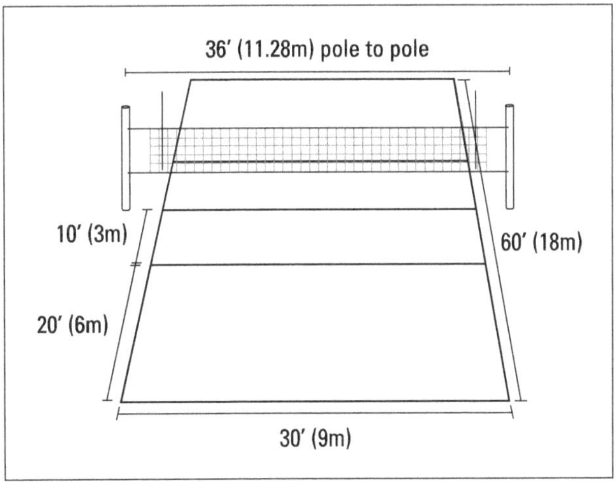

FIGURE 1-1: An indoor court's dimensions.

TECHNICAL STUFF

A women's net measures 7 feet 4⅛ inches (2.24m) in height, and a men's net measures 7 feet 11⅝ inches (2.43m) tall.

Indoor equipment

To play indoor volleyball, you need:

- Twelve people (six on each side)
- A gym or court
- A net
- A ball
- Two *antennas* on either side of the net marking the outer boundaries of the court
- Volleyball shoes and socks
- (Optional) Knee and elbow pads

We get into the nitty-gritty specifics of everything that you need for a game of volleyball in Chapter 4.

Beach

Although similar to indoor in many aspects, beach volleyball is also an entirely different sport with entirely different rules. This section explains the similarities and differences.

Beach rules

Here are the basic rules of beach volleyball:

- **Number of players:** Each team has two players on the court.
- **Number of sets:** Matches are decided in a best-of-three format, in which the first two sets are played to 21 points (and you must win by 2 points). If the match needs a decisive third set, teams play to 15 points (again, needing to win by 2 points).
- **Switching sides:** Teams switch sides of the court every seven points in the first two sets to ensure neither team has an advantage with the wind and sun. In the final set, they switch sides every five points.

REMEMBER

Beach volleyball has only two players per team, unlike indoor's six players (see the section "Indoor rules of play," earlier in this chapter, for how indoor is set up).

Beach court specs

A standard beach volleyball court measures 52 feet (16m) long by 26 feet (8m) wide, divided into two halves separated by the net. The net heights are the same as the indoor net (flip back to the section "Indoor court specifications," earlier in this chapter, for those numbers). Figure 1-2 shows a beach court's specs.

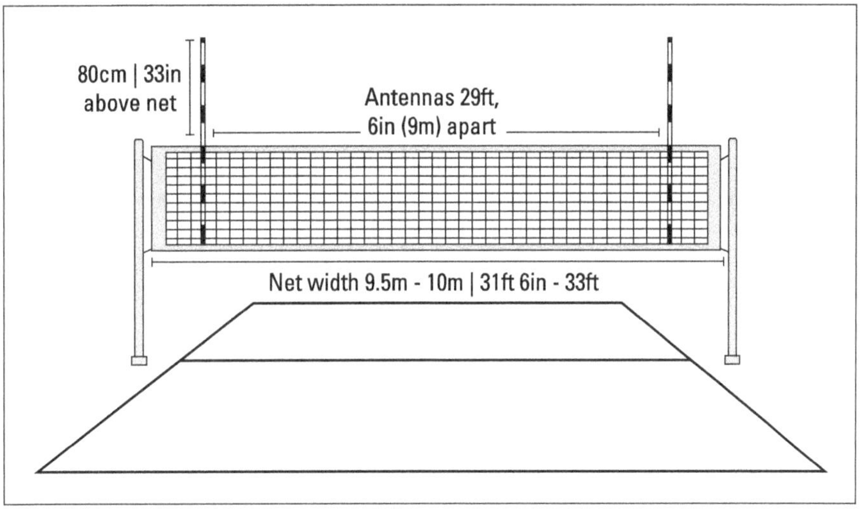

FIGURE 1-2: Beach volleyball court dimensions.

Beach equipment

To play beach volleyball, you need the following:

- Four people (two per team)
- A beach or beach volleyball facility
- A net
- *Lines* to mark the outer boundaries of the court
- At least one ball, although preferably many so that you don't have to *shag* (to chase after) down the beach
- Two antennas
- (Optional) Sunscreen, sunglasses, and a towel

Chapter 4 addresses what you need when playing beach volleyball in detail.

Exploring the Offensive Skills That You Need to Play Volleyball

If defense is said to win championships, offense, by definition, is what allows you to play defense in volleyball. When you score on offense, you then become the defensive team. Without offense, then, there's no defense — and no championships to win. We want you to win championships.

That begins on offense.

The following sections focus on three offensive skills.

Hitting

TIP

Hitting is the fun skill, the one that gets you both acclaim on the scoreboard and on social media highlights everywhere.

Here are a couple of important techniques that you need to master for hitting:

- **Proper approach:** Although you might think we'd begin with the arm swing, that is, in actuality, the last element of the hit that we talk about. Without a proper approach, and proper footwork, the arm swing doesn't matter at all. Hitting a volleyball begins with a pass — on the beach, it's your own pass that your teammate *sets* back to you; indoors, the outside hitters, libero or defensive specialist, pass to a setter, who then sets it to you as the hitter. And your approach to that set determines how well you will put yourself in a position to hit the ball.

  Your *approach* is the footwork sequence you take as you prepare to hit.

- **Arm swing:** Your arm swing is the upper body process that goes into hitting the ball, from drawing your arm back to actually striking the ball. The basic premise is this: To hit a ball with full power, you need an arm swing that maximizes your capabilities as a hitter.

REMEMBER

Chapter 6 looks at the many nuanced differences between hitting indoors versus hitting on the beach, and we — ahem — hit the basic principles that apply to both surfaces. That chapter doesn't just focus on glorious swings that bounce into the heavens or rafters of your gym. It talks about smarts — "hitting it where they ain't," as 1996 Olympic gold medalist Kent Steffes is fond of saying. It's about technique, finding the open space, and scoring in manners both powerful and genius. Hitting a volleyball is far more than thunderous power and physical dominance.

In other words, you can find out how to hit a volleyball and score, no matter your height or physical disposition.

Setting

Do you want to be the most popular person on any volleyball court, be it indoors or on the beach? If so, then master the art of *setting*. Set with your hands and set with your *platform* (the surface you make with your forearms to bump the ball). Set *in-system passes* (perfect passes exactly where you'd want them) and set from the *end line* (the back edge of the court).

TIP

Setting is the most philanthropic skill in the game, the one that allows those around you to shine — and if the crowd is paying attention, you shine just as bright. To riff on motivational speaker Zig Ziglar's famous maxim "You will get all you want in life, if you help enough other people get what they want," a volleyball team can win anything it wants, as long as the setter helps the team's hitters get what they want.

And those hitters want perfect sets, exactly where they prefer them. Perfect setting isn't easy, of course. No skill that demands the type of control that setting does is easy. Setters are like the football quarterbacks, the basketball point guards — the individual through whom the offense flows. A setter needs to be both a cerebral mastermind and a physical talent, making quick decisions and then executing upon those decisions. That brain-and-body challenge is where setters find the fun. Setting is arguably the most dynamic skill in the game of volleyball, and if you appreciate helping others and allowing your teammates — and, therefore, your team — thrive, flip to Chapter 7 to find out how to do exactly that.

Serving

Serving is the boom-or-bust, feast-or-famine, rags-or-riches skill in the sport of volleyball.

REMEMBER

Serving is the only *closed-loop skill* in the game, the one where you control all aspects of it, from the toss to the approach to the final contact. This control makes serving both less complex than any other skill because you control literally everything, and also immensely frustrating — because you control literally everything and therefore can blame only yourself when something goes amiss.

If you play golf and know both the joy and misery of navigating 18 holes against an opponent that doesn't move, you understand the mindset of the server.

You can make the serve, like the drive in golf, an incredible weapon, a virtual non-factor, or your greatest liability. Chapter 8 covers the feast-or-famine nature of serving, where a gigantic Brazilian named Evandro has made his career on serving — and where the 2019 UCLA men's indoor team built a sizable lead and watched it dissolve, almost all because of serving.

Every rally begins with a serve. And whether you hit a float, jump, hybrid, short, or deep serve, you can make it your ally.

Passing

Is passing an offensive or defensive skill? The answer is yes.

When you *pass*, you defend the serve, ensuring the other team doesn't get an *ace* (when they hit a serve that isn't passed), while setting up your offense in the first contact that ideally passes the ball directly into your setter's hands, who then sets the ball to the hitter. (We talk about the pass-set-hit process in the section "Progress of play" earlier in this chapter.)

Passing is the unsung hero of the volleyball world, the gritty, unsexy skill that receives little or no acclaim but is as important as any other. Want to hit a ball on the beach? Better make a pass that your partner can set. Want to stay on the court indoors? You better make sure that you can pass a ball to the setter — otherwise, you have a displeased setter, even angrier hitters, and a scoreboard that you don't much want to look at.

Passing is the very foundation upon which you build a volleyball offense and defense. Chapter 9 explores in plain English the ins and outs of passing and provides tips to help you be a better passer.

Focusing on Defensive Skills

Now you get to the part where you can win those proverbial championships! Defense is a complex process, one that involves both passing and blocking, as well as setting after you've made a dig and hitting those sets in transition — when you're transitioning from defense back into offense after you've made a dig.

Blocking

Rich Lambourne, the 2008 gold medal-winning *libero* (a player who only plays defense) for the United States men's national team, summed up blocking as well as anyone we've heard. He told the viewers on Volleyball TV while commentating a match, "Blocking is about frustration management."

You might think that you should get a *block* on every other point, particularly if you're playing a team or individual who hits the ball a lot as opposed to using more off-speed attacks. But, in truth, blockers actually block very few balls — around two per set for the best men in the world on the beach, one and a half per set for the best women, and about five per match indoors. So, your opponents get a lot more attacks over, around, off, and through your blocks than attacks that go into your block.

WARNING

Frustrating indeed. It's a fickle beast, blocking — full of nuance, timing, and something volleyball players call *hand shape* (how they form their hands when blocking). We dive deep into blocking in Chapter 10.

Playing defense

If you like chess, or a sport that requires thinking on your feet while also reacting quicker than you can blink, then you'll love volleyball defense.

Well, maybe. Because you also have to love getting hit by volleyballs. A lot of volleyballs.

Playing defense is, simply, keeping the other team's attacks from hitting your side of the court, in any way, shape, or form you can. You're doing nothing more than getting hit by the ball, ideally in a manner that controls it to your setter.

That's how Erik Shoji, one of the best *liberos* to ever play the game, rose to the top of the volleyball world. Chapter 11 provides numerous tips for you to become an elite defensive player. If you want to be a great defensive player, you have to accept the fact that your job is, put simply, to get in the way of a volleyball.

TIP

Reverse dodgeball is how Lambourne affectionately dubbed it because, for all intents and purposes, in defense, you want the ball to hit you. Defense requires smarts, determining your opponent's tendencies and making it difficult for them to follow those tendencies. It requires flexibility and a reaction time that would rival any Major League Baseball hitter. It requires angles — both forming them and taking them away.

THE FLOW AND FUN OF VOLLEYBALL

When I (co-author Gabby Reece) think back to volleyball and all that it's given me, it fills me with real gratitude. When I look at my life and anything I've accomplished, so much of it has been built on the shoulders of my early relationship with volleyball.

As a young person, volleyball gave me a place to be big. I was tall early — 6 feet tall at 12, 6 feet 3 inches at 15 — and during a difficult time in my life, the game gave that size a purpose. I was late to it. I didn't grow up dreaming of it. I only started taking it seriously my junior year of high school. I didn't suddenly get good — I got serious. And somehow, that seriousness led me to an athletic scholarship at Florida State University. I never really thought about going to college before that scholarship offer, and volleyball afforded me that opportunity.

At Florida State, I met my coach, Dr. Cecile Reynaud, who became a true mentor. At a time when I was navigating a lot, she taught me accountability and what hard work actually looks like. And the women I played with — both in college and later in the pros — set a standard. They showed me, every day, what commitment and effort feel like in real time.

Being on a team also taught me how to work with people who don't always see things the way that you do and how to celebrate other women's greatness. You realize quickly that together, you can do more. That lesson has stayed with me in every part of my life.

Volleyball also taught me something very simple but very powerful: If I put in the work, I respect myself more. You can't fake it. You can't phone it in. That connection between effort and self-esteem is something I've carried into everything — my training, my work, even how I manage my emotions.

People talk a lot about discipline, but for me, it became a tool. I've used it in sport, in business, and in structuring my life so that I have more time for my family and friends. It also taught me not to feel overwhelmed — to break things down, to stay with the process and the plan.

The game showed me how to set a goal and build a plan to get there. It taught me how to win and, maybe more importantly, how to lose. It gave me the understanding that if I take a risk — personally or professionally — and it doesn't work out, I'll be okay. I'll survive.

And finally, to experience those moments of precision and execution as an athlete is a rare opportunity — to hit a kind of note that you don't often find in day-to-day life. The simplest way to describe this feeling is: to be in flow, not forgetting how fun the game is.

Enjoying the Sport

When Delaney Knudsen — now Delaney Mewhirter, the wife of co-author Travis — first appeared on the popular beach volleyball podcast *SANDCAST*, she mentioned her unofficial mission statement as a beach volleyball player: "If you aren't having fun, then why are you doing it?"

Let this idea be the theme of your volleyball journey, on whatever surface you may be playing it.

Volleyball is fun. It's so fun that writing this book about how fun it is was fun. You can play it:

- Inside and out
- In tiny gyms or beaches that stretch for as far as the eye can see
- In huge arenas or the local park by your house
- With every even-numbered combination, from 12 people to 4 (and even only 2 — Delaney's favorite game in the world is one-on-one volleyball, but she's a masochist in that weird way athletes can be)

Because playing volleyball is so much fun, no place in the world doesn't embrace this sport:

- **The tundra of Nebraska:** Ask the 92,000 fans who showed up to a 2023 women's volleyball match in the University of Nebraska–Lincoln football stadium to watch the Huskers take on the University of Nebraska at Omaha Mavericks.
- **The Swiss Alps:** Ask the sold-out crowd that packs the annual Gstaad tournament on the Beach Pro Tour since 2001.
- **Rio de Janeiro, Brazil:** Chat with the locals there, who line up for hours to watch their favorite teams play both indoors and on the beach.

Have fun with the sport, whether by improving your game, no matter your skill level, or becoming a knowledgeable fan who follows indoor volleyball, beach, or both. Chapter 5 can help. By picking up this book, you just opened up an entirely new realm of fun to have. You can't find a more joyful sport in the world.

THE UNEXPECTED AND WONDROUSLY SANDY LIFE

The winter of 2013–2014 was a brutal one in Maryland, where I (co-author Travis Mewhirter) was raised and where I was living at the time, writing for the *Washington Post,* covering high school sports in the D.C., Maryland, and Virginia area.

My memory has snowfall somewhere around 80 to 90 inches (203–229 centimeters [cm]) that winter, but who knows if that's accurate or me exaggerating (which I'm prone to do). As fate would have it, I got snowed in at my buddy Jason Wheatley's house, and I'd had enough. I decided to apply for every sportswriting job south of Virginia. I grabbed my laptop right then, headed to `SportsJournalists.com`, and began sending out resumes and cover letters.

After a few interviews, I narrowed it down to two opportunities: `ACCsports.com` in Raleigh, North Carolina, or the *Northwest Florida Daily News* in Fort Walton Beach, Florida. I took the latter, location unseen.

After the 18-hour drive from Baltimore to the Panhandle, my parents and I walked to a restaurant called Rocco's Italian Bistro. Our waitress (whom I'd later find out was named Deborah Jewells) noticed I was tall and of a decently athletic build and asked whether I played volleyball. Being from Baltimore, where volleyball is a girls' sport, I gave an easy no. I played it in gym class, but not since. If she knew of any basketball leagues or pickup, I was in.

She didn't know about the hoops scene, but mentioned if I was ever bored, a bar/restaurant down the street named Juana's had six beach volleyball courts and hosted leagues and tournaments pretty much daily. Good scene. Good people. Lotta fun. I should give it a try.

A few months later, I did. I was reading a book, drinking a beer, minding my own business at Juana's, when Ms. Jewells recognized me and asked if I wanted to play on her co-ed fours team that day. I figured, "Why not?"

I can't remember a single day over the next year and a half in which I didn't play beach volleyball.

A man named Judd Smith, whom I call my volleyball dad, noticed me playing one day, saw I was terrible but had potential, and asked if he could work with me. He'd played in AVP qualifiers and won tournaments up and down Florida, and he loved teaching the game. I was awful, hated being awful, and wanted to change the fact that I was awful, so it was an easy yes. After recording a morning radio show in Destin, Florida from six to nine o'clock in the morning, I'd drive back to Navarre, hit the gym, then meet Judd at a bar called Lagerheads on the Gulf, where he had a few courts set up, named Bulldog Beach (after his unbelievably fat bulldog, Tonka).

He'd bring out a bag of those old black and white Spalding volleyballs and set up a trashcan where you wanted me to hit, working on hitting line, angle, and cut shots. Then I'd hit shots into those trashcans until it was time to shower and head into the *Daily News.* There, I worked until 10 or 11 at night — and then headed straight to Juana's, changing in the downstairs restrooms out of my work clothes and into board shorts, and played whatever league, tournament, or pickup was happening that night.

I did this routine for a year and a half, meeting people I'm still close with to this day. Other saints recognized my drive to improve and offered to coach me for free. Scott Allen, Meaghan Allen, Dan Labrador, Matt Rivest, and a host of others all built the foundations of my skillset.

Everyone I met at Bulldog Beach — Judd, Shaun, J.M. Plummer, Matt Blanke, J.D. Hamilton, a blue-nosed kid named Evan Cory, and all the rest — have such a fond place in my heart, and it's not wrong or hyperbole to say that I love them like family.

In 2016, I moved to California, and my life launched at warp speed:

- **2016:** Within six months, I began writing for *Volleyball Magazine* and *DiG Magazine,* covering the sport no differently than I would, say, NCAA basketball's March Madness.
- **2017:** Tri Bourne, one of the best players in the world and a future Olympian, and I launched our podcast, *SANDCAST,* which has since become the most-downloaded volleyball podcast on Earth.
- **2018:** I qualified for my first professional main draw — meeting my eventual wife, Delaney Knudsen, in the process. Five months later, I won my first international medal, a silver on a postcard of an island called Martinique (see the nearby photo of Travis Mewhirter and Tim Brewster winning a silver medal in Cuba).

(continued)

(continued)

- **2021:** I flew more than 100,000 miles, traveling the world, circumnavigating it once — Los Angeles to China to Israel to Moscow to Los Angeles — playing the game.
- **2022:** I jetted home early from a tournament in Mexico to commentate my first match on Volleyball TV, a side quest that would eventually become something of a career.
- **2024:** I coached my first professional teams, Tri Bourne and Chaim Schalk, and Betsi Flint and Julia Scoles. That summer, I signed to coach at Florida State University.

Along the way, I wrote four books (five now, including this one), begat two children, and built a life and family on a foundation of volleyball. A life I could have never imagined. A sandy life I wouldn't change in the least.

IN THIS CHAPTER

- » Recognizing how indoor and beach volleyball are similar
- » Seeing the differences between indoor and beach
- » Dealing with the wind on the beach
- » Deciding to pursue either indoor or beach volleyball
- » Moving from indoor to beach

Chapter 2 Comparing Indoor and Beach Volleyball

Even though indoor and beach volleyball share the same name and do have a lot of similarities, they're quite different when you eye them side by side. This chapter examines the similarities and differences between indoor and beach volleyball in plain English. We discuss each sport's set of rules that influence those differences. After you read this chapter, you can have a good foundation for indoor and beach volleyball rules, whether you're a player, coach, or fan.

Looking at the Similarities between Indoor and Beach

Different as they may be, indoor and beach volleyball share some basic principles related to each action — serve, pass, set, hit, dig, and block — and both build upon similar foundations. You may already have some basic knowledge about the two types of volleyball.

More than likely, you played the indoor version in gym class in elementary and middle school. And you probably watched the beach edition every four years at the Summer Olympic Games — or, regrettably, know beach volleyball only from a particular scene from the movie *Top Gun*.

The following sections inspect what indoor and beach volleyball have in common.

Keeping the ball off the ground

You probably played a game as a kid where you blew up a balloon and tapped it around, doing everything you could to keep it from touching the floor. You'd hurtle yourself over a couch without a moment's hesitation just to keep the game alive. Well, a recurring joke among volleyball players, both indoor and beach, is that they're all just playing a giant game of keep the balloon off the floor. That's the basic premise of both versions of this sport: If you don't let the ball touch your side of the court, you can win an awful lot of volleyball matches.

On the flip side of that, if you can put the ball down on the other team's side of the court, you also can win an awful lot of volleyball matches.

The goal, then, is the exact same for both versions of volleyball: Keep the ball off the ground.

Focusing on the shared skills

At the bare bones, indoor and beach volleyball share some basic skills. Even though each skill has its own nuanced differences, they're all based largely on the same principles. Here are the skills that both indoor and beach volleyball share:

- **Serving:** Both sports have two central types of a serve, a float or a jump serve, which we discuss in greater detail in Chapter 8. Both serves share the same goal: To either score a point by hitting an *ace* (when you score with your serve) or make the ball so challenging to pass that the other team can't easily score on their ensuing hit.
- **Passing:** With the first contact of a rally, you use your forearms — what volleyball terminology calls your platform — to pass (also known as to *bump*) the ball to your teammate. In indoor, this teammate is your setter. On the beach, this teammate is simply the only other person on your side of the court.

  The ideal passing target in both forms of volleyball is close to the middle of the court, a few feet away from the net. Chapter 9 delves into what you need to know about passing.

- **Setting:** The *set* is the second contact of a rally, with the goal of volleying the ball (either with your hands or your platform) to a hitter in such a way that the hitter can attack and try to make the ball hit the floor or sand on your opponent's half of the court. Refer to Chapter 7 for the lowdown on setting.
- **Hitting:** Even though indoor and beach have nuanced differences in hitting, something we explore in Chapter 6, whether playing indoor or beach, you want to hit the ball with enough force and accuracy that the opposing team can't play the ball, so it hits the ground on their side of the court.
- **Blocking:** Indoor and beach have different numbers of blockers — sometimes up to three in indoor, and only ever one in beach — but you have the same aim: To press your hands over the net, effectively creating a wall to prevent the opposing hitter from hitting past you, *stuffing* their attack (meaning the ball never crosses the net). Chapter 10 discusses the ins and outs of blocking.
- **Digging:** Defensive players in both versions of volleyball are essentially professional "keep the ball off the ground" specialists, with their only goal being to keep the ball from hitting the floor or sand on their side of the net. The technique for defensive players in both versions of the sport is the same, with various differences that we dig into greater detail in Chapter 11 — forgive the pun.

Eyeing many of the similar rules

Indoor and beach volleyball have some similar formatting and rules. For example, each rally or point begins with a serve.

Your team gets a maximum of three contacts per rally. These contacts typically follow the format of a pass, set, and hit:

- **Pass:** After a team serves, the opposing team passes to the setter or their partner on the beach.
- **Set:** The second action is typically a set, which is when you position the ball for your hitter to attack.
- **Hit:** The third and final allowable contact is an offensive attack.

  This contact can be a hit, spike, shot, tip, or any other manner of attack. (We talk about the different types of attacks in Chapter 6.)

If you score the point (meaning the ball touches the ground on your opponent's side of the net), you begin the next rally as the serving team. You play both indoor and beach matches in a best-of format, meaning you have to win either 3 out of 5 sets indoors or 2 out of 3 on the beach. (We examine scoring differences in the section "Perusing Scoring Systems," later in this chapter.)

Some moves are illegal in both versions of volleyball:

» You can't touch the net throughout a rally. If you do, the opposing team is awarded a point. In indoor, this rule does have some nuance because it's only an infraction if you touch the net while making a play on the ball.

» You can't lift, catch, or throw a ball throughout a rally. This infraction is known as a *lift.*

» You can't reach over the net and touch the ball before the other team has a chance to play its three contacts.

The height of the net is the same for both indoor and beach volleyball:

» **Men's:** 7 feet, 11 inches tall

» **Women's:** 7 feet, 4 inches tall

The pre-match routine is also the same, in which the captains from both teams meet with the referees for a coin toss. The winner of the coin toss can choose to serve or receive or select a specific side of the court on which to begin.

RULES? WHAT RULES?

We don't mean that there are no rules sometimes — what we mean is that certain organizations play under different rules. The principles across rulebooks are the same, but there are subtle differences in a few, like substitutions in indoor or jersey regulations on the beach.

The organizations that have their own sets of rules are as follows:

- **FIVB:** Standing for Fédération Internationale de Volleyball, this is the governing body that oversees all international play.
- **USA Volleyball:** Typically referred to as USAV, this organization is the national governing body for volleyball in the United States. USAV chooses and supports national teams and promotes volleyball throughout the United States.
- **NCAA:** The National Collegiate Athletic Association (NCAA) is the governing body for collegiate athletics. The NCAA has a rules committee consisting of coaches from Divisions I, II, and III that meet annually to review possible rule changes.
- **NFHS:** The National Federation of State High Schools (NFHS) writes the rules for competition for 15 sports at the high school level, including volleyball.

- **AVP:** The Association of Volleyball Professionals (AVP) runs the domestic beach volleyball tour in the United States and has its own accompanying rules and regulations.
- **Recreational clubs:** Different recreational clubs sometimes have their own rulebook.

Noting Differences between Indoor and Beach

Indoor and beach volleyball have quite a few differences. Table 2-1 lists some of the basic ones.

The following sections discuss some distinctions in greater detail.

TABLE 2-1 How Indoor and Beach Volleyball Differ

	Indoor	Beach
Court size	18 meters (m) × 9m (59 ft × 30 ft)	16m × 8m (52 ft × 26 ft)
Number of players	Six active players, number of substitutes varies on the level and specific rules	Two players, no substitutes
Number of sets	Best of five (best of three in USA Volleyball)	Best of three
Winning a set	First to 25 points (but must win by 2 points); if it goes to a fifth set, first to 15 (win by 2)	First to 21 points (but must win by 2); if it goes to a third set, first to 15 (win by 2)
If a blocker touches the ball	It doesn't count against a team's allowable three touches.	Counts as one of your three allowable touches.
Passing	Players can pass a ball with either their *platform* (forearm) or open hands.	Players can't pass with open hands. You can use your platform, elbow, chest, or foot; and you can link your hands together, making the shape of a taco or tomahawk.
The ball	A heavier, less textured volleyball than beach.	A lighter, softer, and slightly larger ball that's made of a far more weather-resistant material than indoor.
Substitutions	Between 6 and 18 per set, depending on the level of play.	No substitutions. In the case of an injury where one player can't resume play, the injured team forfeits the match.

SUBSTITUTING IN INDOOR VOLLEYBALL

In indoor volleyball, how many substitutions you get per set depends on what association you're playing:

- **Six:** Professional and NCAA Division I men's teams
- **Fifteen:** USAV and NCAA
- **Eighteen:** NFHS

Here are the main substitution rules:

- **Substitution pairs:** A player can sub in at only one particular position during the set.
- **Timing:** Substitutions can occur only between rallies, never during live play (similar to basketball substitution rules).
- **Replacement:** The libero going in is called a *replacement* and doesn't count as a substitution. The libero can replace only a back-row player.

Understanding Rotations

One of the central differences between indoor and beach volleyball involves rotations, which make up one of the most complex features of indoor volleyball. In reality, we could dedicate an entire chapter to rotations — but that would be an awfully boring chapter, so we're going to do our best to make the discussion quick and tidy. Here we give you the basics in plain English about rotations.

Laughing at rotations in beach

TIP

Beach volleyball doesn't have rotations. Hooray! It's a total and wonderful anarchy. Typically, the offensive team has a player who prefers the left side and a player who prefers the right. But as far as the rules go, players can begin each point from wherever they want, and they can switch between positions and sides that they play as much as they want. If you're struggling on one particular side, you can switch to the other. You can even make this switch if you're the server in the middle of serving the ball.

The only rotational element in beach volleyball is that you alternate who serves after you earn the serve back with a *side out* (scoring a point after receiving the serve).

However, when you're playing offense — known as *serve receive* — you have no rules. You can sit down, do jumping jacks, even turn cartwheels (which we saw in a professional tournament in Brazil, no joke). Doesn't matter! Put yourself in whatever position can help you win.

Indoor

Unlike beach volleyball's free-wheeling positions, rotations are a significant part of indoor volleyball. After your team sides out, the six players rotate their starting position clockwise.

REMEMBER

Where you start has little to do with where you can legally finish the play. In other words, you can move into a different position as soon as the ball is served. Your rotation only determines where you begin the point. That said, back row players are still limited to jumping and attacking behind the 10-foot line.

Starting positions

The starting positions in indoor volleyball are as follows:

- **Position 1 (right back):** This is the back right corner of your side of the court. In a typical rotation, the setter begins in this position during the first rotation.
- **Position 2 (right front):** Where the primary outside hitter begins in the first rotation. After the ball is served, the outside hitter typically swaps positions with the opposite hitter (who begins in position 4) because you usually want your outside hitter on the left and your opposite hitter on the right. If you're in serve receive, you go through the first pass-set-hit sequence before players swap sides, if they do at all. If you're serving, they can switch right away, but it depends on the offensive system you're running if you actually do.
- **Position 3 (center front):** In the first rotation, the middle blocker begins in this position, and they remain there throughout the rally, although they can travel along the net in defense to block whoever gets set on the opposing team.
- **Position 4 (left front):** Where your opposite hitter begins in the first rotation. In many (but not all) systems, they switch with the outside hitter after the ball is served.

  TIP

  The opposite hitter always begins in each rotation opposite the setter, who begins the first rotation in position 1 (the back right).
- **Position 5 (left back):** Where the secondary outside hitter, commonly known as an OH2, begins. They stay in the back-left position throughout the rally and can attack from behind the *10-foot line* (also called the *3-meter line;* the line denoting where back row players can attack from).

- **Position 6 (center back):** Where your other middle blocker begins the rally. In most systems, the libero or defensive specialist subs out for this blocker.

  REMEMBER

  If a libero or defensive specialist subs in, they remain in the middle back position because that's the most common area of the court for the opposing team to attack; so those specialists can focus only on digging attacks.

Staying in rotation

Indoor volleyball rotations are complicated, and even the best teams in the world occasionally get called *out of rotation*, an infraction in which a team doesn't line up correctly.

Here are some specific scenarios to help you better understand rotations:

- **Establishing front and back:** When the ball is served, the players in the back row (positions 1, 5, and 6) must begin behind their corresponding front row teammates, and the players in the front row (positions 2, 3, and 4) must start in front of their corresponding back row teammates. For example, the player in position 2 must have at least a portion of their foot closer to the centerline than the player in position 1.
- **Positioning left and right:** For both rows, players on the left must stay to the left of the players on the right. So the player in position 2 must have at least a portion of their foot closer to the right sideline than the player in position 3.
- **Moving:** After the serve, players can move into their preferred positions (see the following section for more specifics about player positions). So, the setter can drift to the front right, the opposite can run over to the right side of the court, the libero can move to the middle back, and so on and so forth.
- **Staying back:** Players who begin in the back row can't attack in front of the 10-foot line, which is a line on the court 10 feet (3 meters) from the net, as long as the ball is above the height of the net.

  REMEMBER

  Beach volleyball doesn't have such a line. Players can attack from anywhere that they so choose, regardless of where they began the rally.
- **Attacking forward:** If a setter chooses to set a player in the back row, it's called a *back row attack* — or, if it's an especially fast set, a *bic* in volleyball parlance (short for *back quick*). They must begin their attack from behind the 10-foot line but can broad jump and attack from well in front of the 10-foot line if they're still in the air. The 10-foot line limits only where you begin your jump, not where you physically contact the ball.
- **Attacking from the back:** If you're an outside hitter and play all six rotations (which many outside hitters do), and you begin in positions 1, 5, or 6, you can

attack only from the back row. If you're a setter and you begin from those same positions, you also lose the ability to attack if the pass is too tight (too close) to the net for you to set.

Figures 2-1 through 2-6 show what the six rotations look like. In these figures, OP = opposite hitter, M = middle hitter, OH = outside hitter, and S = setter.

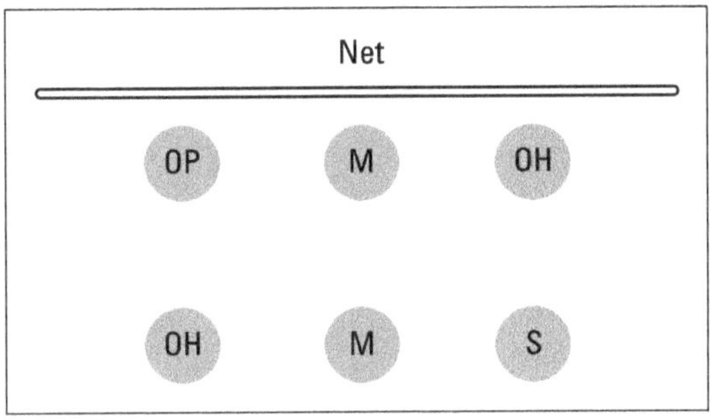

FIGURE 2-1: Rotation 1.

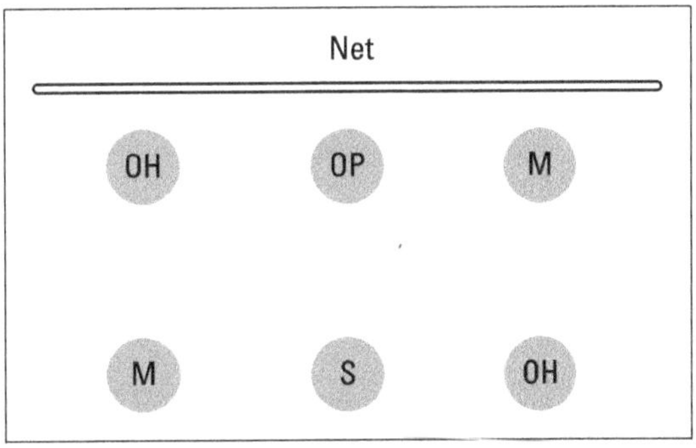

FIGURE 2-2: Rotation 2.

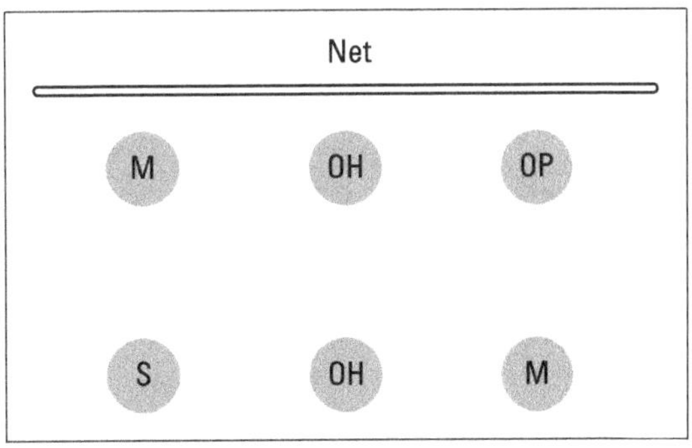

FIGURE 2-3: Rotation 3.

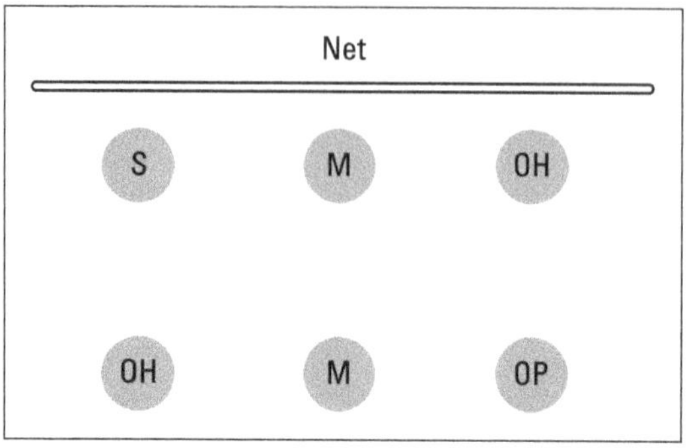

FIGURE 2-4: Rotation 4.

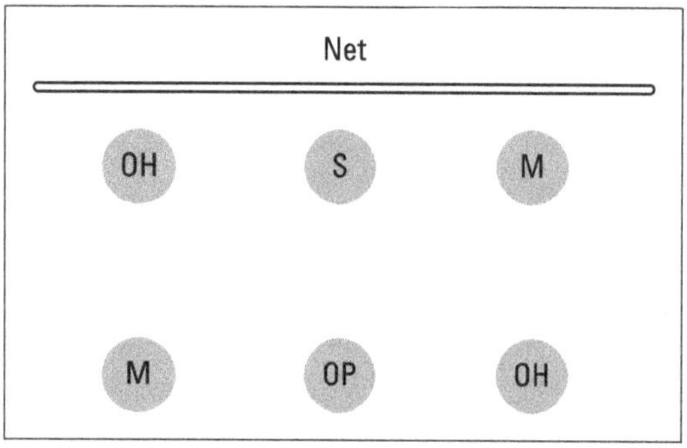

FIGURE 2-5: Rotation 5.

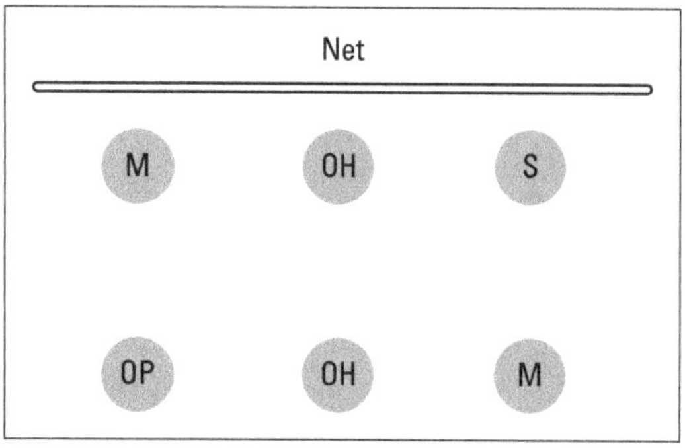

FIGURE 2-6: Rotation 6.

Playing Your Role: Positions

Your position is specific to your skillset on offense, defense, and your ability to block or play at the net, and it comes with specific roles and places on the court you will predominantly play. The following sections break down positions for both indoor and beach volleyball in detail.

Indoor positions

Indoor volleyball has specialized positions. Here's a brief description of each position:

- **Outside hitter:** The main attacker of the offense. Passes serves and does the vast majority of their attacking from the left side of the court. They're the first option for the setter to set.
- **Opposite hitter:** Typically the second option for the setter to set. Also an excellent attacker who does most of their attacking from the right side of the court. Defensively, they block the outside hitter.
- **Middle blocker:** Attack from — can you guess? — the middle of the court, typically on quicker/lower sets. Defensively, they have to block all three potential attacks from the opposing team. They don't often play in the back row, so when they rotate to positions 1, 5, and 6, they sub out with a libero or defensive specialist. They sub back in when they rotate into position 4.
- **Setter:** Sets the majority of the balls on offense. When the setter can't get to a ball that isn't passed well, setting falls to the libero.

  TECHNICAL STUFF

  In a 6-2 system, when one setter rotates into the front row, they become a hitter, while the setter in the back row becomes the default setter. (Often when the back-row setter rotates to the front row, a team will substitute a stronger attacker in that position.) The 6-2 system isn't as common as a 5-1 system (which has five hitters and one setter on the court).
- **Libero:** This player wears a different-colored jersey from the rest of the team and has their own set of rules (see the nearby sidebar for more details). Typically the libero is the best defensive player on the team and also the most accurate passer. They can't attack, attempt a block, or rotate into the front row. Chapter 11 discusses the libero in greater detail.
- **Defensive specialist:** When a front-row player, such as a middle blocker or opposite hitter, rotates into the back row, a defensive specialist often subs in for them throughout the next three rotations in the back row. Like a libero, the defensive specialist is usually one of the team's better passers and defensive players, but they don't wear a special jersey and aren't bound to the rules specific to a libero.
- **Serving specialist:** Often this player comes in for a single rotation and serves, plays the rally, and then subs back out when their team loses the rally. The serving specialist often subs in to serve for one of the middle blockers. After their service ends, they often immediately sub out for the middle who then is replaced by the libero.

Beach positions

Beach has only two positions, commonly known as a blocker and a defender:

- **Blocker:** Positions themself at the net, attempting to block the other team's attack.
- **Defender:** Patrols the area of the sand behind the blocker, attempting to *dig* anything that gets past the blocker.

The most common defensive setup on the beach is called a *line block*, in which the blocker attempts to block the attack straight ahead of the hitter, down the sideline. The defender then covers the angle, or the cross-court attack, from the hitter, to dig anything that gets around the blocker.

Unlike indoor, however, the positions on the beach don't adhere to any rule-specified system, and players can freely switch between positions, even within the same rally (which happens more than you might think). Many teams have both players play both positions, known as *split-blocking*, where whoever isn't serving plays as the blocker and the server plays defense. Beach players can also line up wherever they want, switching sides and positions at any point during the match. (Chapter 10 discusses blocking in greater detail.)

Perusing Scoring Systems

As Table 2-1 lists, indoor and beach volleyball have some slight differences when it comes to scoring a match. The following sections offer the differences in more detail.

Indoor scoring

Professional, college, and most high school varsity matches play best of five sets; first team to 25 points (but they have to win by 2 points) wins the set, with a fifth set (if needed) played to 15 (still having to win by 2 points). USAV modifies its scoring a tad: It plays best of three sets, instead of five, but set scoring is the same.

This system changes depending on the level at which you're playing. Junior varsity (JV) and lower levels play best of three sets. A few states (such as Illinois) play best of only three sets for varsity, as well.

The different governing bodies for indoor volleyball (refer to the sidebar "Rules? What Rules?" in this chapter) have altered when teams change sides. The rules at the time of writing are as follows:

- **USAV:** At the pre-match meeting, the team that wins the coin toss can choose to serve or receive, or they can choose the side that they start on. The teams don't switch sides of the court during the match. If a match goes to a deciding set, the second referee conducts another coin toss. The winner of that toss can choose whether to serve or receive, or select a side of the court.
- **NFHS:** The home team selects its home bench. The teams stay on their respective sides unless a match goes to a deciding set. In that case, the winner of the coin toss for the deciding match can choose to serve or receive or pick a side.
- **NCAA:** Effective starting the 2026 season, the home team selects its home bench. After the second set, the teams change sides. If the match goes to a deciding set, the winner of the deciding-match coin toss can choose to serve or receive or specify the side that they want to play on. In the deciding set, the teams change sides when the first team reaches eight points.

Beach scoring

The standard (and most common) beach volleyball match is best of three sets. The first team to 21 points (if they're up by 2 points) wins the set. If the match needs a deciding third set, it goes to 15 points, again needing to win by 2 points.

REMEMBER

This system changes depending on the level at which you play and the format of the particular event that you're playing. Some formats play one set to 28, others one set to 21. The AVP launched a league in 2024 in which a match includes three sets to 15 points each in a best of three format.

In the most common format — sets to 21, 21, and 15 — teams switch sides of the court every 7 points in the first two sets, and every 5 points in the third set. This switching ensures that no team has a distinct advantage because of the weather conditions (such as having the wind in your face or the sun at your back and not directly into your eyes).

Finding Your Fit

Indoor and beach volleyball are, in many ways, as similar as the name they share. Yet there are also many critical differences that separate them into two distinctly different sports. The weather, equipment, and lifestyle are as different as Nebraska is from Florida.

The best part? You don't have to pick one or the other — there's beauty to both.

Considering the environment: The weather matters

Obviously, you mostly play indoor volleyball indoors, often using a basketball court (although many colleges and professional teams have a specific facility dedicated exclusively to indoor volleyball).

The most notable exception came in August of 2023, when the University of Nebraska built a volleyball court in the middle of its football field when they played the University of Omaha, attracting 92,003 fans, the largest in-person crowd to watch a women's sporting event in United States history. Inspired, the Big 10 and SEC agreed to host an outdoor doubleheader at Wrigley Field in Chicago in 2026, another landmark match.

And you don't have to play beach volleyball on a beach. You can play it anywhere you can haul in sand and build a beach volleyball court, which is a remarkable number of settings.

Even though the most common location for beach volleyball is, simply, on a beach (such as Copacabana in Rio de Janeiro, Brazil, or Manhattan Beach in California), organizers have hosted tournaments everywhere from the base of the Eiffel Tower (2024 Olympics), to tennis centers (1997 World Championships in Los Angeles), to the Horse Guards Parade in London (2012 London Olympics), to parking lots (unfortunately, far too many to count), to even horse race tracks (2012 Preakness in Baltimore, Maryland). Refer to Chapter 15 for some examples of great places to play beach.

Looking good and playing safe: Attire and equipment

Although some equipment is the same for both sports — you need a ball and net, for instance — the attire and equipment for each sport is as unique as the setting on which it's played. Consider this:

» **Indoor:** Jerseys, shorts, shoes, kneepads, and occasionally elbow pads (for protection in case they dive).

» **Beach:** A player can wear whatever they want — you can even find nude tournaments! — although the most common is swimming attire (tops and bottoms for women, board shorts for men).

Chapter 4 discusses the similar equipment and the different attire in greater detail.

Exploring lifestyle differences

Some players (and fans) prefer the orderly style of indoor volleyball — and, for professionals, its massive contracts. And some folks prefer the autonomy on the beach. Beach players like making their schedule, whereas some indoor players prefer someone telling them where they're playing and when. Indoor players like having a coach, beach players not so much. Indoor players enjoy the safety of a contract; beach players enjoy betting on themselves. Indoor players prefer their games in gyms; beach players prefer the wind, sun, rain, and natural beauty.

Beach volleyball is a sport that offers a bohemian lifestyle; it's a rebel sport for the rebels at heart. It's as disorganized and unruly as an ocean tide. Indoor is the far more conventional path, akin to the nine-to-five job, offering a steady salary, stability, and a ladder to climb. Both offer their advantages and drawbacks. Whichever you prefer is a highly personal choice, and you don't have a wrong way to go about it.

THE PROFESSIONAL LIFE

Mike Dodd, Tim Hovland, and Karch Kiraly discovered the perfect hack to their volleyball lifestyles, spending half the year in Italy, making six figures playing indoor volleyball in the highest league in the world, then return to Southern California and play beach volleyball from May through September. Then they'd do it again, and again, and again. For years, they lived this sublime lifestyle, playing both sports simultaneously, reaching immense success in both.

That lifestyle, however, makes sense only in the past. In today's professional — emphasis on *professional* — volleyball environment, you don't really have a way to do both forms of volleyball at the professional level; the only individual currently doing so is Taylor Sander, a two-time Olympian indoors and an AVP champion on the beach. Most players have to choose between the more regimented, scheduled, and

(continued)

(continued)

planned nature of indoor volleyball (with its coaches, training staff, and contracts) and beach, which has its rugged, devil-may-care attitude in which you control all aspects of your career. Sander takes a shorter contract in Indonesia in order to have his summers free.

Taylor Crabb, the 2013 AVCA Player of the Year as an outside hitter at California State University, Long Beach, lasted only nine months on his initial contract to play professionally indoors in France. A Hawaii native, he missed the beach, being outside, and the immense freedom he enjoyed in that lifestyle.

"There was something about living nine months in another country by yourself that wasn't really for me, I guess," he said in an interview with me (Travis). So he returned to California and has since become one of the finest beach volleyball defensive players of his generation, named the AVP's Best Defensive Player five times, the MVP in 2019, and Team of the Year in 2019 with Jake Gibb, his partner at the 2021 Olympic Games.

Like Crabb, Micah Ma'a and Micah Christenson were both raised on Oahu, and the three are good friends. They attended the same powerhouse high school, Punahou, where Barack Obama once roamed the halls. In college, Crabb played at Long Beach, Christenson at Stanford University, and Ma'a at the UCLA, all enjoying tremendous success. But where Crabb found boredom and loneliness in France, both Christenson and Ma'a thoroughly enjoyed their stints playing indoor volleyball in Europe.

In 2021, Crabb represented the United States in the Tokyo Olympics on the beach, while Christenson set for the U.S. indoor team in his second Games. In 2024, Ma'a backed up Christenson, who acted as the setter, and they won a bronze medal in the same year that Crabb was starring on the AVP.

A Significant Difference: Dealing with Wind When Playing Beach

When you're playing indoor, you don't have to be concerned with Mother Nature. However, that's not the case when you're playing beach. The wind can create such a distinct advantage for one team and a profound disadvantage for another. Check out the sidebar "The Rio Olympics and Mother Nature's effect on beach volleyball" in this chapter for a real-life example. The following sections help you navigate the wind when you're playing beach.

Facing the wind

Volleyball players refer to the side of the court that faces the wind as the *good side*. When the wind is in your face, it effectively knocks down the ball. You can swing harder and serve tougher. *Float serves* — serves that you hit with zero or minimal spin — get tossed to and fro, dancing and diving in an unpredictable manner. Facing the wind makes passing a nightmare. If you have the wind in your face, alter your strategies:

- **Serving:** The fun part. You can make all kinds of serves devastatingly effective into the wind. You can up the risk on your serving when serving into the wind because the wind will knock it down, reducing your risk of sending it long, and it'll cause your float serves to move even more.
- **Passing:** Begin a tad farther back than you typically do because the wind carries the ball deeper into the court. Make sure to push the pass a little more to the net because the wind pulls the ball to the back half of the court. Generally go for lower passes in windy conditions because the lower it is, the less time the wind can make an impact.
- **Setting:** Push the set tighter to the net because the wind directs the ball backwards. The biggest mistake teams make when setting into the wind is setting too far off the net, making it difficult for the hitter to keep the ball in front of them.
- **Hitting:** Make sure to wait, wait, and wait some more on your approach. The ball probably drifts back off the setter's hands or platform, so be extra patient. After you approach, swing or shoot deep into the court, using the wind to your advantage.

Playing with the wind at your back

When you have the wind at your back, the ball can sail, often out of bounds. You can struggle to get the ball to the sand quickly because the wind holds it up, allowing the defender more time to chase down shots. Serving becomes more difficult for the same reason. Even setting becomes more difficult: If you don't take the wind into account, the ball can drift tighter to the net, or even over the net and to the other team. For all these reasons, players have dubbed the side with the wind at your back the *bad side*.

If you have the wind at your back, here are some ways that you may want to change your game plan:

- **Serving:** Dial back the risk a bit. Focus more on hitting spots on the court and making the passer move, rather than trying to overpower them. Jump serves don't drop as much as when the wind is in your face and run the risk of sailing long, while float serves don't move nearly as much. Mix up the depths: Hit a high, deep serve to the back of the court or drop a short serve. Aim to make the passer uncomfortable.

- **Passing:** Start a little closer to the net than normal because the wind will knock the ball down. Aim your passing target farther off the net, as well, ensuring the wind can't pull the ball over the net to the opposing team.
- **Setting:** Set a little farther off the net than you otherwise would. The wind will grab the ball and drift it toward the net, so take that drift into account by setting a few feet off the net.
- **Hitting:** The trickiest part of playing with the wind at your back is hitting. Just like in serving, you need to dial back your risk, so reduce the power of your swings by 25 percent or more than you would use in a windless environment. Try quick, fast shots over the blocker or sharper swings that use a little less power than a full swing.

Trying to play in a crosswind

Oftentimes, a beach volleyball match doesn't have a true good side or bad side (see the preceding sections). In events hosted on natural beaches, the wind frequently blows from the ocean inland. If the courts are lined up parallel with the ocean, it makes for a relatively neutral playing field because both teams have a player on the better and worse side. Each player on the oceanside of the court has the more difficult corner because the server can still serve into the wind if they serve cross-court. The opposing team likely targets them, even if they're considered the stronger of the two players. In the event of a crosswind:

- **Serving:** Serve into the wind. Start from the middle or inland side of the court and serve into the wind (see the section "Facing the wind" earlier in this chapter for an explanation of why).
- **Passing:** In front of you, rather than into the center of the court, which you do in a windless scenario.
- **Setting:** Flow your offense with the wind. You can't easily set into the wind or approach a set into the wind (as discussed in the preceding section). Whenever possible, run your set with the direction of the wind to make it as easy on yourself as possible.
- **Hitting:** Hit into the wind (see the preceding section). The wind can help knock the ball down, allowing you to hit with more power, making it more difficult for the defender to make a play on the ball.

THE RIO OLYMPICS AND MOTHER NATURE'S EFFECT ON BEACH VOLLEYBALL

When Phil Dalhausser and Nick Lucena warmed up for their quarterfinal match against Brazilians Alison Cerutti and Bruno Schmidt in the 2016 Rio Olympics, the air was calm. Well, as calm as one can get in the biggest match of their lives, at the base of a stadium on Copacabana Beach packed to the brim with 10,000 screaming, singing, dancing Brazilians, banging drums and roaring their support for the number 1 seed, Brazilians Alison Cerutti and Bruno Schmidt. Both teams had taken their ten minutes of warm-up time on court without a breath of wind, conditions that would promise to deliver a phenomenal match between the top two teams in the world.

But then a curious thing happened: While the emcee announced the players' names, 20-mile-per-hour winds kicked up out of nowhere.

"It was completely different than what we had just warmed up in," Dalhausser recalled in an interview with me (Travis). With the wind blowing directly at the back of one section of the court and into the face of the other, it gave the court a true good side (back to the wind) and bad side (facing the wind).

The scores tell you the story of who began each set on which side: Alison and Bruno (facing the wind) won the first set 21-14; and then, when they were facing the wind in the second set, Dalhausser and Lucena won 21-12. The captains met for the coin toss before the third set, where the winner had the option to either select to serve or receive, or pick a side on which to begin. Brazil won the toss, and it was little surprise that they chose to begin on the good side. Twenty minutes later, Brazil sealed up a 15-9 victory.

Making the Choice to Play Indoor or Beach

For a large percentage of volleyball players, you don't have to choose one type of volleyball or the other. If you live somewhere that has significant differences in seasonal weather, you can play indoor during the cold months and beach during the warm months. That's the beauty of a sport with two such distinct disciplines under the same umbrella.

As a college beach coach at Florida State University — where author Gabby Reece shined as an indoor player — Travis actually prefers when players have a background in both sports because each type of volleyball lends to one another generously, with each requiring different skillsets, movements, and ways of thinking. Only at the NCAA and professional level do you find it nearly impossible to play both indoor and beach at the same time with much success. The sports are, in most cases, too different to do both at once at the highest level of the game.

Moving from Indoor to the Beach: The Tale of Two Kerris

When it comes to the sport(s) of volleyball, if you're great at one version of the sport, there's an excellent chance you can be great at the other, too. The two Kerris illustrate how two former indoor players thought their careers were winding down, until they started playing beach volleyball and found more success.

Kerri Pottharst

Kerri Pottharst (see Figure 2-7) is one of the greatest Australian indoor players ever. Even though the Aussie indoor standout didn't have much experience with the sport of beach volleyball when a knee injury forced her to the sand in 1992, she utilized her indoor skillset to become not only the greatest Australian beach volleyball player of all-time, but one of the greatest of any country. She has two Olympic medals — bronze in 1996 in Atlanta and gold at home in Sydney in 2000.

FIGURE 2-7: Kerri Pottharst and her two Olympic medals.

Published with permission from Kerri Pottharst

She played for ten years on the Australian indoor team, adding a year playing for a club in Bologna, Italy, before her knees made her stop. Her joints couldn't handle one more jump (or, more accurately, one more landing — which we talk about in Chapters 12 and 13) on the hard and unforgiving surface of indoor volleyball.

Someone suggested that she use her versatile skills to go to the beach, which was beginning to boom internationally. Although indoor and beach volleyball have similarities, she soon discovered that beach was a completely different sport (and one much easier on her knees).

Kerri Walsh Jennings

Kerri Walsh Jennings's ego whispered to her not to get on the sand, but she did anyway — and became the most accomplished player in the history of the sport and one of the most dominant athletes of all time.

"My whole entire life I avoided beach volleyball because I would look like an idiot," she told the sports journalist Rich Eisen on his eponymous show in 2018. "I was so ashamed of my skills."

Kerri Walsh? Ashamed of her skills? Here was arguably the greatest high school volleyball player of all time, a three-time state champion at Archbishop Mitty High in San Jose, California, who in 1995 was named the inaugural Gatorade National High School Volleyball Player of the Year. Over the ensuing four years, starring at Stanford University, she

- Became just the second four-time first-team All-American
- Won 90 percent of her matches
- Claimed four straight Pac-10 titles and two NCAA Championships

In 2000, at 22 years old, she competed in her first Olympic Games as an outside hitter — the same Olympics where Pottharst won gold on the beach. Despite this great indoor success, Walsh Jennings was afraid to attempt beach because she thought she'd be embarrassed.

But when a former indoor rival, Misty May-Treanor (a two-time NCAA Player of the Year as a setter for California State University, Long Beach), gave her a call, asking whether the 6-foot-3-inch Walsh Jennings might like to try beach volleyball, Walsh Jennings figured, "I might as well put my ego in check and give it a tryout."

Over the next 12 years, Walsh Jennings (see Figure 2-8) and May-Treanor elevated the sport of beach volleyball into a different stratosphere, winning three consecutive Olympic gold medals, a feat that we doubt anyone can ever repeat. They became household names, inspiring legions of girls to pick up a volleyball, be it indoors or on the beach.

FIGURE 2-8: Kerri Walsh Jennings at the 2016 Summer Olympics.

Kevin Dietsch/Alamy Stock Photo

IN THIS CHAPTER

» Seeing where indoor and beach volleyball began

» Following the rise of volleyball around the world

» Recognizing the modern sport of volleyball

Chapter 3

Appreciating Some History of Volleyball

William G. Morgan and Phil Dalhausser never got the chance to meet. Indeed, Morgan, the man who invented volleyball, passed away in 1942, and Dalhausser, the man who would become one of its all-time greats, was born nearly 40 years after that. Yet the two share an ethereal connection that Morgan both envisioned and never in his wildest dreams could have predicted coming to the fruition that it did.

Standing 6 feet 9 inches tall, Dalhausser is a tall but wiry man. Throughout a career in beach volleyball that includes four appearances in the Olympic Games and a gold medal in the 2008 Games in Beijing, China, Dalhausser would earn the nickname the Thin Beast.

Most any boy in the United States who has a modicum of height and even a hint of athleticism is nudged to play basketball, and Dalhausser was no exception. He tried it and hated it. "Didn't like the contact," he told me (Travis) for my book, *We Were Kings*.

But tennis? Volleyball? Noncontact sports that also favor a long frame and coordinated movements? He was obsessed. "The sports are really complementary," Dalhausser said. "A [tennis] serve is almost the exact same technique as an arm swing in volleyball, and the footwork is really similar. So everything kind of came natural to me and I loved it right off the bat."

Music to Morgan's late ears. Nearly 112 years before Dalhausser would secure that Olympic gold medal in Beijing alongside Todd Rogers, Morgan was working on an alternative to a new sport that had just been invented by his good friend, James Naismith, called basketball. This alternative, volleyball, was for the folks like Dalhausser — the athletes who didn't much like contact.

This chapter follows the history and evolution of volleyball, from its beginnings to where it is today and its funny relationship with its well-known sibling — basketball — and their respective founders.

Beginning with Indoor Volleyball (and Basketball)

Both Morgan and Naismith were students at Springfield College in the 1890s, in Springfield, Massachusetts, a pinprick of a map dot in the world of sprawling universities that boasts just a hair under 3,000 students today. Naismith, the founding father of basketball, and Morgan, the founding father of indoor volleyball, were obsessed with physical education. Primarily, for Naismith: How to make moving and staying fit a fun endeavor, rather than a chore. Or, to be more precise: How in the world to get a classroom of rowdy boys stuck inside during the brutal New England winters to burn some energy.

Naismith's boss at the time, Luther Gulick, the superintendent of physical education at Springfield, gave him an ultimatum: Naismith had 14 days to come up with a game that would help the track athletes stay in shape without being too rough. He surveyed the popular sports in the area — rugby, lacrosse, soccer, football, hockey, and baseball — and grabbed a piece here, stole a concept there, picked up a principle and put it in his own pocket, noticed a flaw and patched it up. He stuck a couple of peach baskets on poles, put them on opposite ends of a court, and dubbed his new game basketball.

You could say basketball has enjoyed moderate success since.

Morgan enjoyed hoops, and he and Naismith enjoyed a productive friendship. Yet Morgan noticed a flaw in his friend's game: Not everyone could play. It was too physical, meant for those rowdy boys and elite athletes in Naismith's gym class and Gulick's track team — not, say, for the old men and women at the YMCA who didn't want to bang in the post or sprint up and down a court all day, chucking balls into peach baskets.

Naismith created a game for those who have abundant energy, physicality, and an appetite — whether small or large — for some physical contact.

In contrast, Morgan envisioned a game for, to be frank, a slightly out-of-shape old man who wanted to:

- Move a bit, but not too much
- Compete, but maybe not be cutthroat about it
- Stay in shape without necessarily sweating a whole heck of a lot

Examining the Early Days: A Game Anyone Can Play

Where Naismith borrowed from the more physical sports to invent basketball, Morgan stole a few concepts from handball, tennis, and badminton for his creation of volleyball. (We talk about these sporting founders in the preceding section.) Like badminton and tennis, Morgan placed a net in the middle of the court, standing 6 feet 6 inches in height, that split a 30-by-60-foot court into two.

Why those dimensions?

It could be played in any gym across the nation that had a basketball court.

The sport started out with rules and regulations that didn't make the cut to today's modern game. Some of those early rules included the following:

- Each match consisted of nine innings (as opposed to the modern five sets, in most cases — although you can find variations all over the world).
- Each inning included three serves per team.
- Teams had no limit on the number of contacts they could make before sending the ball over the net, as opposed to the three contacts allowed today.
- The original game didn't have a limit on the number of players (modern volleyball has six players in indoor and two on the beach).

The sport also started with a different name. Morgan dubbed his creation *Mintonette*, because of its similarity to badminton. That name changed in December of 1895, during an exhibition match to debut the sport before Gulick, Springfield's director of physical education training. A conference delegate in attendance, Alfred T. Halstead, suggested that they change the name to *volley ball* — two words until 1952 — because the main point was to, well, volley the ball between your teammates and eventually over the net.

Seven months later, the North American YMCA Athletic League, where Naismith and Morgan both worked, added the sport to its official handbook.

Looking at the Rapid Spread and Rise of Volleyball

The sport spread like contagion after the YMCA handbook introduced it in 1896 (as discussed in the preceding section). It's not difficult to see why: It was a game meant to be played — and was — by both men and women and wouldn't be formally split between the two genders until more than half a century after the game's founding. A quick history:

- **1900:** Canada adopted volleyball, becoming the first foreign country to accept the game.
- **1908:** China joined in — although they modified it to play with 16 players total to ensure maximum participation per team.
- **1910:** The Philippines, followed shortly by Mexico, South America, Europe, and Africa adopt volleyball.
- **1941–1945:** World War II proved to be an effective vehicle for the sport's spread. American Expeditionary Forces donated an estimated 16,000 volleyballs to the U.S. troops, who introduced the game worldwide.
- **1947:** A governing body, the *Fédération Internationale de Volleyball* (FIVB; International Volleyball Federation — see the nearby sidebar for more information about FIVB), is created by representatives from 14 nations: Belgium, Brazil, Czechoslovakia, Egypt, France, Hungary, Italy, the Netherlands, Poland, Portugal, Romania, Uruguay, the United States, and Yugoslavia who sought to address the issue of creating an international governing body for the sport of volleyball.
- **1949:** FIVB held the first Men's Volleyball World Championships in Prague.
- **1952:** Moscow hosted the first FIVB Women's World Championship.
- **1957:** The International Olympic Committee (IOC) granted volleyball Olympic status, and the sport debuted at the 1964 Tokyo Games with both men's and women's competitions.

The United States had plenty to celebrate about the game and its rapid growth and popularity; it was a wildly popular global sport featured in the Olympic Games barely half a century after William Morgan invented it (see the section "Beginning with Indoor Volleyball (and Basketball)" earlier in this chapter).

VOLLEYBALL GOES INTERNATIONAL: FIVB

Volleyball had grown, and quickly, was sprouting in countries all over the globe. As it grew, 14 countries — Belgium, Brazil, Czechoslovakia, Egypt, France, Hungary, Italy, the Netherlands, Poland, Portugal, Romania, Uruguay, the United States, and Yugoslavia — sought to address the issue of regulating the sport under a sanctioning body, meeting in France in April of 1947.

Prior to those countries taking the initiative, volleyball was, comically, part of the International Amateur Handball Federation.

Let us give thanks to the 14 nations who successfully rectified that situation.

This governing organization became known as the Federation Internationale de Volleyball, more commonly known as FIVB. Check out `www.fivb.com` for more information.

The central goal of the organization was to stage a major international event: The World Championships. In 1949, it did just that, when Prague hosted the first Men's World Championship. Three years later, the Soviet Union hosted the inaugural Women's World Championship, the first of three consecutive World Champs to be won by the Soviets.

Today FIVB has grown to an astounding 222 national associations that participate in a wide range of FIVB-sponsored events ranging from the yearly Volleyball Nations League, Volleyball Challenger Cup, and World Championships to the Olympics every four years. FIVB also has yearly World Championships for age groups:

- Men's Under 21
- Women's Under 21
- Boys' Under 19
- Girls' Under 19
- Boys' Under 17
- Girls' Under 17

FIVB started organizing international beach volleyball competitions in 1987. The first international FIVB-sanctioned event was in Rio de Janeiro, Brazil.

How Men's Volleyball in the United States Evolved

Despite the understandable pride Americans felt at the rise of volleyball as an international sport (see the preceding section), the United States did have one major issue when it came to volleyball: The country didn't have a good team. The Soviet Union, Japan, and the Czech Republic, among other countries, dominated the sport when it was first introduced in the Olympics — a sport that the Americans created.

In 1976, the United States decided to do something about it. USA Volleyball hired a 29-year-old man named Doug Beal to coach the U.S. men's national volleyball team.

Issue was that Beal had never coached in his life.

Humble beginnings

At the time of Beal's hiring as U.S. men's volleyball coach in 1976, the U.S. men hadn't qualified for the Olympics since 1968. Even when they did qualify, the results were little to write home about: ninth in Tokyo in 1964 (the first year volleyball was an Olympic sport) and seventh in Mexico in 1968. Beal was on the team in 1972 that failed to qualify for the Munich Games. Players weren't paid then, or given a per diem for housing or food, a different case than today, when players are paid handsomely, well into the six figures, sometimes into the millions.

A hundred or so players would try out for the U.S. team, train for a week or two, and then, as Beal explained in his book, *Spike!* (Avant Books), "perform to the height of mediocrity and return to wherever we came from. Then we'd wait until the following summer to try it all over again. To expect any kind of success was ridiculous."

Getting professional

So when the unenviable position of Head Coach of the United States National Team opened up, USA Volleyball gave it to a 29-year-old who was an excellent player, yet (as Beal readily admits in *Spike!*) "singularly unprepared to be a national coach and lead a team to the Olympics. I don't know if they really wanted me. But I met enough of their requirements to apply."

Dayton, Ohio, made a bid to become the first National Training Center of the USA National Team, which prompted Beal to quip, "Snowshoes and volleyball don't mix."

Although Dayton didn't provide the ideal location for a training center, the training center allowed the team to work together 24 hours a day, 7 days a week, 365 days a year, which provided the foundation that Beal needed to build a bona fide program.

Those early days in Dayton, fraught with adversity though they were, created something that the national team had long been devoid of: They created a culture.

It seems obvious, in retrospect, that a central location, a training center, offers the optimal way to build a formidable program. But again: These were no easy waters through that Beal had to navigate.

Going to the beach

The low point for the U.S. men came in 1978. After finishing 19th out of 20 teams at the World Championships in Alcona, Italy, Beal decided he was going to quit. He was done coaching.

But in the winter of 1980, he saw a glimmer of hope for the men's Olympic indoor volleyball team. The talent for men's volleyball — both back then and today — comes from a small pool. Beal knew who the best players in the country were Karch Kiraly, Sinjin Smith, Steve Timmons, Tim Hovland, Mike Dodd, Pat Powers, Randy Stoklos, Dusty Dvorak, and Chris Marlowe. (Refer to Appendix B where we explore most of these players and what made them great.)

He knew they lived and competed in Southern California, thousands of miles and a world away from Dayton, and that they frequently played on a radically different surface. The head coach of the U.S. indoor team turned to the beach volleyball players. (Read about beach volleyball's beginnings in the following section.)

Exploring the Start of Beach Volleyball

Beach volleyball doesn't have a clean genesis story in the way indoor volleyball does (see the section "Beginning with Indoor Volleyball (and Basketball)," earlier in this chapter) — no Springfield gym, no founding father, no known date of when and where it began. It's fitting for the rogue sport to be shrouded in roguish myth (see the nearby sidebar in this chapter).

In 1915, the first beach volleyball game took place at the Outrigger Club. The legend goes that a group of bored surfers who couldn't venture out into the ocean due to rough conditions had to wait it out on the shores. The question, then: What to do if they couldn't surf, paddle, or canoe? Well, they put up a net, right there on the beach, and played some volleyball — on the beach.

Californians, meanwhile, scoff at the notion that beach volleyball could have possibly been founded anywhere but Santa Monica, where many claim the sport was born. Hawaiians shrug and point to Outrigger and Waikiki.

Either way, the sport became wildly popular in the West (both in California and Hawaii).

The sport of beach volleyball rose almost hand-in-hand with surfing, and it was the first to represent a niche, offbeat lifestyle, one that didn't care for money or tangible rewards. Players were happy to compete for a case of Pepsi (as they did in 1948), or a kiss from actress Greta Thyssen (as they did in 1954), or something as simple as frozen yogurt or a pitcher of beer (as they did well into the 1980s). The reward didn't so much matter — they just wanted to play.

And they were good. The best in the country.

ABOUT THE ZOO: THE OUTRIGGER'S IMPACT ON BEACH

Some say that beach volleyball began in 1907, on the shores of Waikiki, Hawaii, when a man named Alexander Hume Ford gave the Island of Oahu a visit.

Native Hawaiians called Ford a *malihini* — a newcomer, a stranger. But that *malihini* was no tourist. He was a 39-year-old orphan from South Carolina who loved little more on this planet than to surf. He also wanted to talk business.

The Kaimuke Zoo was defunct by the time Ford began to envision plans for a surf club on the sands of Waikiki. Perfect, really. Ford took two of those grass huts that the old Kaimuke used and relocated them to an acre and a half of newly leased land on Waikiki. He dubbed his new venture the Outrigger Canoe Club, with the purpose, he wrote, according to Matt Warshaw's *Encyclopedia of Surfing*, of "reviving and preserving the ancient Hawaiian sport of surfing on boards and in outrigger canoes."

He designated one hut as a changing area. He used the other as a storage unit for canoes and surfboards. That was the club's mission, anyway — to foster and promote traditional Hawaiian water sports. And it still is. In fact, it's so good at that very thing that through 2024, 40 Outrigger athletes have brought 40 Olympic medals back to Hawaii, success that not even that *malihini* from South Carolina could have ever dreamed.

Ford also couldn't have foreseen that Outrigger would become one of the world's most fertile pipelines of volleyball players.

The Rocky Marriage between Indoor and Beach Volleyball

When Beal began recruiting Californian volleyball players to the U.S. Olympic indoor volleyball team in the 1980s (which we talk about in the section "Going to the beach" earlier in this chapter), he found himself working with a gifted generation of talent (dubbed, by their own team, as the Westies).

But the Southern California lifestyle clashed — loudly and frequently — with Beal's Midwestern ideals, to the point that the only true beach player who remained with Beal and the indoor team for the 1984 Olympic Games was Kiraly. The rest of the beach players returned to a fledgling professional venture called the California Pro Beach Tour.

Both sides enjoyed smashing success:

- **1984:** The U.S. men's indoor volleyball team won their first Olympic gold at home during the Los Angeles Games. (The women wouldn't win their first gold until 2021.)

  That same year, the top beach players and a sports agent named Leonard Armato launched the Association of Volleyball Professionals (AVP), which remains the top professional beach volleyball tour in the United States.
- **1987:** Rio de Janeiro hosted the inaugural Beach Volleyball World Championships, won by the United States.
- **1988:** The United States repeated its men's indoor volleyball gold medal success at the Seoul Olympic Games.
- **1996:** Beach volleyball debuted as an Olympic sport, in Atlanta, and the United States won both gold (Kent Steffes and Kiraly, who returned full time to the beach in 1992) and silver (Mike Dodd and Mike Whitmarsh).

Noting the Most Recent U.S. Successes

The Olympics are, for better or worse, the barometer for a country's success in the sport of volleyball. Even universities classify volleyball and beach volleyball as "Olympic sports."

This has its benefits, as the Olympics are one of the grandest stages in all of sports, a month-long celebration of the mostly under-the-radar sports that only get their due once every quadrennial. There are drawbacks, too, as an off weekend or ill-timed slump will fail to be an accurate representation of the team's true caliber. Such is the nature of Olympic sports, and volleyball as a whole.

Yet the United States has fared quite well — more than well, really. It has been one of the most consistent countries in the world, particularly since the early 2000s, where the sport has seen an explosion in participation. Here we take a closer look at how the United States has performed indoor and on the beach.

Indoor

The United States indoor national teams have been historically one of the strongest federations in the world, collecting a combined 13 medals since the 1984 Los Angeles Olympics. The last Games that didn't feature one of the indoor teams on the podium was 2004 in Athens, a 20-year stretch of dominance for the Americans.

Here's how the women have performed since 1984:

- 1984 Los Angeles Olympics: Silver Medal
- 1992 Barcelona Olympics: Bronze Medal
- 2008 Beijing Olympics: Silver Medal
- 2012 London Olympics: Silver Medal
- 2016 Rio de Janeiro Olympics: Bronze Medal
- 2020 Tokyo Olympics: Gold Medal
- 2024 Paris Olympics: Silver Medal

Here's a look at how the men have fared since 1984:

- 1984 Los Angeles Olympics: Gold Medal
- 1988 Seoul Olympics: Gold Medal

- 1992 Barcelona Olympics: Bronze Medal
- 2008 Beijing Olympics: Gold Medal
- 2016 Rio de Janeiro Olympics: Bronze Medal
- 2024 Paris Olympics: Bronze Medal

Beach

The United States has performed as if the sport was invented here (hint: it was). The women, in particular, have been phenomenal, led by Kerri Walsh Jennings and Misty May-Treanor and their three straight gold medals, followed by April Ross's consecutive medals in Rio and Tokyo. Even though the United States didn't podium in 2024, the women still boasted two of the top-five teams in the world in Kelly Cheng and Sara Hughes, and Kristen Nuss and Taryn Kloth (now Cruz and Brasher, respectively).

When people think of Olympic beach volleyball, they think of the United States.

Here's how the U.S. women have done since 2004:

- 2004 Athens Olympics: May-Treanor and Walsh Jennings — Gold Medal
- 2008 Beijing Olympics: May-Treanor and Walsh Jennings — Gold Medal
- 2012 London Olympics:
  - May-Treanor and Walsh Jennings — Gold Medal
  - Jennifer Kessy and Ross — Silver Medal
- 2016 Rio de Janeiro Olympics: Ross and Walsh Jennings — Bronze Medal
- 2020 Tokyo Olympics: Ross and Alix Klineman — Gold Medal

Here's how the U.S. men have recently performed at the Olympics:

- 1996 Atlanta Olympics:
  - Kiraly and Steffes — Gold Medal
  - Whitmarsh and Dodd — Silver Medal
- 2000 Sydney Olympics: Dain Blanton and Eric Fonoimoana — Gold Medal
- 2008 Beijing Olympics: Dalhausser and Todd Rogers — Gold Medal

The Introduction, and Subsequent Explosion, of NCAA Beach Volleyball

Beach volleyball at the NCAA level began as "sand volleyball," and it started, as most new ventures do — quietly.

Given the rise of beach volleyball at both the juniors and professional level, a small crop of universities sponsored a sand volleyball program, competing under the American Volleyball Coaches Association umbrella and classified as an "emerging sport," which is another way of saying: The NCAA was keeping tabs on it. If more than 40 schools adopted beach volleyball by 2016, it would shed the emerging sport label and officially become an NCAA-sanctioned sport.

It surged past the requisite 40, topping 50 in just three years.

When the NCAA approved to adopt the sport, in June of 2015, it changed the name from sand volleyball to the more widely recognized beach volleyball and it has hosted a National Championship every May in Gulf Shores, Alabama since then.

Beach volleyball at the NCAA level is played differently than at the professional level because it's a legitimate team sport. Each team starts five pairs, ranked in order of ability from one through five. Each pair plays a regular beach match, and the team who wins three of the five pairs wins the overall match.

A THIRD VERSION OF THE GAME: SITTING VOLLEYBALL

In 1956, the Dutch Sport Committee was seeking a fun, competitive way to rehab injured soldiers. Thus, after much brainstorming, was born the sport of sitting volleyball, a combination of volleyball and a German game known as *sitzball,* a sport with no net and seated players.

Sound familiar? It should.

It was invented in a similar manner as its indoor cousin, which was an amalgamation of multiple sports as well.

Twenty years later after beginning as a rehab game, sitting volleyball debuted in the 1976 Summer Paralympics in Toronto as a demonstration sport and was officially added to the medal sports four years later in Arnhem. Women began competing 24 years after that, at the 2004 Paralympics.

Although you can see many commonalities between sitting and indoor volleyball — same number of players on the court, same sequence of play, best of five-set format — there are obvious differences:

- The court is 33 feet by 20 feet, with an attack line at 6.6 feet, rather than the standard 10 feet in indoor volleyball.
- The net stands 3.8 feet high for men and 3.4 feet for women, and if that sounds low, well, remember: The players are sitting.
- Players must have at least one buttock in contact with the floor when they make contact with the ball.
- Front-row players can also block a serve, which isn't allowed in indoor or beach volleyball.

Currently, more than 60 countries compete in a two-stage league system around the world, where nondisabled athletes can also participate. There are now tournaments that feature teams of able-bodied, fully disabled, and combined able-bodied and disabled individuals.

IN THIS CHAPTER

» Figuring out what volleyball equipment you need

» Finding the best apparel for indoor and beach volleyball

» Investing in recovery tools

» Considering what accessories you want

Chapter 4 Choosing the Right Equipment

If a single chapter in this book makes the case that indoor volleyball and beach volleyball are two entirely different sports, this may be the one. Of course, the two versions of the game share their commonalities — you pass, set, and hit a ball over the net, with the intent of scoring — but they're different enough to have their own equipment and attire.

This chapter discusses that essential equipment and attire, as well as some equipment and attire that you don't need but may want, depending on your personal tastes.

Recognizing the Equipment You Definitely Need

Despite indoor volleyball and beach volleyball both going by the name *volleyball*, each requires vastly different equipment — sometimes no equipment at all, in the case of beach volleyball:

- Indoor volleyball calls for padding on joints and other body parts. In beach volleyball, the surface is the padding.
- Indoor volleyball requires a gym. Beach volleyball asks only for decent weather (and even that's optional).

The following sections focus on the equipment that you need for both kinds of volleyball. We explain the clothes in the sections "Considering Essential Apparel for Indoor Volleyball" and "Picking Out Apparel for Beach Volleyball" later in this chapter.

Net and antennas

In both indoor and beach volleyball, you need a net. However, because the courts for indoor and beach have different dimensions, the two types of volleyball require different nets. Chapter 2 discusses the differences between indoor and beach volleyball. In this section, we focus just on the net and *antennas* that mark the outer boundaries of the court.

If you're playing for a club or your school, more than likely, you don't have to worry about a lot of this information because you don't need to find and purchase a net system.

For both indoor and beach volleyball, the net is made of the same materials — polypropylene or nylon netting, or in some cases ultra-fine fiber. Here's the low-down on what you need for your net and antennas, based on the type of volleyball you're playing:

- **Indoor volleyball net and antennas:** The specifications for an indoor net are the same for men's and women's volleyball: 31 feet, 2 inches (9.5 meters [m]) by 32 feet, 10 inches (10m). The top tape is (7 centimeters [cm]) wide, with the bottom tape 2 inches (5cm) wide. Most net systems also have a *net sleeve,* which is the protective covering on the top tape that helps keep the net taut and stable during play. Many governing bodies (such as the NCAA and NFHS) allow for a school name to appear on the sleeve. Some professional leagues like the AVP and MLV allow net sleeve advertising. FIVB sometimes allows net sleeve advertising.

The net height varies depending on the gender of the players:

- **Men's height:** 7 feet, 11⅝ inches (2.43m)
- **Women's height:** 7 feet, 4⅛ inches (2.24m)

The antennas sit directly over each sideline and extend 2 feet 7½ inches (0.8m) above the net.

Jaypro Sports (`https://jayprosports.com`) and Senoh (`www.senoh.jp/english`) are two of the most respected brands if you're looking to purchase a net system. (The antennas come with the net system.)

- **Beach volleyball net and antennas:** A beach volleyball net has the same length for both men's and women's volleyball of 27 feet, 11 inches (8.5m). The men's and women's net heights are the same as for indoor volleyball.

  Beach volleyball antennas have a length of 5 feet, 11 inches (1.8m) and extend 2 feet, 7½ inches (0.8m) above the net.

  Reliable brands for beach volleyball net systems include Cobra and Viper systems, both offered by Cobra Volleyball Nets (`https://cobravolleyball.com`) and Park & Sun (`www.parksun.com`).

TIP

Although indoor and beach referees have a *net chain* that accurately measures the proper height of the net, and *ball pump* that ensures each ball is pumped to the correct PSI, or internal pressure, we suggest that you have one of each tool close for practice.

Volleyballs

Even if you have the best netting system in the world, and all of the requisite players, you cannot play volleyball without an actual . . . volleyball. Below you'll find the correct volleyball to suit your needs.

Using the right indoor volleyball

Different governing bodies require different brands:

- **National Collegiate Athletic Association (NCAA):** All NCAA competitions, both for men and women, use Molten (`https://moltenusa.com`) volleyballs:
  - *Super Touch:* The official ball of the NCAA Women's Volleyball Championships
  - *FLISTATEC:* The official NCAA Men's Volleyball Championships ball

- **National Association of Intercollegiate Athletics (NAIA):** The women use the Baden Perfection Leather Volleyball, while the men use the Molten FLISTATEC.
- **USA Volleyball (USAV):** The same as NCAA.
- **National Federation of State High School Associations (NFHS):** Schools can choose from an option of approved volleyballs, although the most popular include the Molten Super Touch, Molten L2, Mikasa VFC1000, and Wilson NOVA. All balls must include the NFHS authentication stamp.
- **Fédération Internationale de Volleyball (FIVB):** The International Volleyball Federation. The FIVB (and other international competitions) use Mikasa balls (`https://mikasasports.com`).
- **Olympic Games:** Use the Mikasa V200W ball.

Weighing your beach volleyball ball options

Beach, too, has a wide variety of options as far as balls go, but two brands dominate, with a third making a push:

- **Wilson (`www.wilson.com/volleyball`):** King of beach volleyball played in the United States since the early 2000s. It's the ball of the Association of Volleyball Professionals (AVP), as well as its junior circuit, which has exploded since the advent of beach volleyball as an NCAA sport. The vast majority of players use Wilson's OPTX ball, the same ball used on the AVP.
- **Mikasa (`https://mikasasports.com`):** Dominates the international scene in beach, as well as indoor, volleyball because it's the ball sponsor of the Volleyball World Beach Pro Tour. The Olympic Games use Mikasa for beach volleyball competition (like it does for indoor).

  REMEMBER

  Not a lot of players use Mikasa in the United States unless they also compete internationally. At the time of this writing, only Florida State University uses Mikasa as its game ball at the NCAA level.
- **Molten (`https://moltenusa.com`):** Made a push into the beach volleyball scene in 2025, becoming the ball sponsor of NCAA Beach Volleyball, as well as NCAA indoor competitions (see the preceding section). A trickle-down effect means many junior tournaments now use Molten balls because the youth want to prepare for the NCAA. Look for the Molten NCAA Beach Championships Game Ball.

WARNING

Although indoor volleyballs are similar to beach volleyballs in that you use them to play volleyball, don't use indoor volleyballs outside. The material of indoor volleyballs quickly deteriorates if you use them on the beach. On the other hand, beach volleyballs are made to be played in all conditions and weather, and you can use them in a gym — but they play vastly differently than indoor balls.

If you plan to play both indoor and beach volleyball, get a bag of both types of volleyball and use them in the environment for which they're designed.

Volleyball lines

When you play indoor volleyball, more than likely, the facility where you play already has the lines painted on the court. If it's a sports court at a USA Volleyball event or a similar event, the event staff lay down tape to be the lines (see Chapter 2 for an illustration of court markings).

But beach volleyball is a different animal. For a beach court, the court size is 52½ feet long by 26⅕ feet wide (16 meters [m] long × 8m wide) with lines that are between 2 inches and 3⅕ inches (5cm and 8cm) wide.

Park & Sun (`www.parksun.com`) is one of the most reliable brands for all things outdoor volleyball equipment and likely the brand of lines you see on the courts at your local beach or park. The lines should be soft because you don't want to get cuts or bruises from diving or stepping on them (which you do quite a bit).

These lines should also come with anchors that you need to bury in the sand to stabilize each of the four corners of the court.

Considering Essential Apparel for Indoor Volleyball

Some pieces of equipment are optional for volleyball, and some — like the volleyballs we discuss in the previous section — aren't.

The following sections identify some apparel that are non-negotiables for playing volleyball. And because we get into what apparel is best for certain positions, check out Part 2 for the details on the different positions and their roles in the game.

Table 4-1 gives an overview of the following sections so you have all the information in one place.

TABLE 4-1 Essential Apparel for Indoor Volleyball

Apparel	Recommended Brands
Shoes	ASICS, Mizuno, Nike, Adidas
Socks	ASICS, Mizuno, Adidas, Under Armour
Knee pads	McDavid, ASICS, Mizuno, Nike
Spandex and compression shorts	ASICS, Nike, Adidas, Mizuno, Under Armour
Ankle braces	McDavid, Zamst, Med Spec, Shock Doctor

Shoes

Like any sport that has unique demands on an athlete's feet and movement patterns, indoor volleyball has its own specific shoe.

Can a shoe for a similar sport, such as basketball, work? For a time, yes. If you're playing in gym class or just joining a pickup game every now and again, the sneakers you have can do the job — albeit not as well as a volleyball-specific shoe. But if you play volleyball regularly, get a shoe designed for volleyball so that you get the sport-specific support that you need.

Here are some factors to consider when looking for volleyball shoes:

- **Grip:** Volleyball demands no small amount of cutting, change of direction, and quick starts and stops. Get a shoe that has gum rubber outsoles and good grip or traction to keep those changes of direction sharp, with minimal risk of slipping.
- **Cushioning and absorption:** Mostly for the jumping positions — outside, opposite, middle, setter. A shoe that has good cushioning and shock absorption can help lessen the impact of all those jumps and landings. Your knees will thank you.
- **Stability:** Support at the ankles can help reduce ankle rolls and improve lateral movements. The position that you play determines the height of your shoe top:
  - *Low-top:* Liberos, for increased agility and mobility
  - *Mid-top:* Setters and outsides, for balance
  - *High-top:* Injury-prone players, for maximum stability

- **Lightweight and breathable:** You need to move quickly, no matter your position, so look for a lighter shoe. And because you're going to sweat in them, get a shoe that has mesh to stay cool, allowing the heat and moisture to ventilate.
- **Durability:** If you're training or playing multiple times per week, you need a durable shoe so that you don't have to buy a new pair every quarter of the year. A shoe that has strong midsoles can go a long way.

ASICS (www.asics.com), Mizuno (https://mizuno.com), Nike (www.nike.com), and Adidas (www.adidas.com) all offer excellent volleyball shoes. ASICS and Mizuno are the power players in the sport, as far as apparel and shoes go.

Socks

Consider athletic socks — and a lot of them — almost as important as the shoes that you get for volleyball. All the major athletic apparel brands — Nike, Adidas, Mizuno, Under Armour (www.underarmour.com), and so on — have plenty of options for socks. Look for socks that have

- Moisture-wicking material to help pull the sweat away from the skin
- Extra cushioning in the heel and ball of the feet to absorb the shock of jumping and landing
- Breathability so that your sock doesn't turn into a sauna

As far as length goes, that's a personal choice, but the most common type of sock that volleyball players wear reaches to the mid-calf.

Knee pads

In indoor volleyball, no matter your position, you have to dive and slide all over the place on a hard surface. Get some knee pads to protect your joints.

The following list looks at different positions and the types of knee pads that we recommend for each:

- **Liberos:** Look for knee pads that have reinforced foam because you're constantly on the ground, diving for digs and out-of-system passes (moves that we talk about in Chapters 9 and 11).

» **Middles, outsides, and opposites:** Lighter, more flexible knee pads because you need to jump a lot — and these pads make it easier and more comfortable.

TIP

Whatever your position, just make sure to get a knee pad that's the right size so that it stays up throughout a play. A knee pad that requires regular adjusting and pulling up is both annoying and distracting: You don't want to be tugging at your knee pads when you're supposed to be making a dig.

Good brands for knee pads include McDavid (www.mcdavidusa.com), Mizuno, Nike, and ASICS.

Spandex

Male volleyball players usually wear your standard-fare athletic shorts from the usual athletic apparel companies — ASICS, Nike, Adidas, Mizuno, Under Armour — over compression shorts. Women almost exclusively go with spandex shorts without another pair of shorts on top of them.

Spandex allows for a higher freedom of movement for all those jumps, dives, lunges, and various other lateral movement demands. And, perhaps most importantly, they don't move during rallies. You need to constantly adjust looser shorts and material, but spandex stays in place.

Spandex also works well with knee pads (more on knee pads in the preceding section), preventing bunching and reducing agitation on your skin. You can choose whatever leg length covering you want; some women use full-length leggings, whereas others choose shorter options.

You can find good-quality spandex shorts and pants for volleyball from the brands Mizuno, Adidas, Under Armour, Nike, and ASICS.

Ankle braces

A high percentage of indoor volleyball players wear *ankle braces*, which provide stability for your ankles, because the sport puts a high stress on the ankles, with all the jumping, landing, and lateral movement required. A quality ankle brace can reduce sprains, add stability, and help lessen the chances that you reinjure a previously sprained ankle.

To find effective ankle braces, check out the brands Zamst (www.zamst.com), McDavid, Med Spec's ASO (https://medspec.com/product/aso-ankle-stabilizer), and Shock Doctor (www.shockdoctor.com).

Picking Out Apparel for Beach Volleyball

Indoor volleyball includes shoes. Beach volleyball players laugh and say, "What are thoooooseee?"

Here, we discuss some apparel that you don't necessarily need if you want to play beach volleyball, but these items provide no small amount of utility when you're playing outside.

Sunglasses

We can't imagine playing beach volleyball without wearing sunglasses, but some crazy folks do. We don't recommend it. You play this sport outside, during the day, mostly during the summer months (when the sun is out in full force). If you play an all-day, or even all-weekend, tournament and don't use sunglasses, you're going to be uncomfortable, at minimum, throughout the day, constantly squinting and adjusting to keep your eyes out of the sun. Some players, of course, don't like to use sunglasses because wearing them can impact depth perception and they're uncomfortable. On the whole, however, we recommend them.

Here's what to look for in your volleyball sunglasses:

- **Shape:** Look for wraparound sunglasses that hug your face a bit more and shift less when you jump and dive. Aviators might look cool, but they'll fall off your face or move around too much.
- **Polarization:** Polarized lenses tend to help mitigate glare from the sun, sand, and water; but you don't really need polarization because it's a feature designed to reduce glare. In a lot of cases, there won't be a tremendous amount of glare in beach volleyball, so the higher price point doesn't necessitate the use of polarized shades.

If you're looking for premium options, Oakley (`www.oakley.com`) and Roka (`www.roka.com`) dominate the industry, and for good reason: They're the best sunglasses on the market, and the lenses can survive the constant beating they take from the sand.

But you can find solid budget options, too:

- **goodr (`https://goodr.com`):** Offer tremendous bang for the buck because you wouldn't notice much of a difference between them and, say, Oakleys, not right off the bat, anyway. You'll be shocked by what you can get for $25.

» **Blenders (www.blenderseyewear.com):** Another popular pick among beach volleyball professionals who operate on a shoestring budget because they provide exactly what a beach player is looking for — clear vision on a sunny day, and stylistic choices to boot — for an easy-to-buy price.

Men's board shorts

The men have it easy, don't they? The only clothing you really need to play beach volleyball is a decent pair of shorts. Some men choose to wear compression shorts under the board shorts for comfort and, uh, modesty reasons, and some wear just the board shorts themselves. In the end, like most equipment, it's a comfort thing.

Shirts are entirely optional, but if you want to wear one, get a light and breathable one. Cotton clothes can just about suffocate you (the material absorbs all that sweat and becomes incredibly heavy, hot, and miserable). Look for a *tri-blend* (a mix of polyester, cotton, and rayon) T-shirt or tank top because it's light, breathable, and moisture-wicking, so it doesn't become a weighted vest soaking up sweat and sand all day.

The shorts you want to play beach volleyball differ quite a bit from the shorts that you might grab on your family vacation to go sit on the beach, play cornhole, or barbeque.

Key elements that you want your volleyball shorts to have include

» **Stretch:** The shorts need to provide you mobility to jump, dive, and get in all kinds of strange positions that you don't even see in a yoga class. Look for shorts made of a *four-way stretch* material, which is a marketer's fancy way of saying: It's going to stretch and move with you in all of those uncomfortable and strange positions this sport can take you.

» **Moisture-wicking:** You're going to sweat. A lot. Moisture-wicking shorts keep you (mostly) dry and lightweight by not absorbing all of that sweat and sand on your legs and body.

» **Quick-drying:** You don't want shorts made of a super thick material that take forever to dry, otherwise, you get bogged down by heavy, water-logged shorts. A general rule is to avoid cotton, which soaks up everything it can find, becoming heavy, and is a burden to wear.

Mizuno, Slunks (www.getslunks.com), and Hurley (www.hurley.com) offer great men's volleyball shorts, although any major surfing brand, such as Quiksilver (www.quiksilver.com), Volcom (www.volcom.com), and O'Neill (https://oneill.com), offer good volleyball shorts options.

Women's bikinis

The vast majority of female beach volleyball players, from professionals down to the grassroots levels, compete in bikinis designed for athletic movement. Not everyone does, of course. Delaney Mewhirter, wife of co-author Travis, competed on the AVP Tour in onesie suits, and she received exemptions to do so on the World Tour, as well. Brooke Sweat, an Olympian, frequently opted for oversized T-shirts. Some players go for longer leggings, and some don long sleeves. Biker shorts have begun to be popular choices as well. And the NCAA mandates that its athletes wear tank-tops and shorts.

The bikinis that women choose to compete in aren't the same as the ones they lounge around on the beach in. Here are some important factors to consider when looking for a bikini best suited for athletic movement:

- **Snug fit:** Both the top and bottom should fit snugly and provide full coverage. Many athletic bikini tops have racerback and crisscross straps that help prevent slipping during the movements required in the sport.
- **Stretch:** Get a bikini made of stretchy fabric that can move with you while still holding its shape.
- **Durable:** The elements of beach volleyball test every piece of clothing, so you want to make sure it can withstand the constant wear and tear of sand, salt, sweat, diving, stretching, and sun exposure.
- **Minimal accessories:** Keep the decorative hardware, such as rings and metal closures, on your bikini to a minimum because they rub your skin — mixed with sand, which makes it even worse — throughout the match. We get it: You like a little flair. You can add flair — just keep it under control if you want to maximize performance.

All of the major athletic apparel companies — Nike, Adidas, and Mizuno — offer popular athletic bikinis. And some smaller outfits, such as Jolyn (`https://jolyn.com`) and Left On Friday (`https://leftonfriday.com`), have a huge following amongst beach volleyball players.

Sand socks

Yes, on occasion, you may see beach volleyball players wearing socks on the sand. It might not look cool — at all — but on hot, sunny days, where dark sand can become roughly the temperature of molten lava, your feet will thank the heavens that you were wise enough to put on sand socks.

AN OLYMPIAN'S BIKINI STORY

Allow Anouk Verge-Depre, a Swiss Olympian who won a bronze medal at the Tokyo Games, to explain more about why she wears a bikini when she plays.

Less than a year after she became the first Swiss female to win an Olympic medal on the beach, Verge-Depre penned a piece on her Facebook page in May of 2022, headlined: "Let's Talk Bikini!" (The photo shows Verge-Depre in her bikini.)

Volleyball World

"It's my training outfit, my competition outfit and my favorite vacation outfit (ok I like dresses too).

"Since it has been a topic discussed over and over again in the media and on social, I would like to make some statements:

"I love wearing a bikini. I feel strong and powerful wearing a bikini, cause that's how I feel most comfortable to play my sport in the heat, in the sand and at the beach.

"People may think it's uncomfortable to wear a bikini all the time, but I have actually never met a female pro beach volleyball player that does not like to wear her bikinis, yet. Our sport comes from the beach and it shows a great diversity of bodies. Of course, it is an advantage to have a fit body to be able to play our sport at the highest level, but it would be the same wearing long clothes.

"I do think it was very important though to change the FIVB regulations, so every woman has the choice to wear what she feels comfortable with at any particular day. Tights, shorts, bikinis etc., the preference can change according to many reasons like injuries, temperature or for example being on our period. I think it's an important and very good step for our sport that women can choose. Time for people to know this has changed."

Normal socks don't do the trick. You'll rip a hole in them in 10 minutes or less, guaranteed. You may struggle to get TuffSox (`www.tuffsox.com`) on because they fit like gloves with a slot for each toe. But they're the best, most durable sand socks in the industry. Alternatively, if you're looking for cheap but reliable sand socks that can get the job done, many players use the Sand Socks by Vincere (`https://sandsocks.net`).

Naming the Best Recovery Tools for All Volleyball Players

After a long day spent on the court, either indoors or at the beach, your body may yearn for some relief. The following items can help you recover so that you're ready to play again soon:

- **Compression pants:** Slipping on a pair of *compression pants* designed to accelerate muscle recovery, reduce soreness, and increase circulation using dynamic, pulsed compression lets you stay productive while you watch Netflix or that guilty-pleasure rom-com, or just cozy up with a book and something to drink. A lot of science supports their ability to increase blood flow and recovery and professional sports teams across all sports have these pants readily available for their players because, simply put, they work. Compression pants don't come cheap, but if you play a lot of volleyball, it's a worthwhile investment. Check out Normatec pants (`https://hyperice.com/get-normatec`) from the brand Hyperice.
- **Massage gun:** Probably the best recovery tool on the market, this pulsing massager can effectively loosen up your muscles before play, help them cool down afterwards, and bring some relief when you feel tight and sore. It's small and mobile, so you can easily bring it in the car or on a plane (airport security will probably give it an extra look to make sure it's not a real gun — just a heads up). We can't recommend getting yourself a massage gun enough. Reliable options include Hyperice's Hypervolt (`https://hyperice.com/get-hypervolt`) and Therabody's Theragun (`www.therabody.com/collections/shop-theragun`).

» **Foam rollers or massage balls:** Either a foam roller or a massage ball can help break up and loosen tight muscles (even if it feels like mild torture). These tools can get deeper into the muscles than the massage gun, working out the stubborn knots underneath the surface, so they don't feel good in the moment; working out knots is never exactly pleasurable, but your muscles will thank you.

Recovery involves more than just muscles — you also have to take care of the nervous system. Simple breathing practices can help downshift your body from fight-or-flight mode into recovery mode, which improves sleep, reduces stress, and supports overall performance. Structured approaches such as Hamilton House's recovery breathing (`https://hamiltonhouseglobal.com`) emphasize slow, controlled breathing to help athletes reset after training or competition. Even a few minutes of intentional breathing can make a meaningful difference in how quickly your body recovers.

Considering Other Accessories

Whether you play on the beach in 90-degree weather or indoors, you may want these items to enhance your experience:

» **Water bottles:** Self-explanatory. You absolutely need water bottles, especially on the beach, where you might not have readily available water sources like you do in a gym.

» **Backpack or duffle bag:** You need to carry your water bottle, knee pads, snacks, extra shirts and shorts, sunglasses, sunscreen — all of the things — in something. Volleyball-specific backpacks come with a little ball carrier, too, that attaches to the backpack and carries a volleyball perfectly. We recommend those types of bags because it's custom-fit to your exact volleyball needs, but a volleyball-specific bag is a luxury, not a requirement.

» **Towels:** You're going to sweat, no matter which version of the sport you play. If you play indoors, the setters on your team will be grateful if you wipe off those slick forearms so that they don't have to set a ball that comes slicked with sweat after your pass. On the beach, a towel provides the extra benefit of drying you off after an ocean dip, as well, and it gives you something to sit on between matches.

» **Athletic tape:** You jam your fingers constantly in volleyball, no matter which surface you play on or which position you play. Blockers especially need athletic tape available because their fingers are the most exposed to being hit by high-speed swings. Having the tape ready and being able to tape quickly can keep you in the game and keep your fingers and hands in one piece.

IN THIS CHAPTER

» Figuring out whether you want to play or watch (or both!)

» Getting into beach volleyball

» Weighing your indoor volleyball options

Chapter 5

Finding Places to Play and Watch Volleyball

We're guessing that you love volleyball — or someone very close to you is a fanatic about either beach or indoor volleyball. That's probably why you're reading this book. In this chapter, we help you figure out how you can play volleyball, as well as the best ways to simply watch volleyball.

This chapter addresses each type of reader. We discuss where you (or your loved one) can lace up your sneakers, pull up your kneepads (if you want), and hit the court. Or if you'd rather watch in an arena, on a beach, or sit back in your comfy chair, we examine where you can do just that.

Competing or Cheering Them On

We realize that readers of this book come from two camps, the players and the fans:

» **You play volleyball or want to play volleyball.** We have great news for you! You have endless options for playing either beach or indoor volleyball. From your local YMCA and Parks & Recreation leagues to school and club teams, if you're starting out or even have a few seasons under your belt, you have a wide array of choices.

And if you're considering playing volleyball in college or beyond, you may have questions, which we answer in the section "Playing for a beach college team" later in this chapter.

- **You're a fan of volleyball and want to know where you can watch as much of it as you can.** We have more great news for you! While volleyball has become more and more popular, the number of places that you can go in person or via your TV or computer to watch and cheer on your favorite team has steadily increased, allowing you to easily appreciate athleticism at its best.

REMEMBER

The media landscape for watching volleyball on TV and your computer seems to always be changing. We provide a few of the best platforms at the time we're writing in the section "Cheering on Your Favorite Teams" later in this chapter, but we acknowledge that things may have changed by the time you get your hands on this book.

Discovering Where to Play Beach

There are, despite what you might initially think when thinking of "beach volleyball," endless places to play the sport — no beach required. Manmade complexes have been popping up all over the country, from Cincinnati, Ohio to Louisville, Kentucky to New Orleans and Denver and everywhere in between.

You can play beach volleyball in all 50 states, and countries better known for Winter Olympic success than Summer. Taryn Brasher, the best blocker in the United States, grew up in South Dakota. The three best men's teams in the world? From Norway and Sweden.

Seek beach volleyball, and you shall find it.

Hitting the sand for your high school

High school beach volleyball is rare in the United States, and only four states — Florida, California, Texas, and Arizona — offer sanctioned varsity teams for girls (no schools offer teams for boys). Various schools around the country may still offer club or unofficial teams, but the vast majority of players have to either play independently or train with a club.

WARNING

Because boys don't have the option of playing for a high school, they have to participate in any one of the options in the section "Considering where to play beach" later in this chapter.

Joining a beach volleyball club

Beach is a strange sport for a junior player, and even for professionals. It's a team sport — but also not. It's more akin to golf or tennis than it is to indoor volleyball. Wherever you are in the country, whether Florida or North Dakota, you can find a club or group to train with. And that, really, is what a beach volleyball club team is: A training group.

You don't have to play with anyone in your club (at most places, anyway). You can ask anyone in your age group to partner with you at any tournament around the country. Most clubs have regular training with coaches, and then players are free to compete wherever, and with whomever, they want.

Finding a beach volleyball partner

You play tournaments, you meet people, you get their contact info, and you ask them to play in any of the organizations discussed in the following section, which host events year-round, all over the United States.

Volleyball Life (`https://volleyballlife.com`) keeps rankings of players in every organization that we talk about in the following section, so you can easily see who's playing well in your area and who's at your relative level. You'll have a good estimate of what level you're at based on your results in tournaments. If you're winning, it's best to find something more competitive. If not, either stay where you're at or move down until you're ready for more difficult competition.

Considering where to play beach

The best place to find events where you can play club beach volleyball is Volleyball Life (`https://volleyballlife.com`). Here are some of the places you can play club beach volleyball:

- **p1440:** Four-time Olympic beach volleyball Gold Medalist Kerri Walsh Jennings started p1440 (`https://p1440.com`) in 2018 with the intention of making it a professional beach volleyball tour that could challenge the Association of Volleyball Professionals (AVP), while also doubling as a health and wellness digital platform. It quickly pivoted to the juniors market, where it established a thriving organization.

p1440 hosts a Futures Tour year-round, on beaches and in facilities all over the United States. It also hosts camps, clinics, and invitation-only events that are a huge part of college recruiting. Players accrue points at each tournament that they play, and the players who have the most points earn spots in the prestigious regional and national competitions.

- **Association of Volleyball Professionals (AVP):** The biggest name in beach volleyball, the AVP (`https://avp.com`) is the main grassroots organization when it comes to juniors beach volleyball. Although its name refers to professionals, it also hosts events all year long all over the United States for age groups and skillsets across the spectrum. Don't let the name scare you, either: Players at all levels can get their start here, even if you haven't competed yet. Players build up points, based on their finish, to the AVP regional and national championships.
- **Amateur Athletic Union (AAU):** Although many people know the AAU for its robust basketball circuit, it also hosts events year-round all over the U.S. in beach volleyball (`https://aausports.org/volleyball`). Like p1440 and the AVP, you accrue points in every AAU-affiliated event that you play, and you can build up to the regional and national championships.
- **Beach Volleyball National Events (BVNE):** Another reputable organization that hosts events around the country, year-round. Go to `https://bvne.org` for more information.
- **USA Volleyball:** USA has a vast ecosystem for players at all levels, from youth beginners to Olympic athletes, to train and compete. It hosts a USA Volleyball Beach Tour, with 40 USAV regions for junior volleyball players, culminating in the USA Volleyball Beach National Championships.

TIP

- **Local tournaments:** You can find at least one beach volleyball facility or site in every state in the U.S. Often these facilities have their own tournaments and leagues during the week and on the weekend. Many of them host their tournaments on Volleyball Life (`https://volleyballlife.com`), but you may have to look for some at the facility itself. You might need to do some digging around, asking neighbors and other players in the area.

Playing for a beach college team

If you develop your game well enough at the juniors level, competing in one or all of the organizations that we talk about in the preceding section, college coaches notice you — and they may want you to play for their program — and often for free, because schools offer scholarships and potentially even cash in the form of name, image, and likeness (NIL) deals.

USA Volleyball, too, may take note and invite you to their National Training Development Program, which is a big honor. Congratulations!

Here are the two main college routes that you can go.

Going to the beach with the NAIA

The National Association of Intercollegiate Athletics (NAIA) is a governing body for smaller schools and athletics programs. If you're not a top talent, you want an extra two years to develop, or have another personal reason, aim for this level. You can always transfer to a higher-level school if you develop your game. If not, that's totally fine! Enjoy competing at this level while you can.

REMEMBER

Currently the NAIA is the only college-level athletic association that offers men's beach volleyball as a collegiate sport, so this is the only route for males.

Getting your NCAA beach game on

The NCAA is the gold standard for women's collegiate beach volleyball. Although the NCAA traditionally has three tiers for its sports — Division I, Division II, and Division III — in beach volleyball, the NCAA has two levels:

- **Division I:** The highest level of competition
- **Divisions II and III:** A combined category of small schools

Introduced in 2009 as an emerging sport, beach volleyball was sanctioned as an NCAA Championship sport in 2016 and has since become the fastest-growing sport in the history of the NCAA. Currently, more than 100 NCAA schools have beach volleyball programs.

Only women can play at the Division I NCAA level, as there are no offerings for men's beach volleyball for a variety of reasons — scholarship rules and finances being the primary drivers.

Having some beach fun with other adults

Where can you play just for fun, or maybe even some cash? You can find nearly limitless options to continue playing as an adult. Volleyball Life (`https://volleyballlife.com`) has the full smorgasbord of events all over the country, all year. Here are a few of the most consistent, reputable organizations:

- **Association of Volleyball Professionals (AVP):** While serving as the flagship professional tour (`https://avp.com`), the AVP also has lower-level events that anybody can play in. These events take place all over the country, all year long, and offer various prizes, from decent cash payouts, to volleyballs, to towels, to items of whatever company is sponsoring the tournament. Sometimes, the prize is just fun and quality time outside playing with friends, as Figure 5-1 shows.

FIGURE 5-1: You can enjoy a beach event as an adult.

Photo by Travis Mewhirter

- **California Beach Volleyball Association (CBVA):** The CBVA runs hundreds of tournaments up and down the West Coast for players at all levels, from juniors to beginners to bona fide professionals. It also has a respected ranking system, so players who earn a top finish in one category move up to the next, so you're never playing someone who's too high in level. (Sandbaggers beware!) Check out `https://cbva.com` for more information.
- **Sunshine State Outdoor Volleyball Association (SSOVA):** The SSOVA is the Florida equivalent of the CBVA. If there's an adult tournament in Florida, SSOVA (`www.ssova.com`) is likely running it.
- **East End Volleyball (EEVB):** The EEVB has been running beach volleyball tournaments since 1977 and hosts tournaments all up and down the East Coast. Check out its website at `https://eevb.net`.
- **Great American Volleyball (GAV):** Based in New Jersey, and like East End, the GAV hosts events on the East Coast of the United States. It also hosts regularly at indoor sand facilities, keeping events going all year long. Go to `www.greatamericanvolleyball.com` for more details.

TIP

You can find dozens, if not hundreds, of other organizations that put on tournaments on Volleyball Life (`https://volleyballlife.com`), the hub of nearly every volleyball event imaginable.

Knowing Where to Play Indoor

Volleyball is quite literally everywhere in the United States. Gyms? All over. Arenas? You bet. Football stadiums? That's happened. Baseball fields? Oh, yes. If you can fit a volleyball court into a given space, someone will find a way to do it. That's how big the sport has grown — and continues to grow.

Knowing where to play can get tricky, however, with all of these options, which is why we present this section for you, explaining where you can make your entry into the game, no matter your age or level.

Weighing your juniors indoor options

You have a lot of opportunities to play volleyball when you're younger than 18. Here are some of the main ways.

Playing on indoor volleyball school teams

Your main option is to play for your student team, whether you're in elementary, middle, or high school. In fact, for nearly a decade, indoor volleyball has been the most popular high school sport for girls in the United States, overtaking basketball for the top spot. Nearly every high school has a team, and a school team gives you the easiest way to get into the sport.

REMEMBER

Even boys are beginning to have options because 36 states — as of this writing — have at least one school that has a high school boys volleyball team. It isn't a huge school sport for boys by any means, but it's growing, and quickly.

Joining indoor volleyball clubs

When the school season ends, many volleyball players look to continue or supplement their training by joining a club. Clubs are literally all over the United States, and Volleyball Club Hub (`https://volleyballclubhub.com`) does an excellent job of compiling clubs in every state. Because the school season takes place in the fall, clubs often run in the winter, spring, and early summer. Summers are mostly left to the individual players' devices because they can participate in camps or play beach volleyball — or take some time off and vacation with the family.

Most clubs have multiple age groups, from 12U (12 and under) all the way up to 18s (seniors in high school), and they typically practice two to three times per week and play in one to two events per month, if not more.

Because your options for high school boys volleyball are limited if you're male (25 state athletic associations sanction the sport at the time of writing this book), club is definitely a way to go for males looking to get into the sport. If you're looking to get recruited to play in college, you almost have to play in clubs, which compete in a variety of different governing organizations.

Certain clubs will travel more — and therefore cost more — but offer more opportunities to play. Others travel less and are more affordable, but those club teams play fewer tournaments. There are tradeoffs to both, so weigh your options according to your goals as a volleyball player and your budget.

Going to college for indoor volleyball

For some, high school or juniors club volleyball is as high as they want to go. Others may still want to climb higher, into the college ranks. The NCAA, NAIA, and National Junior College Athletic Association (NJCAA) have options for both men and women, although the number of women's programs vastly outnumbers that of the men, mostly due to scholarship and financial reasons.

Here are the various pathways to competing after high school:

- **NCAA:** The NCAA is the main pathway to the next level of volleyball, with three divisions varying in size and competition level. There are literally hundreds of programs for women, where only a few for men. Here are the options at the NCAA level:
  - **NCAA Division I:** The highest level of the sport, Division I features the cream of the crop of collegiate volleyball players. The sport has grown to the point that not only do most Division I schools offer a full scholarship, but many offer cash on top of that. Outside hitters have been known to command well into the six figures in NIL payments from their respective sports as volleyball explodes in popularity. (NIL is a whole other topic; check out `https://www.ncaa.org/sports/2021/7/9/name-image-likeness.aspx` for more information.)

    As of 2024, 347 of the 365 Division I schools sponsored a volleyball team.

- **NCAA Division II:** With nearly 300 Division II schools offering volleyball as a sport, this is another excellent option. Although you won't find nearly as many scholarships available, most schools are able to offer at least some money in terms of scholarships.
- **NCAA Division III:** The lowest rung on the NCAA ladder, there are more than 400 schools that offer volleyball as a sport. Students who choose to play DIII often do so because they want a balance of athletics and academics, which gives them the change to experience the all of the college experience while still competing.

» **NAIA:** NAIA is a college sports governing body for smaller, primarily private or faith-based universities in the United States. Approximately 220 NAIA schools sponsor women's volleyball teams, and more than 60 have men's volleyball.

» **NJCAA:** The NJCAA is the governing body for two-year college athletics in the United States. This is an excellent option for athletes who are still developing and want to take two years to compete while having their eyes on finishing their careers at a bigger school. It's also an outlet for athletes who want to save money on tuition in their first two years because NJCAA schools are much cheaper than most NCAA schools, before finishing their careers at a four-year institution.

The men's offerings in college are limited, like in school. The number of colleges offering men's indoor volleyball ranges per year while different colleges add or cut programs, but between 28 and 34 Division I schools field a team, and almost all schools offer a club team. The NCAA Division III sanctioned men's volleyball in 2015, so more than 150 institutions now have teams.

Playing club in college

If you're in college and want to compete and play volleyball, but don't want to do so on your college's team, you still have an option. The most common route for college students to continue competing after the high school level is on a college club team. Most major universities offer a club volleyball team option, and they often operate in a similar fashion as a varsity sport, with tryouts, a coach, travel to national championships, and tournaments. It isn't unusual for a club player to be a genuinely elite volleyball player. The NCVF (`https://ncvf.org`) organizes playing opportunities and a national tournament for collegiate club volleyball players (see Figure 5-2).

FIGURE 5-2: You can play club in college.

Photos by Fayna Zeng and Catherine Dzanski

Playing recreational and semipro indoor

You have several options if you're an adult and want to play indoor volleyball:

- **USA Volleyball (USAV):** If you're looking for something more competitive, USAV (`https://usavolleyball.org`) has regional associations all over the country with divisions for every skill level. These associations compete, culminating each year in the wildly popular USA Volleyball Adult Nationals.
- **National Volleyball Association (NVA):** The NVA resides in a murky midway point between semiprofessional and professional. It's a legitimately high-level league that offers modest pay, but it isn't full-time. If you're a talented player but not quite good enough to play overseas, but you also want to keep your playing career somewhat alive, the NVA might be the perfect landing spot for you.
- **YMCA and other rec leagues:** Many cities in the United States have rec leagues that range from "I just want to have fun" to "I want to compete and win." Just search online for local volleyball leagues in your area.

Professional

More than likely, unless you're the next Lloy Ball, you won't be playing professionally; instead, you probably want to watch professional volleyball. Refer to the sections "Watching the Pros Play Indoor" and "Watching the Beach Volleyball Pros" later in this chapter for more information about pro leagues.

Cheering on Your Favorite Teams

With the ease of streaming matches online, following your favorite team, no matter the level, is easy. Even beach volleyball has live scoring for independent tournaments over the summer, which you can follow online at `volleyballlife.com`.

That said, we can't begin to list every way that you can watch your team on TV or on your computer. Because the media landscape is always changing, we include a sampling of sites and platforms that you can use at the time of writing but do some online sleuthing yourself to see what's out there. Also, ask your fellow fans whether they have a site they recommend for you to follow your team.

Rooting on your school team

If you have a son or daughter playing volleyball and want to support them, go in person to watch them play! Tickets are cheap, if not free, at most places, including NCAA Division I matches, and there's nothing like a volleyball atmosphere.

Attendance records have been falling like dominoes every year: Nebraska, Creighton, Michigan, Indiana, Cincinnati, and more all set new attendance records in 2025 alone, and it seems to be simply the tip of the iceberg.

Volleyball is, simply, put, having its breakthrough moment.

If you're not able to cheer them on in person, look into the following:

» **VBTV:** Volleyball TV began as a streaming serving for professional volleyball, both indoors and beach, but also began televising Big 10 matches in the NCAA. Head to `https://tv.volleyballworld`.tv to get a subscription — you'll have more volleyball than you can possibly watch.

» **ESPN+:** This is the most common outlet for college matches, including the National Championship for both NCAA Division I beach and men's indoor volleyball.

- **Big Ten Network/Big Ten Plus:** Specific to, you guessed it, the Big 10 conference in the NCAA, you can subscribe to watch Big 10 matches.
- **SEC Network:** The SEC isn't just about football! It's also one of the strongest volleyball conferences in the country and televises matches on its name brand SEC Network.
- **Your school's stream:** Tricky to find, yes, but each school sometimes stream its own matches in its own way. Many go live on YouTube, and some have a private link specifically for parents and alumni who want to watch online. Check in with the coach, an administrator, or player on the team.

As the popularity of collegiate volleyball has skyrocketed, so has viewing opportunities. Check your local listings like Fox Sports and ESPN for high-profile matches that are broadcast during the weekends.

Watching the Pros Play Indoor

For decades, there was a dearth of professional offerings for volleyball in the United States — and then, suddenly, there were three leagues happening at once. It has been a boom for volleyball players in the United States. Of course, with that boom has come confusion on where and how to follow each one. Here we have you covered.

Staying in the United States — indoor domestic leagues

What a time to be writing this portion of the book! By the time you read this, it might very well be outdated — the U.S. volleyball landscape is rapidly changing. While we write, you have three options in the United States to watch women's professional volleyball:

- **League One Volleyball (LOVB):** Founded in 2020, with a start date of 2025, LOVB is one of the two major indoor leagues in the United States. As of this writing, there are six franchises — Atlanta, Austin, Houston, Madison, Omaha, and Salt Lake City — with two more announced as expansion franchises in San Francisco and Los Angeles. You can find their website at `www.lovb.com`.
- **Major League Volleyball (MLV):** Formerly called the Pro Volleyball Federation (and found at `https://provolleyball.com`), the MLV played its first season as the MLV in 2025, and were led by the Omaha Supernovas, which were the

biggest television and attendance draw in the sport. You can find franchises in these cities:

- Atlanta
- Columbus
- Dallas
- Grand Rapids
- Indianapolis
- Omaha
- Orlando
- San Diego (now defunct)
- There are another three expansions announced in Northern California, Washington D.C., and Minnesota.

REMEMBER

LOVB and MLV operate as standard professional sports — including franchises, coaches, general managers, drafts, and all the rest. We don't think the pro volleyball ecosystem can support two professional leagues for long, so in ten years or so — if not less — we bet only one league will remain.

» **Athletes Unlimited Pro Volleyball:** This is an entirely different world of professional sports, based more on individual performance of the 44 professionals in the league (`https://auprosports.com/volleyball`). Teams change week to week, and an individual is crowned the winner at the end of the season based on their individual stats.

ESPN carries most Athletes Unlimited matches, and for the sake of staying up to date in a rapidly changing television landscape, the best resource for information on where to watch each league and team is the respective websites.

Going overseas — indoor international leagues

Volleyball has been a hugely popular professional sport in Europe and Asia for decades, and the vast majority of the top talent aspires to play on one of those two continents. Italy is the gold standard, with its SuperLega for men and Serie A1 for women.

Other top leagues include Poland, Turkey, Brazil, Japan, Russia, France and China, all of which offer high salaries to attract top talents around the world.

If you want to watch the world's top professional players, international leagues — both women's and men's — are your best bets. Search for those individuals leagues online.

Tuning into the Olympics

Volleyball, both indoors and beach, has been deemed an "Olympic sport" because that's when most of the world tunes in to watch. Volleyball (indoors and beach combined) is the biggest event for both versions of the sport, the one most all players put on their vision board. An Olympic medal is a legacy-making achievement.

NBC, and its streaming app, Peacock, provide tremendous coverage of the Games, and you can watch every single match, on demand, if you have the app. NBC also televises the premier matches in primetime on its flagship channel.

Watching the Beach Volleyball Pros

If you're an avid fan of beach volleyball, then you have several options to follow the professionals do their thing. Here are your main choices:

- **Association of Volleyball Professionals (AVP):** Founded in 1983, the AVP has been the beach volleyball equivalent of the Professional Golfers' Association (PGA), National Basketball Association (NBA), National Hockey League (NHL), and Major League Baseball (MLB). Up-and-coming players aspire to play in the AVP, and it's the best domestic tour in the world. Check out `https://avp.com` for more details.
- **Volleyball World Beach Pro Tour:** The international circuit for professionals. Overseen by FIVB (International Volleyball Federation), this tour features Olympic qualifying and the best players in the world. You can watch all matches on the Volleyball World TV (VBTV) app, which has been one of the most significant developments in the sport this century. Check out `https://en.volleyballworld.com` for more information.
- **Other independent events:** Here are some rogue events unaffiliated with any of the major organizations:
  - *Seaside:* A festival of beach volleyball on the stunning coast of Oregon, Seaside (`https://seasidebeachvolleyball.com`) is the largest annual

gathering of volleyball players in the world. With divisions ranging from co-ed fours, to juniors, to professionals, and featuring a huge prize purse, Seaside is an absolute must on every beach volleyball player's bucket list.

- *Motherlode:* One of the longest-running tournaments in the sport, the Motherlode (`https://letsgovolleyball.com/mother-lode-aspen`) has been hosted on Labor Day weekend in Aspen, Colorado, for decades. Like Seaside, it offers every type of division and age range, and players from all over the world always block it off on their calendars.
- *Fuds:* If Seaside is a festival of beach volleyball, Emerald Coast Volleyball Week (known as Fuds; `https://emeraldcoastvolleyball.com`), hosted bi-annually in Fort Walton Beach, Florida, is its raging, fun-filled sibling. Fuds is the party scene for the party player, a fours tournament that has divisions and ages across the spectrum, with nightly costume and themed parties. That said, it also hauls in some of the world's best talent to win the professional fours tournament and is always an incredibly entertaining event.

2

Finetuning Skills to Play Volleyball

IN THIS PART . . .

Explore the fun skill of hitting and how to successfully score on the beach and indoors.

Discover how to become the best teammate, by understanding the ins and outs of setting.

Find out how to manage the risk-reward of serving and explore the many different options that you have as a server.

Use passing as your greatest weapon and improve your passing game.

Discover the ins and outs of blocking, as well as how to block your opponents off the court.

Realize that digging isn't just for shovels — it's for your defense, too.

IN THIS CHAPTER

» Identifying the traits of a good hitter

» Understanding point of preparation

» Moving your feet and arms for a proper hit

» Hitting with brains or brawn

» Completing your attack

» Doing some hitting drills

Chapter 6

Focusing on the Attack: Hitting

We start Part 2 by highlighting hitting, which kind of breaks all the rules. We're not supposed to start with hitting. Hitting should come last because it's the final contact of your offensive sequence, right?

But hitting is fun. Hitting is, for the most part, what people come to this sport to do. The outside hitters are the heroes, the Thors of this sport's story, with their muscles exploding out of their muscles. Great teams are built around hitters, and they're the central figures in every writer's story when covering a team.

Hitting is fun. And volleyball is fun. So, fun is where we begin. This chapter explores what you need to know about hitting, including the point of preparation, spacing, footwork, timing, arm swing, and more. We examine a few of the best hitters in the world of volleyball, and how great hitters can come in all shapes and sizes — and how you, no matter your physical makeup or athletic ability, can become an effective hitter, too.

Understanding What Makes a Great Hitter

A great hitter, well, hits. Not only that:

- **Indoor:** You act as the rock of the team, the player whom your setter turns to when they need a point, the linchpin whom everyone relies on to score, no matter the scenario. Tight in the fifth set? No problem — as the hitter, you can get the ball, and everyone in the gym knows it.
- **Beach:** No opposing team wants to serve to you or attempt to dig or block your hits. You strike fear into opposing defenses. Down 13–14 in the third set? No problem — you know that you can put the ball away — terminate the rally — and give your defense a chance to win the match.

In either type of volleyball, you're an elite hitter.

But how do you become this elite hitter? What exactly makes your run-of-the-mill hitter elevate to greatness? The following sections identify the traits that make a hitter stand out.

Having confidence

In June of 2018, Taylor Crabb, standing all of 6 feet tall, took a mighty swing against Phil Dalhausser, one of the greatest blockers the sport of beach volleyball has ever seen. It didn't go well. Dalhausser blocked the swing straight down for a point. This play in itself wasn't unusual. But Crabb's reaction was: He stared at Dalhausser through the net, as if he couldn't believe that Dalhausser had the gall to block him. On the very next point, Crabb took another huge swing, unbothered by the block, and scored a point.

That's what excellent hitters do: They respond to getting blocked — which happens to the best of the best — with no drop in confidence. They know getting blocked or dug is simply part of the game, and they continue staying aggressive with their swings and hits, trusting their ability to score.

Playing smart

The best hitters can identify the line between confidence (see the preceding section) and outright stubbornness, and they adjust to what the defense is doing, changing their tactics based on the options available to score. If swinging crosscourt doesn't work because the team is blocking well in that area, an elite hitter quickly adjusts to swing down the line. If the opposing team has trouble digging roll shots or tips, the best hitters notice their struggle and adjust accordingly.

An open area on the court always, always, always exists. The best hitters find it.

Staying high

The net for the women stands 7 feet 4 inches tall, and for the men a hair below 8 feet. The best hitters rarely hit the top of the net — called *the tape*, in volleyball vernacular — they want to stay high with all of their contacts. If they do get *stuffed* at the net — another term for being blocked straight down — at least the net itself doesn't do the stuffing. When a hitter contacts the ball at the peak of their jump, arm fully extended above their head, most blockers find it very difficult to stop that hitter.

With this book, we hope that we can help you become that hitter.

Managing risk

Despite the best efforts of your setter, you don't always get the perfect set:

- **Indoor:** The setter may have to deal with an errant pass and have to set from a less-than-ideal position (too low or high, too close to, or far off the net).
- **Beach:** Wind or rain can affect the set, as can the simple fact that moving in sand is difficult.

Regardless of the cause, you can't get every set perfectly where you want it. The best hitters recognize this fact and change the type of attack from what they initially planned. If you can't safely hit a full-power swing into the court, adjust to a shot or tip. If you think the set drifts too far inside and you can't get your feet in an optimal position for a full approach, take a little pace off.

The best hitters read the situation and adjust accordingly, making the other team beat them — because they don't beat themselves.

Getting to the Point of Preparation

You do the majority of your work as a hitter without the ball. It begins after the pass, with a concept called the *point of preparation*, also referred to the *batter's box* and the *point of hesitation*.

The term you prefer doesn't matter; they all cover the same basic principle, which is the rough starting point for where you begin to approach hitting a set. For this book, we use the term *point of preparation.*

TIP

Every hitter approaches a set differently, depending on size, position (for indoor), and various conditions such as wind or rain (for beach). Consider the following when finding a basic point of preparation:

- **Beach:** Start at arm's length from the net. Take two big steps toward the end of the court, and then a little hop, like you're going to rise up and hit a ball toward the end line.
- **Indoor:** You don't have a uniform point of preparation indoors in the same way that you do on the beach. Indoor has multiple hitting positions (middle, outside, right side, and back row), so your point of preparation depends on a few factors, including the offense that your team runs.

Wherever you end up becomes your rough point of preparation. For bigger individuals, make your point of preparation a bit farther back from the net than smaller players. After you pass, hustle to your point of preparation, pause for a moment to prepare for your approach, and then, right before the ball leaves the setter's hands, slowly — slowly — begin your approach.

The following sections examine your point of preparation and roughly the distance that you want to keep between yourself and your setter, as well as the crucial role of timing.

Determining your distance from the setter

The distance from your setter or partner provides a crucial aspect of your preparation to hit. How you determine the correct distance depends on whether you're playing beach or indoor.

Beach distance

On the beach, whether you're on the left or the right, hitting left-handed or right-handed, start roughly 4 or 5 feet (1.2–1.5 meters) from the setter. This distance gives you enough wiggle room to chase a set that drifts outside or to hustle to one that dies inside. In that position, you greatly increase the odds of getting an easy set to hit. It's a simple setup, and simplicity often gives you the most reliable way to stay a consistent player.

Figure 6-1 illustrates a standard point of preparation on the beach.

FIGURE 6-1: A hitter waiting at their point of preparation, ready to begin making their approach.

Photo by Travis Mewhirter

Indoor distance

In indoor, the specific position that you play largely determines where you find your point of preparation:

- **Opposite hitters:** Attack at the right side of the net and approach that way regardless of where the pass is
- **Outside hitters:** Attack the left side
- **Middles:** Attack from — you guessed it — the middle

Indoor involves much less thinking when it comes to point of preparation because you're a specialist at your given position. You operate in a specific system, so you don't really need to worry about where the setter is setting from: You're going to your specific spot, at your specific time, regardless of the setter's position.

Getting your timing down

You can sum up much of hitting in one word, which you might not expect: Timing. By *timing,* we mean approaching and jumping at the best moment to meet the set in the air. If you approach too early, you end up under the ball and can't get your best hit on it. If you approach too late, you have to deal with the ball too far in front of you, and you can't get your maximum jump and hit. You have to time your approach with your set in both indoor and beach volleyball, although the methods of that timing differ based on whether you're inside or on the beach.

Indoor timing

Timing for indoor hitting is everything because each team customizes each offense to its setter and hitters. In many cases, the coach designs this system. But the hitters and setters must be able to communicate with one another when a set is too high, too low, or in that Goldilocks zone of juuuuust right. When the setter touches the ball, you (as the hitter) must be making a certain step on your approach; otherwise, you throw off the timing of the set and approach — and you have a very unhappy setter and likely a vocally displeased coach.

Depending on your position or your specific system, you make your second or third step when the setter touches the ball. Regardless of your position, however, you always approach a particular spot — because setters *drill out* (practice) location and timing, location and timing, location and timing, over and over and over and over and over and over again.

REMEMBER

The process of perfecting timing is, at the same time, incredibly complex and totally simple. You can't find a formula for developing timing because each setter and hitter, and each offense, develops different timings based on the physical abilities of the players involved. To improve upon your timing, you simply have to rep it out (repeat it) over and over again in practice. Work on every set until it becomes automatic. Work on the offense when everything is perfect — *in system*, as the volleyball lingo goes — and work on the offense when everything is a bit chaotic (called being *out of system*). You want to rep your timing until you need little or no communication with your setter — you just know exactly how the timing works from every position on the court.

Beach timing

Beach requires a much more dynamic range of movements than indoor (which we talk about in the preceding section). You can't expect the ball to go to the exact location at the exact trajectory each time — nor should you — because of the myriad factors that come with playing outdoors (wind, sun, rain, and so on), as well as the fact that you have four fewer players on your side of the net.

REMEMBER

Where indoor hitting focuses primarily on timing, you hear on the beach the three-word phrase *feet to ball* constantly, which refers to getting your feet exactly where you need them in order to jump and hit the ball with all of your offensive options available to you.

HITTERS COME IN ALL SHAPES AND SIZES

Becoming an excellent hitter in volleyball doesn't have a singular path. If you want a rule or a formula to become elite, or even passable, in volleyball, you won't find it here (or anywhere else, for that matter).

Whether you're 5 feet 6 inches or 6 feet 7 inches tall, you can find success using the same principles of attacking that we discuss in this chapter, no matter the surface on which you play.

Consider these big indoor hitters:

- **T.J. DeFalco:** This 6-foot-4-inch hitter (who's listed as 6 feet 5 inches tall on the USA Volleyball website, but you can file that in the category of generous) has a long, languid arm that cracks like a whip. From a pure height perspective, this American is vastly undersized, several inches below your average outside hitter at an Olympic Games. What he lacks in height he atones for in an arm swing that resembles a sort of beautiful violence, extending back, back, back — and then, blink-and-you-miss-it, suddenly it's lashed forward, the ball whistles by your ear and tags the floor, and the United States scores a point. Defenses are left wondering what in the world just happened. He mixes speeds, tempos, and angles. He hits it where the defender isn't, plain and simple.
- **Wilfred Leon:** A Cuban who won a silver medal at the 2010 World Championships, defected to Poland, then won a silver medal at the 2024 Paris Olympic Games. He's 6 feet 7 inches and a towering presence. His arm swing is fast, yes, but nothing like DeFalco's. Volleyball circles describe his swing as heavy. The ball simply explodes off his hand, often detonating on the poor soul in the way. He cares not where defenders stand; he often aims right for them. Where DeFalco relies on deception and variety when it comes to speeds and locations, Leon leans on an astonishing power that he knows no one can defend against if he's not blocked.

These two players play the same position and are considered mostly equals, despite the vastly different approaches they take to accomplish the same goal: hitting the ball and scoring a point as a result of doing so. We talk more about these styles of hitting in the section "Considering Deception versus Power: "Hit It Where They Ain't!"" in this chapter.

If you're here for beach volleyball, allow us to provide two more contrasting success stories, who make up the top-ranked team in the world in women's beach volleyball as of 2025 and offer the sport's most unsolvable riddle:

- **Kristen Nuss:** Nuss is a 5-foot-6-inch sparkplug of a human being. When she graduated from Louisiana State University (LSU) in 2021, she did so as the winningest player in the history of NCAA beach volleyball.

(continued)

(continued)

If you serve to Nuss — and therefore defend her on the third contact — you face a player who seems to see and know everything you're doing before you do it. She hits it where you're not, every time. She's a sniper, a craftswoman. Her shots hit every line and find every gap. She's crisp in her shot placement because she must be.

- **Taryn Brasher:** Nuss's partner, who stands 6 feet 4 inches, is a bruiser. Formerly Taryn Kloth, she played indoors at Creighton University before finishing her collegiate career on the beach at LSU. Brasher and Nuss won their first Association of Volleyball Professionals (AVP) event in Atlanta in 2021 and did the same internationally, in Australia, at a Beach Pro Tour event with the *Fédération Internationale de Volleyball* (FIVB; International Volleyball Federation).

  Brasher's passing isn't as steady as Nuss's (although that's an unfair standard — nobody's passing is as steady as Nuss's). But on a majority of her passes, Brasher is *in system* — the volleyball term for a mostly perfect pass, roughly 3 feet off the net, in the center of the court. For a player her size, she has remarkable control of the ball. Like indoor hitter Wilfredo Leon, Brasher doesn't worry so much about avoiding the defender or the blocker; in fact, she often seeks the hands of smaller blockers and intentionally hits it right off them. She sees defenders standing across from her and blasts it in front of them.

Where Nuss avoids, Brasher seeks. Where Nuss chooses peaceful shots, Brasher chooses power. Same result, different means.

Approaching for the Hit

Your hitting approach is, for the most part, a four-step process, and it comes with two basic general rules: Move slow, faster, fastest; and move small, bigger, biggest.

REMEMBER

Your approach to your point of preparation is the most critical aspect of timing, which we discuss in the section "Getting your timing down" earlier in this chapter. A correct approach gives you optimal timing, and optimal timing leads to optimal hitting, and optimal hitting leads to points scored, and points scored lead to winning.

Everyone loves winning.

The following sections walk you through these steps.

Step 1: Start with a timing step

For right-handed hitters, start with a small step on your right foot, called a *timing step*, which helps you either slow down your approach (if the set is higher than you wanted), speed up (if it looks lower than you initially anticipated), or allow you to stay in cruise control if it's just right. Figure 6-2 shows the first step in a four-step approach.

FIGURE 6-2: A hitter takes a small timing step when beginning the approach.

Photo by Travis Mewhirter

REMEMBER

If you're left-handed — like co-author Travis — take these steps and simply use the opposite foot. So, if a right-handed hitter begins their approach by making a small step with their right foot, you, the lefty, take that timing step with your left foot.

Step 2: Step with your left foot

Take a slightly bigger step than your timing step (see the preceding section) on your left foot, called a *momentum step*. (You can see the momentum step in Figure 6-3.) Now that you see the height of the set, you can begin building your momentum into approaching the ball to maximize your speed and the height of your jump. During this step, bring your arms forward to build upon that momentum and begin your arm swing.

FIGURE 6-3: A hitter takes a momentum step.

Photo by Travis Mewhirter

Step 3: Get your feet to the ball

The step that follows the momentum step (discussed in the preceding section) is known as the *directional step*, which allows you to get your feet to the ball (see Figure 6-4). In a perfect world, you get the set exactly where you want it, every single time. Alas, you don't live in a perfect world.

Even indoors, where you don't have to worry about wind, rain, and sun, the ball doesn't end up in the exact same location every single time, and hitters enthusiastically (and affectionately, of course!) inform their setters when the setters miss their spots. This directional step allows a hitter to take off with their left foot and hop to wherever the set goes. If the ball drifts outside of the intended location, you can use this step to chase it outside; if the set falls short of the target — it's set too far inside, in volleyball parlance — you can use this step to get inside.

The directional step goes hand-in-hand with your ability to *track the set*, meaning observe the trajectory of the ball. If you see that the ball is higher than you anticipated, you must use this directional step to slow down; if the ball is lower, you speed up. If the ball is inside the target zone, you adjust and step into the court; if it's outside, you adjust and move outside. You make all of these adjustments by using this step.

Photo by Travis Mewhirter

FIGURE 6-4: The hitter makes a directional step toward the set.

TIP

Your upper body's position also comes into play. On this directional step, you want your arms to go back, nice and loose, swinging like a pendulum, which keeps your arms loose for the hitting arm swing, as well. (We talk about how to use your arms effectively in the section "Exploring Arm Swing Mechanics" later in this chapter.) Figure 6-5 shows an example of the peak of the jump, with the player's arms loaded correctly prior to hitting.

Step 4: Transfer your forward momentum

In the *gathering step* (which follows the directional step, discussed in the preceding section), you transfer all of that forward momentum that you generate in the preceding three steps into the ground so that you can jump as vertically as possible.

The directional step (Step 3) is a bit of a hop, and here (on your gathering step), you land from that hop slightly staggered, right foot in front of the left. Crouch down, coiling like a spring, gathering all of that momentum, and explode upwards, swinging your arms up as high as you can and then hitting the ball (see the following section). Figure 6-6 illustrates the gathering step.

FIGURE 6-5: The peak of the jump, with the hitting arm cocked back and opposite arm straight out in front.

Photo by Travis Mewhirter

FIGURE 6-6: The gathering step.

Look at the hitter's legs, how they're gathering all of the momentum, coiling down like a spring.

Photo by Travis Mewhirter

THE GOOFY (OR NOT-SO-GOOFY) FOOTED APPROACH

Not all approaches are created equal, or exactly the same. Bigger, more athletic players might begin farther back from the net than shorter, less explosive (they don't jump as high) players.

And some prefer an opposite-step footwork known to most as *goofy-foot.*

A goofy-footed approach is when a right-handed hitter approaches like a conventional left-handed hitter, and vice versa. Why it's called goofy-footed, nobody really knows — it's just different from the norm, so it looks a bit goofy, we suppose.

But the results can be anything but.

Here's a collection of the greatest offensive players in beach volleyball who have approached goofy-footed (and the list could go on):

- 1996 Olympic Gold Medalist Karch Kiraly
- 55-time tournament winner Jose Loiola
- 2025 World Champion Tina Graudina
- 2021 Olympic Silver Medalist Oleg Stoyanovskiy

You might be asking: Do I need to fix my approach if I'm goofy-footed?

Not necessarily, despite what many coaches would have you believe.

As you can see, plenty of successful players have proven you can score while approaching goofy-footed. Let the results guide you: If you're able to score, and your body feels comfortable approaching in a goofy-footed manner, carry on.

Again, we're firm believers in the mindset that there's no one way to do anything — the "right way" is what's uniquely best for you and your body.

So if you're goofy, embrace the goofiness!

Exploring Arm Swing Mechanics

When you envision a perfect arm swing, think about an archer drawing back an arrow: right hand back, elbow cocked, left hand straight ahead. (If you're left-handed, reverse this image.)

If that image doesn't give you a clear idea, think of the Greek god Zeus throwing his thunderbolt.

When you think of the arm swing, you probably picture only the product at the peak of it, when you're the archer about to release their arrow or Zeus about to throw the thunderbolt.

In reality, as we explain here, the arm swing involves much more than that moment. Each step of your approach involves your upper body, as well — particularly, your arms. You don't approach by using just your feet; you use your arms to both build momentum and prepare to use your arm as a weapon ready to hit the ball and score.

Breaking down the arm swing

As you begin your approach (see the section "Approaching for the Hit" earlier in this chapter), your arms drift slightly forward with your momentum step, creating force throughout the *kinetic chain* (your body's sequence of movements) while you get into your directional step, as shown in Figure 6-7 — refer to the section "Step 3: Get your feet to the ball" earlier in this chapter.

With the directional step, your arms swing backwards while you coil down, preparing to explode and rise up for the hit (see Figure 6-8).

REMEMBER

While you rise, you do so with both arms raised into the air (see Figure 6-9). One of the most common mistakes that new volleyball players make happens when they leave their opposite arm hanging down. With that arm down, they lose a tremendous amount of torque that they need in the arm swing for both power and accuracy.

While you get closer to the peak of your jump, you become the archer/Zeus, pulling your right arm back, with your elbow staying about the same height as your ear, forming a roughly 90-degree angle between your hand, elbow, and shoulder. Meanwhile, your left hand remains straight out in front of you. Refer to Figure 6-10 to see all of this positioning put together.

You're now prepared to hit.

FIGURE 6-7: The arms drift slightly forward while they build momentum.

Photo by Travis Mewhirter

Look at the hitter's arms, how they've gone all the way back to harness all the momentum they've built in their approach.

FIGURE 6-8: Arms drift backwards while the hitter coils down into their approach.

Photo by Travis Mewhirter

FIGURE 6-9: Both arms come up while you make your jump.

Photo by Travis Mewhirter

FIGURE 6-10: The hitter at the peak of their jump, ready to hit.

FP Creative Stock/Adobe Stock Photos

Becoming a whip

Many new or uninformed players view the arm swing as a club, with all the power coming from the arm itself. Instead, think of the arm swing, and your body, like a whip: The handle of the whip is your hips, while your fingertips form the edge of the whip.

You initiate the swing, then, not with your right arm, but with your hips and left arm (the hips pull and the arm's movement crunches the body down), starting the kinetic chain of the arm swing. While you tuck your left elbow down, your right arm naturally rises, staying relaxed, in the same way that the head of a whip stays relaxed when swinging.

TIP

Ever try to whip a hotel towel? It works best when everything is relaxed, relaxed, relaxed — until you're ready to snap and crack it on your unsuspecting roommate. Your right arm is the hotel towel. And while you extend higher, you want to get your full hand on the ball, wrapping over top of it to create the topspin that makes it fly true to its target, finishing with that hotel-towel crack.

Taylor Crabb, a 2021 Olympian on the beach and the 2013 American Volleyball Coaches Association (AVCA) Player of the Year indoors as an undersized outside hitter, estimates that 70 percent of the power of your arm swing comes from your core, not the arm itself. That's the power of the whip.

After you contact the ball, you can allow your right arm to finish naturally near your left hip, where your pocket might be in a pair of pants, following through without resistance.

Shaping your hands

At this point, perhaps you're feeling a bit like Ricky Bobby in the movie *Talladega Nights*, doing his first interview, wondering what in the world he's supposed to do with his hands during an interview.

TIP

New volleyball players often ask how they're supposed to shape their hands when they hit. Think of ball-shaped hands. Hit the ball with your dominant hand, maintaining contact with the ball, so that the ball goes into your non-dominant hand and comes to a stop. Now, take your dominant hand away, keeping the shape of it after it hit the ball into your other hand. Figure 6-11 shows you how to shape your hand while hitting.

That's roughly the handshape to use when you contact the ball: not with a fist, karate chop, or club, but with a ball-shaped hand.

FIGURE 6-11: What a well-shaped hand looks like prior to hitting a ball.

Photo by Travis Mewhirter

WHAT'S WITH ALL THE GRUNTING?

If you tune into the Olympics every four years to watch beach and indoor volleyball, as tens of millions do, you hear quite a bit of grunting after serves and big swings. What gives? Is that player being showy, bombastic, or just kind of obnoxious?

In fact, when a player lets out a grunt, that generally means that their breath and arm swing are connected, so at the point of contact, they exhale all that oxygen at once.

So, in that case, grunting is a good thing, even if it makes you self-conscious.

This grunt scenario goes across virtually all sports in which a player makes a form of explosive contact: those hissing piston sounds of boxers after landing punches, the grunts and screams from tennis players, the guttural roars from shotput and discus throwers.

If the oxygen is coming out of you so quickly that you feel the need to grunt after a swing or jump serve, you're on the right track.

Considering Deception versus Power: "Hit It Where They Ain't!"

Kent Steffes is one of the greatest beach volleyball players of all time. But he's a realist, and physically — standing 6 feet 4 inches, with a decent but mostly average vertical leap and a hitting power that could best be described as okay — Steffes was no freakish specimen of size that you often see in the sports world. What, then, set him apart? What put the fear of God in his opponents to never, ever, ever let him touch the ball if they could help it?

"Volleyball's a simple game," Steffes told co-author Travis Mewhirter. "Just hit it where they ain't." He's being coy, yes, but he also has a point.

Table 6-1 breaks down some of the differences between attacking on the beach versus doing so indoors:

TABLE 6-1 Attacking in Beach and Indoor Volleyball

Volleyball Type	Number of Opponents	Play Area	Style
Beach	One blocker and one defender	A beach that has a lot of open area	A finesse game, with looping shots into corners or chips around the defense
Indoor	Up to three blockers and three defenders	A gym that has precious few open spots	Mostly a power game

To hit it where they aren't, you must know where the defender is and where they aren't. That's no easy feat when considering all the steps that you have before you: Approach for the hit, track the set, take a peek to see what's on the other side of the court, jump — and then make the right decision on top of all that.

Meanwhile, the opposing team does everything that they can to throw you off. They start in one position and, at the last second, dart into a different one. They make hitting it where they aren't as difficult as possible. (Chapter 11 discusses defense in greater detail.)

So, how do you know where they are and where they aren't? The following sections explain how to see the defense and find the open spaces on the court to score.

Finding the seams and avoiding the block

You need to have vision, the ability to see what's happening on the other side of the net. Vision, of course, begins with the pass, which we discuss in Chapter 9.

If you pass in front of you, between 2 and 4 feet off the net, then everything involved in the play remains in front of you, which you need so that you can see the defense (which is, of course, in front of you). Pass behind you, and now you have to track a ball that's coming from the back half of the court, which means you lose sight of everything on the other side of the net — all the information that you need so that you can know where they are and where they ain't.

After you pass in front of you, you begin your approach. When you reach your point of preparation (which we talk about in the section "Getting to the Point of Preparation" earlier in this chapter), you can take a look at the other side of the net, determining how the defense is setting up, which gives you an indicator of their base defense. Where the blocker and defender begin can tell you an awful lot that you want to know:

- If the defender begins in your angle, or across the court from you, the blocker is likely blocking your line attacks.
- If you have the defender in front of you or down your line, the blocker is likely blocking your angle or cross-court attacks.

While you approach (discussed in the section "Approaching for the Hit" earlier in this chapter), you can keep most of your attention on your setter and the ball, but out of your peripheral vision, stay aware of any movement on the other side of the net.

REMEMBER

Although observing where the other team's players are sounds simple (really, it is), it's perhaps the most difficult offensive skill in the sport of beach volleyball, requiring tremendous passing control, the ability to observe two things at the same time (the ball and the defense), and the quicksilver decision-making to take in all that information and make the right choice — all in tenths of a second. You have to hit it where they aren't — or you can take a page out of the indoor playbook: Just hit it.

Playing the waiting game

As a hitter, you have to keep the ball in front of you. If you overrun the set, so the ball is behind your head, you lose all sight of the defense and also lose much of your power — a nightmare scenario for an offensive player. If you can keep the ball slightly in front of you, directly over your hitting shoulder, you can see everything you need. So to become an elite offensive player, you have to wait, wait, and wait some more on your approach, and then get your feet to the ball.

TIP

Here's a helpful saying for keeping the ball in front of you in beach volleyball: At the beach, when you're late, you're on time. This saying means that you should wait longer than you think necessary to begin your approach.

If you keep the ball in front of you and don't detect movement out of your peripheral vision, simply hit it where they ain't, based on the information you gathered at your point of preparation (discussed in the section "Getting to the Point of Preparation" earlier in this chapter). If you do detect movement, do the opposite: Hit the ball where the defender started because you know, based on their movement, that they're no longer there.

THE DREAM OF AN OUTSIDE HITTER

Mike Lambert thought he was dreaming. The best kind of dream, and one that would reoccur every time he touched the ball when he made the switch from indoor to beach volleyball in 2002. He had to face only one blocker.

From 1995 through 2000, Lambert was one of the most feared indoor volleyball outside hitters in the world, making his first Olympics in 1996 while still competing for Stanford University, where he won a National Championship in 1997 and was named Most Outstanding Player. He made another Games in 2000, in Sydney, while playing professionally in Italy, in the highest league in the world (SuperLega). His reputation preceded him, as it does with most Hall of Fame hitters, and teams respected his abilities, routinely sending at least two, usually three, blockers to attempt to stop him. Even then, it typically didn't go well for the defense.

"I'd be thrilled if I got to go against a two-man block and then a one-man block. It's 'Oh, this is a freakin' dream — I can go here, I can go there,' when you go to the beach and that's all you have to hit against," he said on the *SANDCAST* podcast with me (Travis).

On the beach, you have to contend with just one blocker and one defender. You can find generous swaths of court in which to put the ball.

Indoor? Not so much. With six total players, and sometimes three blockers to work around, indoor attacks are less about finesse and more about power. So everything about offense in indoor is slightly, but not entirely, different than beach.

Finishing the Attack: The Step Close

The final phase of a volleyball hit is called the *step close*, the final step of your approach, where you gather all of that momentum and harness it into your best attack, one that you hope scores.

Like anything in life, you can have the strongest start and the best middle section, but if you don't finish strong, it's all for naught. The same goes for your approach: You can have the most patient point of preparation, the smoothest steps, the perfect arm movement — but if you don't finish with a strong step close, you don't put yourself in a position to score.

The following sections show you how to step close with power and efficiency.

Attacking with power

In beach, your final steps — the *step close* — maximizes your potential for vertical height and contacting the ball at the highest point that you can. Given that the surface (the sand) is moving and resisting your every step, you have to minimize *broad jumping* (when your vertical jump involves forward motion and takes height out of it); ideally, you jump almost straight up and down, so your feet land in the very footprints they left when you launched yourself up.

If you go too broad on your broad jump — the biggest mistake indoor players transitioning to beach make — you lose height on your jump and hit the ball too low, either bringing the blocker into play by giving them a low swing or hitting the ball into the net.

REMEMBER

On the beach, broad jumping can cripple your game as a hitter. Indoors? You can use it as a weapon.

In indoor, broad jumping adds velocity and power to your approach. Indoor players in the back row may take off from behind the 10-foot line (also known as the 3-meter line, which separates the court in terms of front and back) and contact the ball just a few feet off the net, harnessing all that forward momentum and kinetic energy, and whipping it into an explosive hit. Players in the front row don't need such an extended broad jump, but they follow the same idea: You want your jump to push you forward, adding momentum into the swing to increase power.

Attacking with purpose

The most common attack in indoor is a high, deep swing into the back meter of the court. ***Remember:*** You have multiple blockers in front of you, so the opposing team will block anything low either on your side of the net for a point or in a controlled manner to make it a *transition play* (moving to an offensive play) — also likely resulting in a point for the other team.

Keep your swing as high as possible, aiming for the deep corners of the court or the *seams* (the *gaps*) in between the defenders and blockers.

Beach players can get their purpose in attacking from the section "Considering Deception versus Power: "Hit It Where They Ain't!"" earlier in this chapter.

Mixing things up with off-speed shots

Make powerful swings your first option. And make them your second and third options, too. Powerful swings set up your *off-speed attacks,* which are tips, roll shots, or anything that comes with less pace — and, ideally, more precision — than your powerful swings.

Off-speed and deception attacks are mostly used in beach volleyball (which we talk about in the section "Considering Deception versus Power: "Hit It Where They Ain't!"" earlier in this chapter).

TIP

In indoor, a properly timed off-speed attack, either a tip shot or a roll shot (see the following sections), gives you an excellent way to keep the defense on guard, not knowing exactly what to expect.

Think about a baseball pitcher who throws a 100-mile-per-hour fastball: Although he uses that pitch as his foundation, when hitters prepare for that speed, it sets up his change-up or other off-speed pitches effectively because they're expecting and preparing for a different ball.

You can also use these off-speed attacks when you don't have your set where you want it, you're off balance, or something in the play goes imperfectly and you need to dial back the risk.

The tip shot

The most commonly used off-speed shot is the *tip shot,* where the hitter tips the ball by using their fingertips to an open area of the court, usually just over or around the blockers.

Say that the set is too tight, so the opposing team will likely block a swing: You can open your hand and simply tip the ball anywhere you want. Typically, you can effectively tip the ball short around the wall of blockers because the defense now anchors deep, anticipating more of all those deep swings you've been hitting.

REMEMBER

Indoor and beach volleyball have a big difference: In beach volleyball, you aren't allowed to tip. Tipping gives far too big an advantage on the beach because you have so much space to work with and fewer opponents to defend. Tipping the ball with your open hand provides an extremely controlled attack deemed too easy on the beach, so the FIVB made tipping illegal, which organizations in beach volleyball have widely adopted since. The FIVB replaced tipping with a play called the *pokie,* where you use your knuckles instead of your fingertips to poke the ball around the block.

The roll shot

You can use a roll shot, another off-speed attack designed for precision, as a tool that you set up by using power as your first option. In a *roll shot,* you perform the set up and execution of your hit the same as when you use your big, powerful swing: You have an explosive approach, swing your arm so that it looks like you're cranking back for a mighty spike — but then you roll your hand over the top the ball and attempt to drop it into the middle of the other side of court, over the blocker and just in front of the defense (who is ideally ready for a big swing).

A key difference in hitting a roll shot versus a regular attack (see the section "Attacking with power" earlier in this chapter), involves how you contact the ball. With your regular swing, you use your whole hand — and specifically your palm — to produce power. With a roll shot, you use the pads of your fingers to roll over the ball, aiming for the upper third, making the ball travel in a softer, slower arc. It's not about power, but about placement and finesse.

Incorporating Hitting Drills into Practice

At the end of the day, becoming an excellent hitter isn't rocket science. The more volleyballs you hit, the better you become at hitting a volleyball. Simple as that. We have a couple of drills that we love that can both improve your hitting skills and make for a ton of fun while doing it.

H-O-R-S-E

You may be familiar with the game that people play on basketball courts all over the world, H-O-R-S-E. You can play the same game (and have a lot of fun) on a volleyball court, as well. You can play indoors or out, and with any number of players (even just one if you're competitive enough with yourself!).

Follow these steps for a two-person volleyball H-O-R-S-E game:

1. **Pick a shot or swing that you want to hit.**
2. **Make a target zone on the court.**

   You can use a cone, hula hoop, patch of sand, T-shirt — anything that denotes the target.
3. **Toss a ball to the other player.**

   That player sets the ball to you.
4. **Attempt to hit the ball into the target.**

   If you miss the target, you get a letter (an H in the first round), and you jump to Step 6.
5. **If you hit the ball into the target, the other player has to also hit the ball into the target.**

   If they miss, they get a letter.
6. **A player chooses a new target.**

   Which player gets to choose depends on whether a player missed the shot in this round:

   - The other player gets to choose if you missed in Step 4 or if you both hit the target.
   - You get to choose if the other player missed in Step 5.
7. **Repeat Steps 1 through 8 with a new target to hit each time.**

   The game ends when someone loses by spelling out H-O-R-S-E.

You can modify this game so that, rather than getting a letter if you miss, you get a point if you hit the target. Play to however many points you want.

TIP

If you want to level up the drill, have a third player serve the ball to you, and then you have to pass to the other player and then hit that player's set to you. This variation makes the game much more difficult and more like playing an actual volleyball game.

Wall ball

For this drill, which you can do by yourself, you need only yourself, a ball, a hard floor, and a wall that can take some hits. Follow these steps:

1. **Stand about 10 to 15 feet (3–4.5 meters) from the wall.**
2. **Toss a ball to yourself.**

   Act like you're setting yourself.
3. **Hit the ball into the ground in front of you.**

   Contact the ball as high as you can. You want the ball to bounce off the floor and hit the wall so that the rebound off the wall acts as a set to you.
4. **Hit the rebound from the wall back into the ground.**
5. **Repeat Step 4 until you're satisfied.**

This drill has a number of benefits:

- » You can get a lot of repetitions without needing an entire bag of balls.
- » You have to work to get your feet to the ball, tracking the rebound off of the wall to put yourself in a position to hit the ball again.
- » Your hand contact on the ball becomes excellent in the span of 10 to 15 minutes of practice.
- » You get more hits during this solo drill than you do in most full practices with a team.

IN THIS CHAPTER

» Appreciating the need for setting

» Making yourself a great setter

» Setting in ideal (and less-than-ideal) situations

» Examining the different types of sets

» Improving your setting with important drills

Chapter 7

Assisting Your Hitters for the Kill: Setting

You can make a firm argument that setting is the most important skill in the game of volleyball, whether in indoor or beach. A *set* is the second contact in a traditional three-contact offense that includes a pass, set, and hit. In other words, you, the setter, get your hitter ready to make a successful attack by using either your platform or hands to put the ball in the optimal location for your hitter to terminate the rally, score your team a point, and get the kill.

This chapter goes into both the value of being an accurate and consistent setter, as well as how to become that individual for your team. Nothing can make an offense flow better than a reliable setter because they can take a pass — any pass — and still put their hitter in a position to score a point. And nothing can make an offense stop in its tracks like an unreliable setter can.

The good news? By reading this chapter and showing the initiative to improve your game, you're well on your way to becoming the reliable setter every team needs.

Understanding Why Setting Is Essential

Being able to effectively *set* — taking the pass and either using your forearms or hands to send the ball to the hitter in a position so that they can get a kill — makes you a great partner on the beach or an excellent teammate indoors.

You can argue that setting is the most important skill for a volleyball player to have because a bad setter can botch even the best pass, whereas an excellent setter can capitalize on that perfect pass, clean up sloppy passes, and bring the hitter back *in system,* which is the precise location where they want the set to go. (We discuss setting in system in the section "When everything's going as planned — in-system setting" later in this chapter.)

Everyone — literally everyone — wants to play with a good setter. And everyone — literally everyone (middle blockers included) — needs to be able to set.

And if you're an exceptional hitter (a position that we talk about in Chapter 6), on the beach, you have no choice but to also become an exceptional setter. You can be the most spectacular hitter on the planet and still be an objectively bad beach volleyball player if you don't also have setting skills that allow your partner — and therefore your team — to score on a consistent basis.

Opposing teams see you annihilate balls in warmups or hear of your reputation as a hitter of Herculean power — and they simply don't give you the ball. They serve your partner in beach, and suddenly you — the big imposing hitter, armed with your 40-inch vertical and massive spikes that have indefensible power — get taken out of the game. The opposing team laughs because you get no chance to use all of that power.

All you can do is set.

Don't feel discouraged if you find yourself in this situation. It's a beach volleyball story as old as time. You have a simple — although not easy — fix to this universal problem: Become an elite setter. Develop something to threaten them with by developing into a consistent setter who helps make your partner as good on offense as you are. Do your job as setter well enough, and you might even see a few serves yourself.

Recognizing the Traits of a Great Setter

Setters are more than just athletes. They act as the nucleus of the team; everything flows through them. Hitters are only as good as their setters, and teams are only ever really as successful as their hitters. An elite setter doesn't necessarily need to make phenomenal, highlight-reel sets all the time — although those kinds of sets are nice — they mostly have to avoid mistakes. *Consistency* describes the best setters because a consistent set allows a hitter to make a consistent approach to the ball, and a consistent approach allows for consistent hits, and consistent hits allow for consistent scoring, and consistent scoring allows for consistent winning. Here are some traits that we notice in great setters.

Leading the team: The quarterback of the offense

A great setter needs to have the ability to run the offense and earn their team a point. The setter runs the offense by deciding which player to set (after identifying which hitter is hot or which hitter will get the weakest block from the opposing team) and figuring out which tempo or height of set can most likely lead to a kill. In indoor, players often refer to setters as the quarterbacks of the offense because they make the tricky and vital decision of whom to set.

Like a quarterback on a football team, the indoor volleyball setter has their primary target (the outside hitter), their secondary option (the opposite, also known as the right-side hitter), and a power option (the middle). (We talk about these positions in Chapter 5.) In indoor volleyball, think of the back-row hitter like a quarterback's running back. And like a quarterback who can also run, setters can choose to go on offense themselves, making dumps and attacks of their own on the second contact. In volleyball terminology, when the setter attacks on the second contact, that decision is called *options* because the setter has the option to set or attack.

REMEMBER

Whether the setter is the official captain of a team doesn't so much matter because setters are, without question, the leaders of the team. This role is as much emotional as it is physical. If a hitter is struggling, the setter needs to both emotionally regulate the hitter and put their sets in even more precise locations so that the hitter can be in the best position to succeed. If the back row passers are struggling in indoor, the setter needs to hold them accountable and maneuver them in a way to bring the passes back to a consistent location.

The setter acts as the brains and the heart of the team, both the CEO and the janitor cleaning up the mess.

Being the brains of the team

A great setter needs brains. Setters are stereotyped as smarter than their hitting brethren, mere Neanderthals who see ball, hit ball. Setters need to know where to set the ball — where the defense is weakest — putting their hitters in the most advantageous position to get a kill. To be a setter, you need to be both mentally and physically tough. A slightly inaccurate set to the optimal hitter who has only one blocker in front of them is vastly better than a perfect set into a *triple-block*, where the hitter faces three opposing blockers.

In beach, you don't have as complicated decision-making when it comes to setting. Only one player can set, which makes setting equally important and, depending on your view of things, more difficult. A setter on the beach must put a ball into a target the size of a basketball hoop in wind, rain, sun — and, yes, even snow every now and again — while moving on a surface that changes and resists their every step.

Attacking as a setter

Another important trait that a great setter has is the kill mentality. When they're in the front row, they not only see themselves as having the option to get a kill, they also can and will take aggressive swings as powerful as any hitter, often with only a single blocker or no blockers at all in front of them.

Consider Camryn Haworth's stat line from her final year at Indiana University in 2024. At first glance, you might understandably confuse her for the second outside hitter or an opposite. She left the school as its all-time leader in aces and, in her final season, finished third in kills. As a setter.

You may be thinking, "Isn't her job to facilitate the offense, to set the hitters?" Yes, but the setter can be as effective a hitter as anyone on the court, as evidenced by Haworth's stat line (see Figure 7-1).

If the setter begins in the front row, they can jump and attack:

- **The dynamic option of a lefty setter:** A lefty such as Haworth becomes extra dangerous because the ball doesn't have to travel across the plane of her shoulders before she hits it on the second contact; she can pick it off quickly, before the defense has time to make a read on her.
- **Taking the option:** If the pass is too tight to the net, a setter frequently hits on their own — called an *option attack* — as opposed to setting their hitters.
- **Dumping the ball:** Often, setters don't even need to hit the ball to score; they can perform a *dump,* in which they rise up and put both hands on the ball, looking like they're going to set. Instead of setting, however, they redirect the ball over the net to find an open area of the court.

FIGURE 7-1: Camryn Haworth attacking as a setter.

Published with permission from Camryn Haworth

REMEMBER

Indoors, a setter can attack only if they begin in the front row. If they're in a back-row rotation, they can't attack with the ball entirely above the height of the net, so they're really only a threat to option when they play in a front-row rotation.

THE FOUNTAIN OF YOUTH

Adam Roberts is, at the time of this writing, a 49-year-old man who looks 27 — and will probably look 27 if you pick up this book ten years from now. He has found the fountain of youth, and that fountain of youth is beach volleyball.

A big part of what's keeping him forever young is playing with good setters. Hear us out.

Roberts played his first professional event in 1998. In 2025, he was still playing roughly the same style of game he started with nearly three decades prior. He's 6 feet 1 inch and athletic — he played basketball at Elon, a small university in North Carolina. But, like any great athlete, he also understands the limits of his own game. Offensively, he has what can be described as a limited hitting window, meaning if his teammate doesn't place the ball exactly where he needs it, he has a hard time scoring.

(continued)

(continued)

There's no shame in this limitation. A *hitter's window* is the rough area in which the setter can set a ball and the hitter can get a kill out of it, no problem. Some hitters, such as Wilfredo Leon (whom we talk about in Appendix B), have a window roughly the size of the gym in which they're playing. Other hitters, such as Roberts or the 5-foot-6-inch dynamo Kristen Nuss, don't have such a luxury. Instead, they have elite setters who play alongside them — because if they don't have that support, they don't last long.

At the beginning of one season, Roberts polled a few players, asking their opinions on whom he should play with. A bigger, up-and-coming talent was recommended, Andy Benesh. Came with a huge serve. Was such a force offensively that nobody would dare serve to him. Adam smiled and wondered the all-important question: Can he set?

Oh, could he. Benesh has had success with every partner (including Roberts) because, absolutely, he can hit with high efficiency, but he's always, always, always making his partners better by being an elite setter. Here's a photo with Roberts and co-author Travis Mewhirter after winning a tournament in Myrtle Beach, South Carolina.

Setting a Volleyball: The How-To

No matter whether you play indoor or beach, the how-to for setting is the same. If you're using your hands to set — which happens 99 percent of the time indoors and becomes a personal preference on the beach — you want the ball to ideally come at you so that it would hit you square in the nose if you dropped your hands and let the ball through.

REMEMBER

The most important piece of advice when setting in indoor volleyball is simple: Keep the ball slightly in front of you because it allows you to push the ball any direction that you choose with relative ease. This positioning keeps all your options open: the outside, the opposite, the middle, and the back row. These options, in turn, keep the defense frozen and unable to read which hitter you're going to set.

On the beach, this positioning also keeps your options open, whether your hitter is running to the far end of the court, behind you, or just a few feet in front of you. Because your weight is still behind the ball, you can also push the ball through the wind if you need to.

The following sections walk you through how to execute the two ways to set: the hand set and the bump set. We also discuss the importance of practicing setting.

Using your hands: The hand set

Hand setting isn't much different than shooting a jump shot in basketball, and the balanced use of both lower and upper body is much the same. In the same way that you don't see any basketball players beginning their shot from behind their heads — we leave that to soccer throw-ins — you don't see setters starting their set from behind their heads, either.

You use a hand set when you're *in system* — when the passer passes the ball to an ideal location and your offense is running the way it's supposed to.

Here are some tips to help you hand set:

- **Keep the ball in front of you.** This positioning allows you to use your weight to maintain your full range of setting possibilities and ensures that you can make your sets as accurate and consistent as possible.
- **Shape your hands like you're holding a ball.** You can get what volleyballers call *ball-shaped hands* by grabbing the ball from the sides and wrapping your hands around it, then dropping the ball without moving your hands. Use that hand shape when you set; like the hands shown in Figure 7-2.

FIGURE 7-2: Shaping your hands like you're holding a volleyball.

Photo by Travis Mewhirter

- **Find your comfortable position.** Some players set with their elbows wide, some do it with their elbows narrow and tucked. It's mostly a matter of personal preference, and your hitters don't really care what you look like, as long as you get the ball into the proper location. Test out what elbow position works best for you.

TIP

Grab a ball, find a wall, and set the ball into the wall, experimenting and exploring all the various positions. Find what works for you. And then practice. Set 100 balls before you fall asleep. Set while watching movies (like beach volleyball great Phil Dalhausser did — see the sidebar "Quiet setting: The Phil Dalhausser path to mastery," in this chapter). Set as much as you can until you find your sweet spot. Volleyball (like all sports) is both highly personalized and highly technical, and although we can give you a general fundamental principle to a skill such as setting, the exact answer for each athlete is an infinite range of movements. Find what works for you when you use ball-shaped hands and have the ball slightly in front of you when you hand set.

An excellent and common cue for setters is to grab the ball and act like you're about to drink a 2-liter of soda (see Figure 7-3). That positioning can provide you with a reliable indicator of how to hand-set.

Addressing illegal contacts

If you want to make someone angry or stir the pot for a fiery conversation, just whisper the word "double" into a setter's ear and see what happens. You can't easily find a more contentious topic in the sport of volleyball than doubles and lifts:

- **Double:** When the ball enters and leaves your hands at uneven times, one hand before or after the other. By rule, the ball must come in and out of both hands simultaneously.

FIGURE 7-3: Set like you're drinking a 2-liter bottle of soda.

Photo by Travis Mewhirter

- **Lift:** When the setter catches and effectively throws the ball to their hitter. Rulebooks also use the term *prolonged contact,* but the common vernacular is, simply, *lift.* Refs typically judge a lift by whether the ball comes to a complete stop in the setter's hands before they release it for the set.

The referee gets a lot of room for interpretation when it comes to whether a ball is double contacted (or lifted) or not, and a lot of that room is quite vague. The double contact rules grew vague to the point that, in 2024, the NCAA mostly removed double contacts on the second contact (as long as the ball stays on the offense's side of the net). Lifts are also a gray area, and every ref will call it differently. In indoors, lifts are called very strictly, while on the beach, setters are given more leniency with how long the ball can legally remain in their hands.

The Beach Pro Tour experimented with changing the double contact rule briefly at three professional events in 2025. Needless to say, the reaction on social media to the proposed change was almost universally opposed. Players brought out their pitchforks and torches, and they rioted — figuratively speaking, of course — to get the rule restored to its usual form.

WARNING

In reality, describing any double contact rule in a print publication is difficult because whatever we write here will likely be outdated by the time you pick this book up.

Let us make a clear distinction between indoor and beach volleyball in regards to double contacts:

- **Indoor:** Multiple contacts in one attempt are legal, as long as the ball stays on the team's side.
- **Beach:** Multiple contacts, regardless of the play situation, are highly illegal on the beach and always qualify as a double. Because you have so much more open space on the beach, this rule prevents an unfair advantage because the setter could redirect the ball with both hands in so many different ways.

Here are a few other differences between indoor and beach volleyball when it comes to double contacts and lifts:

- **Tipping:** Indoor setters can tip the ball across the net by using one hand; beach players can't.
- **Dumping:** Indoor setters can dump the ball across the net by using two hands; beach players can't.
- **Holding:** Beach players can hold onto the ball for a beat longer than indoor players can; indoor setters must essentially flick the ball or risk being called for a lift.
- **Calling doubles:** Indoor setters have more lenient rules on what gets called a double; beach standards are traditionally much stricter, although the two are getting closer because beach continues to get more lenient at the time we're writing.

Playing with no setting rules

One of the biggest, if not the biggest, hindrances to up-and-coming players learning to hand set is the fear of being called for a double contact (discussed in the preceding section). If we were the czars of indoor and beach volleyball across the United States, we'd simply remove the double contact rule until the varsity level of high school so that kids could learn how to set fearlessly. Beach volleyball legend Phil Dalhausser, a 2008 Olympic gold medalist and one of the greatest players of all time, learned to set so fearlessly because he didn't have the shadow of doubles hanging over him.

When Dalhausser, who we identify in Appendix B as one of the game's greatest, and his teammates trained in Myrtle Beach, South Carolina, Adam Roberts, the leader of the group, put a rule in place: No doubles would be called. This freedom allowed the team members Dalhausser, Nick Lucena, and Matt Heath to experiment with their hands without fear. They tested the range of their abilities, when they could get a ball to come out clean and when they couldn't. They pushed the perimeters of their comfort zones, finding touch from all areas of the court, setting from all sorts of angles that they'd never try otherwise.

However, you do have to set with the intention for it to come out clean. It just doesn't matter, in that training, whether it actually is a clean play or not. If you're simply throwing up anything and everything without a care, you're not improving; you're just goofing.

So when you're going out to play with your friends on the beach, give it a try: Drop the double rules for a few games — then put them back in place and see how it goes. You'll improve, guaranteed.

Relying on your platform: The bump set

The same principle of setting that applies to hand setting (see the section "Using your hands: The hand set" earlier in this chapter) — the transfer of energy from back to front — applies to bump setting, too. *Bump setting* is simply passing the ball with your *platform* (your forearms) to the hitter's preferred location.

To bump set, follow these steps:

1. **Keep the ball in front of you.**

   If you have the ball in front of you, you can step into the ball to set, allowing for the transfer of energy from back to front.

2. **Position your body in relation to the ball.**

   Unlike hand setting, you don't want the ball to land on your nose. Position yourself for a bump set so that if you stick your arms out straight, the ball would land in your hands.

3. **Crouch slightly down, moving the energy from your back leg to your front leg, and have the ball bounce off your platform to your target.**

   You form your platform in the same way that you pass (see Chapter 9 for more on passing).

   Figure 7-4 shows how a bump set looks.

REMEMBER

You usually see a bump set indoors in relatively desperate times — when the offense is *out of system*, meaning the pass is well off the intended target. (We talk about out-of-system setting in the section "Transitioning and out-of-system setting" later in this chapter.) The team is scrambling, and whoever makes the second contact uses a bump set, rather than a hand set, either because they physically can't get their hands on the ball (if they're diving, for example) or the distance the ball needs to travel is too far for the limited power of a hand set.

FIGURE 7-4: A bump set.

allejo123/Adobe Stock Photos

QUIET SETTING: THE PHIL DALHAUSSER PATH TO MASTERY

Phil Dalhausser will go down as one of the greatest players to ever play beach volleyball. Standing 6 feet 9 inches tall and weighing less than your average broomstick, his peers in professional beach volleyball dubbed him the Thin Beast. We mention his accomplishments in Appendix B.

Dalhausser wasn't always good at volleyball, or really even passable. He was big, yes — but like many big athletes entering a new sport, he was unrefined. Adam Roberts (see the sidebar "The fountain of youth," in this chapter, for his story) saw the massive potential in Dalhausser and his usual partner, Nick Lucena, when they began to enter small-time tournaments up and down the East Coast in the early 2000s. (Lucena would eventually compete in two Olympics himself, both with Dalhausser.) So Roberts invited them to move in with him in Myrtle Beach, South Carolina, where they could train together every day.

Dalhausser dropped his job working construction and made the move. But he's a fidgety guy, Dalhausser, and not one to simply sit with nothing to do. And here he was, now living with a trio of roommates — Roberts, Lucena, and Matt Heath — who, after training a couple hours each day, could (and would) hang out and watch movies the rest of the day and night. So they'd put on a movie, and Dalhausser would fidget. With a volleyball.

But he's also a nice guy, so he would do his best to set as quietly as he could to avoid disrupting the viewing experiences of his buddies. Imagine the compound interest of doing that practice, day after day after day, all after training for two hours every morning.

Dalhausser focused on quiet setting throughout his decorated career. When the ball smacks into your hands, making noise, you probably bobble it, resulting in either a double or just a mishandled and therefore inaccurate set. But if it comes in quiet, both hands softly corral the ball and release it together, without a sound, which indicates that you have a soft — and, most likely, accurate — touch.

Playing In and Out of System

Ideally, you want to be *in system,* meaning you get a perfect pass right in your hands. This type of pass presents you with your full array of options as a setter. However, you certainly can't always be in system because opposing servers do what they can to make a pass not ideal. If you're setting, you sometimes get a pass somewhere other than exactly where you want it, meaning you're now officially *out of system.*

TIP

As a setter, you must always aim to *better the ball,* meaning improve on the pass, no matter what kind of pass you get.

The following sections take a closer look at the ins and outs of in-system and out-of-system setting.

When everything's going as planned — in-system setting

In-system setting is the ideal environment in which to set, when the pass is perfect and you have all of your options available to you as a setter. All of your hitters are making their approaches, knowing that a perfect set is much more likely, because you have the ball right where you need it to set them up for a thunderous swing.

In indoor volleyball, a setter's starting location also called the *base position* depends on the rotation they're in. Regardless of rotation, however, they remove themselves from most any possibility of passing. After all, the setter wants to set the pass, not pass it themselves. The setter ends up in the same location, regardless of rotation, to put themselves in the best position to play the second contact of an offense:

- A few feet off the net
- On the right side of the court
- A few feet in from the antenna

This position allows for maximum flexibility in whom the setter sets.

The setter stays on the right side of the court because they

- » Face the outside hitter, their primary target, which makes for an easier, more consistent set.
- » Can defend, blocking the opposing team's outside hitter. For this reason, a setter needs good blocking skills.

In beach, neither player knows, until the other team serves, who will pass and who will set. If you see that your partner is getting served, follow these steps:

1. **When you see that the opposing team is serving to your partner, get to a position roughly in the middle of the court.**

   Position yourself perhaps 10 feet (3 meters) off the net and halfway along the net so that you can get to any pass, whether it's in system or out.

2. **Angle your chest or core to face your target.**

   Keep the ball in front of you.

3. **Place your net foot forward.**

   Your *net foot* is the foot closest to the net. If you're on the left side of the court, you can more easily set with your left foot forward and your right foot slightly back. If you're on the right side of the net, flip that: Your right foot slightly forward and your left foot slightly back.

4. **Follow through to set your partner where they (politely) requested it.**

   After passing, hitters call where they want the set — how high and where along the net. Finish your set by following through, so your momentum moves the ball toward the hitter's specified target.

TIP

Picture your chest, belly button, or core as a flashlight that you want to shine on your intended target (see Figure 7-5). Perhaps imagine yourself as Ironman, with that enormous arc reactor on your chest. That guiding light lets your teammate (or teammates) know where you intend to send the set. Not only does this body movement show your hitter where you intend to set the ball (which they find enormously helpful for their approach), but it also produces a much more consistent set by minimizing any errors that they make when setting. Consistency is gold when it comes to setting because hitters can approach more aggressively if they know that the setter likely can get a set where they want it.

In a perfect world — and playing volleyball, like all sports, isn't perfect — you can face your target every single time; which happens when you're in system.

FIGURE 7-5: The setter facing their core to the target.

Augustas Cetkauskas/Adobe Stock Photos

Transitioning and out-of-system setting

What happens when you don't get a perfect pass or your defensive teammate(s) make a dig, and you have to scramble to set the ball?

Having to set in less-than-ideal circumstances is called *out-of-system setting* (or, when it happens after a dig, *transition setting* because you're transitioning from defense to offense). At the same time, setting out of system is more complicated and much simpler than in-system setting:

- **More complicated:** You, the setter, have to scramble to get to an errant pass, meaning you have a lot more work to do to get yourself to the ball.
- **Much simpler:** You have greatly limited options when you're out of system or in transition, so you have a hugely reduced range of decisions to make. You might be able to set only one of your hitters indoors, usually a high set. On the beach, if you typically have a variety of different locations along the net where you can set, when out of system, you might be limited to just one.

Transition setting is important. Vitally so. Three-time Olympic gold medalist Karch Kiraly — four-time, if you include the 2021 Olympic gold he won coaching the U.S. women's indoor team — referred to transition setting as flecks of gold because of how important and rare those opportunities are.

Here are a few commonalities of transition and out-of-system setting for both indoors and on the beach:

» **Get in the right position.** Get your core around the ball and face your target when you can to show your hitter where you intend to set. You can't always get positioned properly but do your best to shine your proverbial light on your target (we talk about this imaginary flashlight in the preceding section).

» **Don't move too much.** If you can't get in the ideal position, simply aim the shoulder closest to the net toward your target and lob the ball high and over that shoulder, keeping your upper body still and balanced. The most common mistake setters make in this situation is swinging their platform, which makes for a highly inconsistent set that your hitter finds nearly impossible to read. Aim your net-side shoulder to the target and lob the ball over that shoulder.

» **Set high.** Out-of-system and transition setting likely calls for higher sets than when you're in system because you have to set from farther off the net or in chaotic situations in which you need to give your hitter time to approach the ball. Make sure to lob the ball and give it a nice peak, like a rainbow.

» **Use the bump set.** The more off-balance and rushed you are in getting to the ball, the more trouble you have making a consistent set by using your hands.

Indoors especially, everyone needs at least a rough understanding of how to set for when you find yourselves in an out-of-system situation. If the setter can't get to the ball, setting duties fall to the libero. If the libero also can't get there comfortably, it goes to whoever's closest and able to make the best possible set (even you, middle blockers).

THE SETTING GAME

Mark Knudsen is the patriarch of one of the more successful volleyball families in the United States. A native of Southern California, he was raised playing the game, earned a spot on the UCLA indoor team, won a few National Championships under the legendary coach Al Scates, won a few more as Scates's assistant coach, and proceeded to play professionally on the beach. He met his wife, Diane, at a tournament in New Jersey, and together they had four children who went on to play Division I volleyball:

- Delaney won a National Championship on the beach for Pepperdine University and enjoyed a solid professional career.
- Lindsey became St. Mary's College's number 1 outside hitter.

- Kelsey was a digging machine of a libero for St. Mary's College, Brigham Young University (BYU), and California State University, Northridge.
- Jake, the youngest, set the kills record for Moorpark College before moving on to Jessup University.

This is both a short and long way of saying: They know how to play, and teach, volleyball — at all positions and on both surfaces.

Although this pro-volleyball family do play board games together, they also regularly play a game that the patriarch himself dubbed The Setting Game.

It's a simple game, requiring one ball, a basketball hoop, and any number of players. They line up behind one another at the free-throw line. The first person in line tosses a volleyball to themself and then sets that ball into the basketball hoop. If the ball goes in the hoop, that player wins a point and goes again. If the ball misses the hoop, the player behind them then sets the ball, either off a bounce from the court or without the use of a bounce, again attempting to set the ball into the hoop. If that player misses, the player behind them attempts to set the ball into the hoop. Whenever someone puts the ball in the hoop, that person then begins the next round by tossing to themself and setting from the free-throw line.

Critically, players actually want to play this game, they look forward to playing. That goes a long way. Because I (Travis) married Delaney and therefore ended up in this volleyball dynasty, I've played this game for hours, and it never gets old.

Over a few rounds of The Setting Game, you set a ton of balls from many different angles, requiring many different types of touch and loft on the ball. You back set with your platform, side set with your hands. You attempt one-handed scoop sets, poke sets, jump sets. There will be some sets from deep, some from short. Some sets require you to lob it with a lot of height, some require less.

The best part: The Setting Game is perfect for beach and indoor players alike; you can play during inclement weather and — vitally — it's fun.

Recognizing the Types of Sets and How to Do Them

The following sections discuss the details of some actual sets that you can use in games and matches. These four are the most common sets that you see while watching volleyball and that you set yourself while playing the game. There are other more advanced sets, but here we stick to the basics.

Setters typically use hand signals, numbers, or a team-specific type of sign language to inform hitters what location, height, and speed they can expect. Others use a coded verbal system, typically numbers, or simple words such as hut or blue, to inform the hitters.

Four

The four set is the most common set in indoor volleyball because the setter sets to the outside hitter most frequently. To set a *four* (also known as an *outside*), the setter lobs the ball high to the left side of the court, just in front of the antenna, to give the outside hitter time to get a full approach, jump, and swing.

Five

A five set is virtually the same set as an outside (see the preceding section), only you direct it to the right side of the court — to the opposite hitter. The height and tempo are virtually the same as an outside: a high lob of a set, which gives the opposite hitter time to make a full approach and swing.

One

Every middle blocker loves the one set. Why? Because the one is for them and them only. The *one set* is as quick as it gets, designed only for perfect passes right into the setter's hands. With a one set, the middle blocker is already jumping before the set even leaves the setter's hands, a speed designed to keep the opposing blockers out of position, giving the middle blocker either no block or a late and out-of-position block. It's one of the most difficult sets for opposing teams to stop.

The most common variation of a one is . . . a two, which is the same set in terms of location on the court, but just a tad higher.

Pipe

The *pipe set* is designed for a hitter coming out of the middle in the back row — right down the pipe, you could say. The setter sets the ball just inside the 10-foot line, leading the back row hitter (most likely your second outside hitter on the court), who has to jump from behind the 10-foot line in order to attack.

WARNING

If the back row hitter takes off from in front of or on the 10-foot line, that's a violation and results in a point for the opposing team.

A DIFFERENT MINDSET

Kylie DeBerg is 6 feet 4 inches and was a three-time All-American outside hitter at the University of Missouri in the 2010s. She graduated from the school in 2020 as the all-time leader in kills and points per set and finished in the top 10 in total kills and aces. She saw that she could get her master's degree for free if she used her final years of college eligibility to play beach volleyball. She transferred to Louisiana State University (LSU), which had a reputation for developing indoor converts into excellent beach players. See the following figure of her in action at the net.

Photo by Mark Rigney

Acclaimed as she was indoors, she was so bad that first semester at LSU that every day she'd do nothing but set with her coaches for an hour.

Her teammates, intrigued by this new and potentially tremendous — but at that moment awful — player, watched DeBerg from the office windows, amused and likely concerned that they'd have to play with her.

(continued)

(continued)

"One of my teammates would watch, and she'd go, 'Wow, she sucks at setting,'" DeBerg said on the *SANDCAST* podcast. "I was that bad. It's a different mindset of not being served every time and not getting to hit every time. Indoor, I didn't really talk to my teammates. I didn't have to. I was out there and did my job. Beach, it's just you and your partner."

And in order to be a good partner, in both versions of volleyball, you must make those around you better. You can most effectively help your teammates by becoming an excellent setter.

The height of a pipe is slightly lower than that of a four or five (see the preceding sections), but not by much: You, the setter, are giving your hitter time to make a full approach and jump.

Trying Different Drills to Improve Your Setting

The most efficient way to improve your setting is to set — a lot. The following sections offer some drills that can work to improve your setting for both indoor and beach volleyball.

REMEMBER

The most important element of any setting drill, of course, is to set as many balls as you can while retaining your focus on quality reps over quantity. As soon as you feel the quality of your set slipping or faltering, slow down, take a break, and try again.

Triangle setting

Triangle setting is quite possibly the most-used drill among professional beach volleyball players and beginners alike. It's simple, and it includes the three main elements of beach volleyball: hitting, passing, and setting.

For this drill, you need at least three players: One to hit the ball, one to pass, and one to set back to the hitter. If you have a fourth player, you can add them as an extra setter.

In this version of the drill, position all players on the same side of the net:

- Player 1 stands at the net straight in front of Player 2, who's in a serve-receive position.
- Player 3 starts in the other passing position next to Player 2.
- If you have a Player 4, you can add them as another setter.

With everyone in position, follow these steps:

1. **Player 1 tosses or hits a ball to Player 2.**
2. **Player 2 passes to the middle of the court.**

   They should have a target location of 5 or so feet (about 1.5 meters) from the net.
3. **Player 3 sets back to Player 1.**
4. **Player 1 catches the ball and then hits it back to Player 2.**
5. **Repeat Steps 2 through 4 for ten reps.**
6. **Switch positions.**
7. **Repeat Steps 1 through 6 until everyone has had the chance to set.**
8. **Switch sides of the court.**
9. **Repeat Steps 1 through 7 on this side of the court.**

   After ten reps in all positions on both sides, using both bump and hand sets (discussed in the section "Setting a Volleyball: The How-to" earlier in this chapter), you can quickly improve your setting touch.

You can level up this drill in a couple of ways:

- Have the hitter (Player 1) hit from the other side of the net, so the ball goes over the net. This change makes it a more advanced drill for both the passer (Player 2), who's now passing a more difficult serve, and the hitter who has to hit the ball over the net.
- To make the drill even more challenging, have the hitter back all the way up to the service line on the other side of the net and hit full-length serves.

Solo setting

If you don't have a ton of friends readily available to play or do drills, that's no problem! You can easily improve on your setting skills by yourself, as long as you have a ball. (Just check out the sidebar "Quiet setting: The Phil Dalhausser path to mastery" in this chapter; Dalhausser practiced setting while his roommates watched movies.)

To do solo setting practice, follow these steps:

1. **Lie down on the floor with your knees bent so that your feet are flat on the ground.**

   This positioning allows you to focus only on what you're doing with your arms and hands.

2. **Hold a ball in your hands and then set the ball toward the ceiling.**
3. **Catch the ball and lower it.**
4. **Repeat Steps 2 and 3.**

   Do as many reps as you want to, trying to make your sets — the catch and release — as quiet as you can, working on those soft hands.

Here are a couple of variations on this drill:

- Do this same drill while standing.
- Increase the difficulty by adding spin on the ball when you toss it to yourself to set.

IN THIS CHAPTER

- » Seeing the offense and defense of the serve
- » Figuring out what makes a great server
- » Getting yourself ready to serve
- » Trying different types of serves
- » Finding your personal best serve style
- » Doing some service drills

Chapter 8

Putting Your Team in the Best Position to Win a Point: Serving

The serve is the first contact of a volleyball rally — and also one of the most polarizing topics in volleyball, both indoors and out. Are you on offense or defense? Should you go all out with your serve, attempting to score a point with an ace, or play it safe and allow the other team to have an easy ball to pass?

Like nearly all debates in sports, these questions have no correct answers. In this chapter, we examine serving in all of its nitty-gritty detail. We cover what traits make a great server and what types of serves are most effective. We also examine whether you can miss serves in the name of aggression and pressuring the opposing team and still win games. And we consider this weighty question: Are aces really that important to your defense?

Serving as Offense or Defense

The *serve* — in which a player hits the ball from their endline over the net to the other side of the court — is the first contact of a volleyball rally.

The big question: When your team serves, do you consider your team on offense or defense? An unscientific poll, but a poll nonetheless, that we conducted scoured more than 1,000 volleyball players, coaches, and fans via social media and asked this simple question. Both responses have valid arguments:

» **Offense:** The 56 percent who responded that they viewed serving as an offensive contact clearly understand that the quickest, most calorie-efficient manner in which to score a point is an *ace* (when the server hits a serve that the opposing team can't return). Scoring a point is an offensive trait (ignoring, of course, that you can also score in a single contact on defense by using a block or a well-placed dig, which we talk about in Chapters 10 and 11).

» **Defense:** The 44 percent who responded that serving is defensive because the serving team is sending the ball to the awaiting offense in serve-receive position have a valid case, as well. In some instances, teams view serving as the first contact to set up the defense. If a team struggles when the setter has to chase a pass to the left side of the court, doesn't handle short serves well, or has limited options when the passer (whether an outside hitter, a libero, or one of the two players on the beach) is pushed deep, the team doesn't necessarily have a point-scoring mindset. They're more focused on defense to increase their percentages of earning a point.

We lean a tad on the offensive side. The ball is in your hands, and you can score a point. That's offensive enough for us.

Exploring What Traits Make a Great Server

Becoming an elite server is simple — but simple doesn't mean easy. Just because you don't have an opponent blocking you or a teammate who might set you poorly doesn't mean serving doesn't have its challenges. Oftentimes, players feel intimidated by serving because you control the only action happening on the court while you serve. But here are two traits that, when mastered or developed into a proficiency, can make you one of the best servers on any court that you step on:

» **Consistency:** You absolutely need consistency in your serve if you want to become an elite server. Not only do you want to simply serve it in bounds on a consistent basis, but you also want to make it challenging to pass. The ability to manage risk and reward involves attempting an aggressive serve that the opposing team finds difficult to pass while ensuring that you put the ball inbounds. This balance is no easy feat, and so many teams struggle to consistently apply pressure (which we talk about in the sidebar "Live by the jump serve, die by the jump serve" in this chapter). If you can consistently hit difficult serves in bounds, your opponents will see you as a menace that they have to deal with.

- **Accuracy:** Accuracy is a skill far greater than power when it comes to the serve. And you can apply it consistently. Hitting open spaces, which makes the opposing passers move, accurately provides a valuable skill for serving. Couple accuracy with consistency, and you can become a point-scoring machine.

REMEMBER

The preceding list doesn't include power, which might surprise you. But power is, in reality, quite far down the list of great serving traits. Only a few genetically blessed individuals have enough pure power to simply overwhelm opponents with speed, and speed only.

Getting Ready: The Pre-Serve Routine

Serving is called a *closed-loop skill,* meaning that you control every aspect of it, from where you serve, to how you serve, to the routine, toss, and hit. It's the only such skill in volleyball. Only when you're serving do you have control over everything, from what happens before you serve, to your toss, to how you hit the ball and where. Common comparisons present serving as akin to a free throw in basketball or a shot in golf: You control everything. Especially what happens before you even begin to serve.

TIP

We can't overstate the importance of a pre-serve routine. If breakfast is said to be the most important meal of the day, the pre-serve routine is, almost inarguably, the most important aspect of the serve.

You don't need to make your pre-serve routine complex. You also don't need to have rituals, although many players do have them, such as:

- Bouncing the ball three times
- Holding the ball high above their head, staring at it
- Bouncing the ball off their fists to themselves

» Rolling the ball around their arms

» Doing a brief line dance

» Blowing a kiss to the heavens and offering up a prayer to the Serving Gods (we're exaggerating only slightly with this one)

Whatever their ritual, they follow it up by taking a breath, identifying their target, tossing the ball, and then ripping the serve.

Geena Urango (who played indoor and beach volleyball at the University of Southern California [USC], has won two Server of the Year Awards from the Association of Volleyball Professionals [AVP], and was named the MVP of the 2024 AVP League) described her pre-serve routine in a video on *The McKibbin Brothers* YouTube Channel: "Toss the ball between my hands, hold the ball up to my face, take a deep breath, relax, then hold my hand out for the toss. Two things I like to ask myself are where and where? Where am I serving on the back line? Where am I serving, the exact location on the other side of the net?"

The two elements that every pre-serve routine should have: breathing and target identification, which the following sections discuss. Anything else is up to you. Figure 8-1 shows a pre-serve routine.

FIGURE 8-1: The calm before the serving storm: The critical pre-serve routine.

Dziurek/Adobe Stock Photos

TIP

A mediocre server who has a pre-serve routine can accomplish significantly more than an elite server without one because that server is far more consistent. Maintaining your pre-serve routine allows you to serve just as well at 24-23 in the third set as you do at 0-0.

Taking a deep breath

Before you serve, take a long inhale, followed by an even longer exhale. Doing so helps you reset both mentally and physically, lowering your heart rate and switching your focus from the externalities of the match and point to you and what you control.

Focusing on your target visually

Whatever your target, you absolutely must identify it. A serve without a target is a road trip without an end destination, a sailboat without a harbor. The server needs to identify a target that can make the passers move.

Find a spot on the floor, a shadow on the beach, a spot where you can see the line ticked up just a notch, or a logo — something so small that if you miss it, you can still make a good serve. Think of this targeting as the opposite of the "shoot for the moon, and even if you miss, you land among the stars" maxim — aim for a dime and you can get a half-dollar.

TIP

Ideally, your targets will be the *seams* (the gaps) between the passers or the space between the passers and the lines of the court. Seams are the most effective places to serve because serving to those locations forces passers to move or adds the possibility of miscommunication between passers.

If you can focus on your target, you can become a serving genius. Even if you hit a serve that has wicked speed and movement, if you hit it directly at the passer, that serve isn't terribly effective. Your serving targets are nearly as important as your serving technique itself.

Especially when hitting float serves (see the section "Executing a Float Serve" later in this chapter), focus on making the passers move:

- A short serve or deep serve makes the passers move, sometimes to the point that they even wind up on the ground, but either way, in making the passer move, you have disrupted their approach.
- Serve in between the seams of the passers or the seams between the passers and the lines to make the passers move and cause disruption.

REMEMBER

Often in indoor volleyball, a coach will suggest to the player a zone, an area of the court to serve (see Figure 8-2). The zones correspond to the six positions on the floor. So, if a coach wants the player to serve to zone 1, they may give a 1 signal to the server.

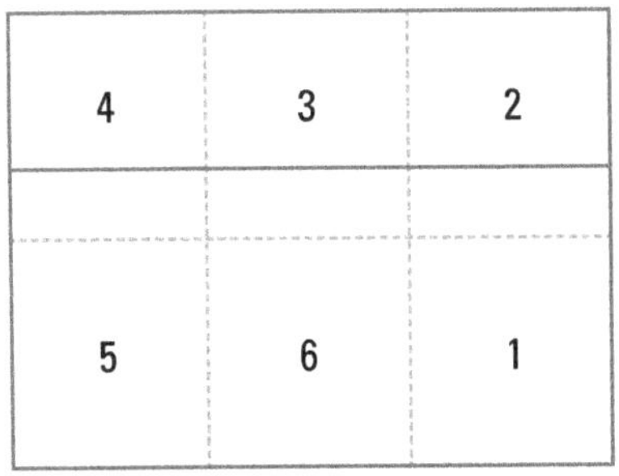

FIGURE 8-2: Serving zones.

Refer to the section "Cornhole serving" later in this chapter for a drill that you can do to work on hitting your targets.

MAKE IT MOVE

Like your authors, coach Andrea Becker conducted a somewhat unscientific study on serving, although she went far beyond the reaches of social media (which we did) and instead looked deep into months of data. (We talk about our study in the section "Serving as Offense or Defense" in this chapter.)

A former sports psychology consultant for the U.S. Men's National Team — the team that won a gold medal at the *Fédération Internationale de Volleyball* (FIVB; International Volleyball Federation) World League Finals in 2014 — Becker's sweet spot lies in the cross-section of her two specialties: volleyball and psychology.

Boasting both a bachelor's and master's degree in kinesiology and sport performance, as well as a PhD in Sports Studies just for fun, Becker also helped University of California (UC) Irvine win the 2012 NCAA Championship before she moved to UCLA and, finally, full-time for the USA Men's National Team.

During a stretch of practices one summer in 2015, she came armed with a radar gun, a notebook, and a question: What makes for the most effective serve? Which serve leads to the most out-of-system passes, aces, and, in the end, defensive points scored?

"I noted for each serve where the server started, what type of rotation they put on the ball, whether it was jump spin, whether it was a float, whether it was a hybrid, where the ball went, and what the passing number was," she said on the *Coach Your Brains Out* podcast in 2018. "Out of that, the data suggested that movement was the most important thing. That's what made the serve the most difficult. If you could put some kind of movement that's difficult to detect, that's where most of the out-of-system balls came."

In some cases, Becker noted, if a server can rifle a ball in more than 73 miles per hour — this sort of speed comes almost exclusively on the men's side — then pace provided quite a good deal of out-of-system passes. But not everyone has the ability to hit such a fast serve.

Everyone, from a fifth grader just learning the game to the 65-year-old grandpa who's still playing pickup, can make the serve move.

Executing a Float Serve

A *float serve* sacrifices speed for movement; you make the ball travel with zero spin on it, thereby increasing its unpredictable movement. This type of serve is the simplest serve to hit and master, as well as one of the deadliest — an excellent combo. You don't need an abundance of power to hit an effective float serve, you just need the focus necessary to hit a ball with minimal spin — and maximum movement.

The most effective float serves have the following characteristics:

- Speed — not as much as a jump serve, but enough to get on the passer quickly
- A trajectory that looks like a line drive, barely getting over the top of the net
- Minimal to zero spin, thereby creating the devastating *float effect*, making the ball move in an unpredictable, hard-to-read manner

John Mayer, the coach for Loyola Marymount University (LMU) beach volleyball (see the sidebar "Hitting the three-point serve," in this chapter, for more on Mayer's career), advocates for a serve with the following characteristics: fast, flat, floating. Accomplish all three, and you have a devastating serve. This rule, like nearly all rules when it comes to volleyball serving, applies to both indoor and beach.

So what makes a fast, flat, floating serve stand out? You can't easily distinguish which of the three elements — fast, flat, floating — is more important than the other. Each has a legitimate argument, although speed might have the best of the bunch.

Here's a closer look at the three elements of this serve:

- **Fast:** You can't, by definition, make a serve flat if it doesn't have speed; it simply can't get to the desired target.
- **Flat:** The ball travels mostly in a straight line, rather than a loopy arc.
- **Floating:** You can make the float effect all the more effective by the *pace* (speed) that you put on the ball. When you combine pace with zero or minimal spin, then a float serve becomes dangerous.

Although you can hit a float serve in a number of ways, the following sections guide you in the most effective method.

Preparing to hit a float serve

In order to hit a float serve fast, you must transfer your energy from back to front. Here's how to execute a one-step serve:

1. **Stand a few feet behind the baseline (also known as the endline).**

   Positioning yourself here means that you don't *foot fault* (when your feet touch or cross the baseline while you serve).

2. **Make a letter V with your body.**

   Position your opposite foot slightly forward, opening toward your hitting shoulder. Have the majority of your weight — maybe 65 to 70 percent — on your back leg.

3. **Load your hitting arm with your elbow back and your hand near your head.**

   Put your hand in a position where, if you wiggle your fingers, you might be able to tickle your ear.

   TIP

   Some players like to visualize pulling their elbow back like a bow and arrow; others prefer to feel like they're pinching their shoulder blades together. Either method works, so choose the one that makes sense to you.

4. **Make your dominant hand (the one you hit with) firm and open (see Figure 8-3).**

   How firm and open? Try clapping your hands together without using your fingers, essentially banging your palms together to create that satisfying pop.

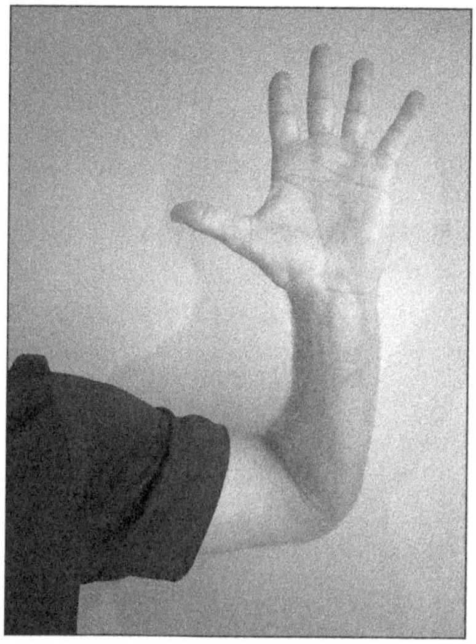

FIGURE 8-3: An open hand for serving a float serve.

Photo by Travis Mewhirter

TIP

As Mark Burik, a longtime professional and founder of the instructional company Better at Beach, describes it: "We want all hamburger, no French fries." Your fingers, in this case, are the French fries, and you don't want them included in your float serve meal. Hamburgers (palms) only, folks.

Finding your Goldilocks zone with a float toss

High-level volleyball players point to the toss as the most vital aspect of a serve. The toss of a float serve determines whether you can make it fast and flat and produce the float effect.

With a float serve toss, you need to find the right toss that places the ball slightly higher than your head, but not too high so that you don't get under it. Everyone has a different *Goldilocks zone* — not too high or too low, but juuuuuust right. Find yours by hitting as many float serves as you can against a wall or over a net to find that zone:

REMEMBER

- **Up and down:** If you have to wait for your toss to come down, it's probably too high. And if your toss is too low, you have to hit up at the ball just to clear the net — and there go your fast and flat categories of the three-point serve.

  Think about a float serve toss not as tossing the ball at all but presenting it to your dominant hand.

- **Front and back:** If you toss too far in front of yourself, you have to reach to hit the ball — thereby losing power and likely your flat trajectory. Too far behind, and you have to hit up at the ball, which also loses power and trajectory.
- **Left and right:** Tossing the ball too far to the left or right means that you have a difficult time hitting your desired target because you don't have the ball on your hitting shoulder, which you want. You have to adjust, either with your feet or your arm swing, and these adjustments can cause inconsistency.

Refer to the later section "Goldilocks toss" for a drill to practice your toss.

Hitting the float serve

After you get in position and perfect your toss (discussed in the preceding sections), you're ready to actually hit the float serve. Just follow these steps:

1. **Step forward, bringing your dominant foot in front.**

   Transfer the energy from back to front with this step.

2. **Contact the ball just above eye level, following through forward.**

   Create that flat trajectory that all servers love.

3. **As quickly as you can at contact, freeze your arm and hand.**

   Minimize your contact time with the ball while you drive through the center of the ball. The ball should pop off your hand. This minimal contact maximizes the float effect because it reduces the possibility of your hand turning over the ball and creating spin.

WARNING

To create the float effect, you need a firm hand. If your hand is too relaxed, it naturally takes the shape of the ball and creates topspin, removing the float effect and making for an easy pass. (A jump serve, which we talk about in the section "Hitting a Consistent Jump Serve" later in this chapter, uses topspin to add a downward trajectory to the serve.)

Practicing your float serve

When practicing your float serve, imagine a line that connects the top of the antennas on either side of the net, forming a rectangle (the net serving as the bottom, the imaginary line at the top, and the antennas on the sides). If you can hit your serve with some pace (fast), within that rectangle (flat), and with zero spin (float), you have an effective serve that has all sorts of unpredictable movement. You can take string or construction tape and physically tie it to each antenna, creating the rectangle.

HITTING THE THREE-POINT SERVE

John Mayer is a man known for many things at this point in his volleyball career. Currently, he's the head coach of the Loyola Marymount University (LMU) beach volleyball program, where he started in 2016. He turned around the losing program (it was 4–11 and had only a single winning season in its history when he inherited it). By 2025, he had built it into a bona fide powerhouse, making the finals of the NCAA Championship. He is, at the time of this writing, the six-time West Coast Conference Coach of the Year, owner of six straight conference titles, and the 2025 American Volleyball Coaches Association (AVCA) Coach of the Year.

He has built beach volleyball into the best sports program, period, of any sport in LMU history. One element of his LMU teams — and the many professionals he's coached along the way — stands out above the rest: They have one of the best serving games in the country.

Out of the dozens of elite servers whom Mayer has coached, not a single one of them relies on a jump serve (which you can read about in the section "Hitting a Consistent Jump Serve" in this chapter). Across the board, the float serve (discussed in the section "Executing a Float Serve" in this chapter) stands as the most reliable weapon of Mayer and his pupils, from Betsi Flint (three-time AVP Best Server; see the accompanying photo of Flint serving a float serve), to Emily Capers (2017 AVP Team of the Year), to Billy Allen (a three-time AVP champion), to Mayer himself (he was the 2015 AVP MVP and Best Defensive Player).

Serving is the easiest skill to practice on your own because you don't need a teammate or opponents. All you need are some volleyballs and a net (or even just a wall if you can mark the rectangle at the appropriate heights). You can use tape on a wall or string to connect the antennas on a net, and you can work on your technique until you're hitting a truly nasty serve.

Leveling Up to the Jump Float

A *jump float serve* is slightly more advanced than a standing float (see the section "Executing a Float Serve" earlier in this chapter), and like anything in life that comes with more rewards, it also comes with a higher risk of missing.

You can do a two-handed toss or one-handed toss on your jump float serve, which just comes down to personal preference and which toss you can use to produce a more consistent and accurate serve.

Serving a two-handed jump float

Follow these steps to do a two-handed jump float serve toss:

1. **If you're right-handed, begin with your left foot behind you.**

   If you're left-handed, do the opposite.

2. **Take a step forward with your left foot and toss the ball with both hands in front of you.**

3. **Take two more steps forward while you put your arms in a hitting position.**

   REMEMBER

   The *Goldilocks zone* is important — not too high nor too low, not too far in front nor too far behind, not too far to the right nor left — just right.

TIP

Toss the ball only as high as your highest reach. Think about setting yourself a quick set, also known as a *one*, in which the ball barely clears the height of the net.

Doing a one-handed jump float

You can do a one-handed toss, which is just as common as a two-handed toss (see the preceding section). In a one-handed jump float serve, you follow the same procedure outlined in the preceding section, except that you put your arms up earlier.

This more advanced serve can keep your opponents on their heels. Try it by following these steps:

1. **Cock back your dominant hand in the same position that you have your arm prior to hitting a ball.**

   We talk about the proper form to hit a ball in Chapter 6.

2. **Present the ball in front of you with your opposite hand.**

   Hold it roughly eye level, perhaps the height of your forehead.

3. **Take a step forward with your left foot, toss the ball, and use your dominant hand to hit.**

   REMEMBER

   You need some time to find the rhythm, the height of the toss, the spacing between your steps, and the timing of the sequence, so do many repetitions and find what works for you.

Hitting a Consistent Jump Serve

A *jump serve,* when you toss a high set to yourself and hit it like you're spiking a ball from the end line, may be the most intimidating skill in the game — even more intimidating, perhaps, than a hitter who can spike with the power of Thor. Players simply can't avoid Evandro Goncalves (see the nearby sidebar), or any other elite jump server. You know, when the rotation turns their direction and the ref hands them the ball, it's their serve. You can't do anything about it, as compared to hitters, against whom you can use certain strategies and techniques to help avoid or mitigate their abilities. A jump server is just going to serve — it's simple as that.

But if ball movement other than in a straight line is the most reliable source of out-of-system passes (which we talk about in the sidebar "Make it move" in this chapter), what makes a jump serve so dangerous? In a word, power. Think of a jump serve like how a hitter attacks a set on offense. It's the highest velocity serve that a player can hit.

Statistically speaking, when a player can bring enough power and pace with their jump serve, it has the highest probability of producing an ace, which is the quickest way to score a point.

The steps for a consistent jump serve are nearly identical on the beach and indoor. To start, you need the same first two components in a jump serve that you do for a float — the pre-serve routine and toss. The following sections get into the specifics of the jump serve routine and toss. (For more on these components for a float serve, refer to the sections "Getting Ready: The Pre-Serve Routine" and "Finding your Goldilocks zone with a float toss" earlier in this chapter.)

The following sections walk you through the steps to hitting a consistent jump serve, including advice from Paul Lotman, a 2012 indoor Olympian who played professionally both indoors and on the beach.

Getting your routine down

Just like a float serve (which you can read about in the section "Executing a Float Serve" earlier in this chapter), any jump serve requires the same pre-serve routine: centering yourself with a breath, identifying a target, and focusing on that target.

EVANDRO GONCALVES AND THE POWER OF A JUMP SERVE

No single individual evokes more fear when at the service line than Evandro Goncalves (see Appendix B for more). From 2017 through 2025, the 6-foot-11-inch Brazilian was voted by his peers on the Beach Pro Tour and the *Fédération Internationale de Volleyball* (FIVB; International Volleyball Federation) Best Server in the World eight times, a record. Still only 35 years old at the time of this writing, he'll go down as the greatest server in the history of beach volleyball. He didn't accomplish this prowess with any tricks or sneaky tactics — just power, and power alone. Goncalves hitting a float serve (discussed in the section "Executing a Float Serve" in this chapter) is as rare as snow in his hometown of Rio de Janeiro. He climbed to the top of the serving Mount Everest by using the most-feared weapon in both beach and indoor volleyball: The jump serve.

During a tournament in Recife, Brazil, in 2024, he hit 37 aces en route to a gold medal — more aces than the next three best servers combined. This stat doesn't consider out-of-system passes produced (meaning the opposing team had an errant pass), which helped his partner, Arthur Lanci, capitalize on numerous opportunities to score defensively.

At the 2025 World Championships in Adelaide, Australia, Goncalves again led the field in aces, despite finishing fifth and playing two fewer matches than the four teams that advanced into the semifinals.

Paul Lotman says, "Routine is obviously a huge component; that's a given. To each his own, whatever works without overthinking what you want to do with your serve. I always try to clear my mind and focus on the important aspects of a good serve."

He should know: His jump serve was so dangerous that he came to the 2012 London Olympics primarily to do just that — serve — on the indoor team. Eleven years later, *Volleyball Magazine* named him the 2023 Server of the Year — on the beach.

Finding your jump serve Goldilocks toss

To do a consistent, quality jump serve, keep these tips in mind for your toss:

- **Toss the ball high.** Go significantly higher than that of a float or a jump float (which we talk about in the sections "Executing a Float Serve" and "Leveling Up to the Jump Float" earlier in this chapter). The higher the toss, generally, the more velocity you can put on the ball.

WARNING

But the higher the toss (especially on the beach, where the wind can take the ball and disrupt your rhythm), the higher the risk.

- **Don't toss it too high.** Make your toss high enough that you can still jump to your full height, but not so high that you get out of rhythm or allow the elements to have an effect. A lower toss generally results in a more consistent jump serve, but one that comes with less power. This is the first Goldilocks zone of the jump serve: Find a toss that isn't too high or too low, but just right.
- **Lead yourself with your toss.** "Toss well in front to be as dynamic as possible and get momentum into the serve," Lotman told me (Travis) in an interview. But, you might be asking, "What if I foot fault?" Therein lies the balance, the second Goldilocks zone, of the jump serve.
- **Don't go too far forward.** Toss enough in front of you that you have the ball in front of you, but not too far so that you either *foot fault* (when you step on or over the endline while serving) or broad jump so much that you lose height on your jump.

Approaching your toss and hitting on your way up

When you hit the jump serve, you use the exact same technique that you do when you hit a spike on offense (refer to Chapter 6), but you're obviously farther from the net when you serve. Generally, players use one of two practiced approaches for a jump serve. Players at all levels use both approaches equally. It all comes down to personal preference:

- **Four-step approach:** Co-author Travis Mewhirter used a four-step approach because the walking step helped him build momentum into the serve.
- **Three-step approach:** Others, like indoor Olympian T.J. DeFalco, use a three-step approach because that's what he's most comfortable with.

TIP

If you're a beginner, try both types of approach and find what's comfortable for you.

Follow these steps to make a four-step approach:

1. **Begin with a small walking step.**

   Take just a little step to build momentum into the serve.

2. **Toss the ball.**

   See the preceding section for advice on getting your toss right.

3. **Take a medium-length step toward the toss.**
4. **Take a long stride so that you get closer to the toss and build momentum.**
5. **Take a short step while you gather all of that momentum and prepare to jump.**
6. **Jump and hit the ball at the highest point that you can.**

On a three-step approach, you simply skip the first step; toss, take a medium-length step, a long stride, a short step, and then rise and hit your serve.

Preparing for the service hit

WARNING

The gravest mistake you can make as a server is hitting the serve into the net. If you hit the serve into the net, the passers don't have to decide whether to pass the ball or let it go out of bounds. Hitting your serve into the net is an automatic point for the other team — no decision to be made, nothing.

If you're going to miss, *miss long* (meaning the ball goes out of bounds behind the other team's endline, which is why you want to hit it on your way up and drive it over and across the net, rather than attempting to hit it at a downward angle).

When you contact the ball during your serve, keep your arm and hand relaxed and loose so that your hand wraps around the ball and creates the topspin that makes a jump serve move and dive as quickly as it does. (See the section "Working on topspin" later in this chapter for a drill into topspin.) Although you want your hands firm for a float serve to create zero spin (as discussed in the section "Executing a Float Serve" earlier in this chapter), have your hands looooose and acting like the end of a whip when you hit a jump serve so that you can create as much spin as possible.

Keeping your swing smooth

Paul Lotman's advice on a jump serve's swing may seem a bit counterintuitive: "Don't over-swing. Good jump serves with the right amount of pace and movement should feel smooth and fluid, 75 to 85 percent of whatever your max power is — no more and no less. If you don't hit that range, you're probably serving too easy or making an error."

Of course, the point of a jump serve is to bring power and pace. That's why it's so dangerous. But it's only dangerous if you hit it in bounds.

You'd be amazed at what you find when you attempt to hit a jump serve with only 75 to 85 percent of your power. Not only can you be more consistent in your serving than when you try to use all your power, but you don't actually lose as much speed as you might think on your serve.

Finding Your 90-Percent Serve

Different athletes have different serving capabilities. Some, such as Evandro Goncalves (discussed in the sidebar "Evandro Goncalves and the power of a jump serve" in this chapter), can hit a jump serve as well as anyone has ever hit a jump serve. Some players, such as John Mayer (whom we talk about in the sidebar "Hitting the three-point serve" in this chapter), are masters of the float. Your goal as a volleyball player is to try as many different serves as you can until you find the one that works for you most of the time, what we call the *90-percent serve.*

You'll miss when serving. And you should! If you don't miss a serve every now and again, you likely aren't serving aggressively enough.

But if you're missing more than about 20 percent of your serves, or your ace-to-error ratio is beyond the 1:1 that effective servers seek, dial the risk back a notch. The easiest way to reduce the risk is to simplify. For example:

- If you're a jump server (see the section "Hitting a Consistent Jump Serve" earlier in this chapter) and miss a few, reduce the complexity of your serve to a jump float (which we talk about in the section "Leveling Up to the Jump Float" earlier in this chapter).
- If you hit a jump float and you're missing, try a standing float (flip to the section "Executing a Float Serve" earlier in this chapter).
- If you're already hitting a standing float, seek to hit a spot on the floor, rather than attempting to make your serve as flat as possible.

TIP

Oftentimes, simply making a passer move out of their lane can produce an out-of-system pass.

But, you might think, "What about my aces? Isn't that the easiest, quickest, most calorie-efficient manner in which to score a point?" Indeed. But we particularly like a motto espoused by Rob Browning, who coached St. Mary's College of California women's indoor team for 20 years. Hit your serve, he'd tell his players, and aces will happen.

He preached for his players to find a serve that they could hit in bounds 90 percent of the time. If you can do that, you get your points. When you find your 90-percent serve, you find your aces.

LIVE BY THE JUMP SERVE, DIE BY THE JUMP SERVE

If you can hit a jump serve with enough pace and power, you can't find a more threatening tool. But it doesn't come without its risks. Just ask former UCLA men's volleyball coach John Speraw.

Speraw had preached risky serving since he was hired back to his alma mater in 2012. That approach had led the Bruins to the NCAA National Championship match in 2018. Serving was the sword he had chosen to live by and, at times, die by.

With the score tied 17–17 in the third set in the championship match, which pitted UCLA against top-seeded California State University, Long Beach, the match was tied one set apiece. UCLA's 6-foot-4-inch junior Dylan Missry had the ball in his hands.

UCLA's game focused on serving, which won them the second set primarily because of it. In particular, jump serving. To be even more precise, Missry's jump serve. Missry continued bombing one jump serve after the next, igniting a 6–0 run that put the Bruins up comfortably, on their way to sealing the set.

Half an hour later, with the score tied 20–20 in the fourth set, the Bruins needed only five points to be crowned National Champions. They missed a serve into the net. At 21–21, they missed another serve into the net. At 22–22, they missed a serve long. At 23–23, Missry — arguably the most dangerous server in the country — missed his serve into the net.

Three points later, Long Beach sealed up the fourth set by using an ace of their own. Twenty minutes later, Long Beach won their first National Championship in 27 years.

The jump serve can propel you to greatness, onto the very doorsteps of a National Championship — and it can be your most inconsistent weapon, giving the opposing team points at the most critical junctures.

Practicing Serving with Drills

Serving is, by far, the easiest skill to improve because you need only yourself, a ball, and somewhere to serve. In the following sections, we describe a few of our favorite serving drills, which can help you improve your serving in no time.

And we like drills that can double as games. Games are fun and keep you coming back because you want to, not because you feel like you have to.

Goldilocks toss

Follow these steps for one drill that can help you perfect your service toss in the Goldilocks zone:

1. **Toss the ball to yourself.**

   Toss the ball as if you're about to serve.

2. **Catch the toss instead of hitting a serve.**
3. **Repeat Steps 1 and 2 eight more times.**

   You want to do the toss-and-catch a total of nine times.

4. **Repeat Step 1.**
5. **Actually hit the serve.**

   This repetition turns your toss into an automatic process, rather than something that you have to consciously think about every time it's your turn to serve.

6. **Repeat Steps 1 through 5.**

   Rep out your toss — over, and over, and over again.

Working on topspin

A jump serve is centered on *topspin* and its ability to wreak havoc on opposing teams. Topspin helps the ball drop to the ground faster, which means that you can hit it harder while still keeping it in bounds. It's a tremendous tool.

You can work on adding topspin simply by standing, no jump necessary. Just follow these steps:

1. **Stand 10 feet (3 meters) back from the net.**
2. **Toss the ball to yourself.**

3. **Hit the ball over the net by wrapping your hand over the ball while you hit it.**

   Think about your hand hitting closer to the bottom of the ball and coming over top of it while you complete your serve and swing. As your hand wraps over the ball — *snapping,* you'll hear players say a lot — you'll create the topspin.

4. **Repeat Steps 2 and 3 until you can consistently add topspin to your serve.**
5. **Take a step backward on the court.**
6. **Repeat Steps 2 through 4 until you have topspin down from this distance.**
7. **Repeat Steps 2 through 6 until you're successfully hitting topspin serves from the endline.**

Zombie passers

With your serve, you want to make the passers move. In this drill, the passers physically can't move — tell them they're zombies! Follow these steps to practice this effective drill:

1. **Set up passers in the typical positions of an opposing team during serve-receive.**

   These zombie passers can't move their feet for the remainder of the drill. As the server, you want to avoid the zombie passers, hitting serves that the zombies would have to move in order to hit — only they can't!

2. **Hit a serve.**
3. **Score the serve.**

   Here's how the scoring breaks down:

   - **You get a point.** The zombies can't touch the serve without moving their feet.
   - **The zombies get a point.** They touch the serve without moving their feet.
   - **The zombies get two points.** They pass the serve by using their platforms without moving their feet.

4. **Repeat Steps 2 and 3 until either you or the zombies reach 15 points (or however many you want to play to).**

This drill emphasizes the importance of making the passers move their feet. The more you force the passers to move and get out of position, the better chance you have of forcing an errant pass, which could be anything outside of the court, more than 10 feet off the net, over the other side of the net, or into the net itself.

If you don't have enough players to use as zombies — or if you don't have anyone at all to drill with — set up immobile targets, such as trash cans, that can stand in at the passers' positions.

Cornhole serving

This drill is akin to the popular tailgating game of cornhole. Instead of a board and bean bags, however, you use a volleyball court and balls. Just follow these steps:

1. **Denote your target and a smaller target within that target.**

   These targets are your version of the cornhole board and the cornhole itself. You can use cones to mark your targets, but you can just as easily lay down a T-shirt or backpack to mark your targets.

2. **Go to the endline on the other side of the net from your targets.**
3. **Serve, aiming for your targets.**
4. **Award yourself points based on where your serve lands.**

   Here's the scoring structure:

   - **Zero points:** You miss both targets.
   - **One point:** Your serve hits the bigger target (your board).
   - **Three points:** Your serve hits the smaller target (the cornhole).

5. **Repeat Steps 3 and 4 until you reach 21 points.**
6. **Move your targets to a new spot on the court and play again.**

IN THIS CHAPTER

» Seeing what makes for a great passer

» Gathering the components of an effective pass

» Going back to geometry class

» Finding the passers on your team

» Passing different kinds of serves

» Using an overhead pass

Chapter 9

The Meat and Potatoes of Volleyball: Passing

This chapter is all about the meat and potatoes. The bread and butter. The very soul of a volleyball offense, no matter the surface.

Hitters get all the glory, the headlines, the post-season awards, and the gaudy numbers. Setters, too, get much of the praise when an offense is humming the way it should. Both hitters and setters provide vital, critical ingredients to make a successful offense, being competent offensive players.

No type of player gets to shine without a pass.

Neophytes call a *pass* (the first contact of the offense) a bump, referring to part of the old bump-set-spike traditional sequence of a volleyball offensive play. But no one in serious volleyball circles describes it as a bump. It's a pass. Drop *bump* from your vocabulary, unless you're describing a *bump set* which is when you use your platform to set your hitter.

Without an accurate pass, your team is in an awful sorry state. You make your setter or partner upset if you constantly send them chasing passes into the cheap seats or down by the ocean.

Your hitters — or you, if you're on the beach — will be furious if they never get an in-system set, when everything is going smoothly.

REMEMBER

You'll find it nearly impossible to beat a team that regularly passes in system.

This chapter shares what makes a great passer and focuses on the different ways to pass the ball and what you need to know in terms of moving your feet, creating space, and finishing. With these fundamentals and a ton of practicing, you can start *passing dimes*, whether you're indoor or on the beach.

Identifying What Makes a Great Passer

Passing is where everything begins. Your team will have trouble siding out if you're passing inaccurately, and if you can't side out, you can't play defense, and if you can't play defense, you can't score and win matches. Everything begins with the pass.

Here are a few traits that make excellent passers:

- **Consistent:** Almost anyone can get hit with a ball and it'll end up in the location in which you want to pass. But to pass to that location on a consistent basis? That's what you're looking for. Consistency is everything when it comes to passing. No team is more difficult to beat than one who passes perfectly almost every time. Conversely, no team is easier to beat than the one who can never seem to pass in system.

  Be the former. Be consistent.
- **Calm:** If you're the one doing much of the work in serve-receive, when your team is passing, then you're going to be under a lot of pressure. You might be getting pinged with devilish float serves or getting bombed by massive jump serves. No matter, you must stay calm and be ready for every type of serve. The calmer you are and looser you are, the more consistent you're going to be as a passer.
- **Smart:** The ball knows one thing and one thing only: Angles. It will only go the direction you tell it to via the angle in your platform (see the next section). The best passers are smart and know how to angle their platforms so it's always facing their target.

Forming a Platform

A *platform* is the term that describes the flat, solid surface players create with their forearms to either pass or bump-set a volleyball. A solid, consistent platform can make all the difference between being an accurate passer and not. Here, we explore the two main ways to form a platform:

- Fist-in-palm
- Thumb-on-thumb

Which is superior? The answer to that is both.

Both forms are common and correct, and both operate under the same principle for success, which involves making your platform surface as flat, even, and solid as possible, while getting your elbows as close together as you can, which makes for a flatter, more even surface.

REMEMBER

Everyone's body is unique, and some passers prefer one way to form a passing platform, some prefer the other, and some even form a variation of the two. At the end of the day, aim to create the flattest surface with your forearms that you can, which leads to the most consistent results. You want consistency. Use whatever technique helps you form that consistent, flat platform.

The following sections walk you through how you can form a platform that works for you.

Going with a fist-in-palm platform

To form the fist-in-palm platform (see Figure 9-1) — the most common type of platform — follow these steps:

1. **Make a loose fist with your nondominant hand.**
2. **Wrap your dominant hand around that fist.**
3. **Lay your thumbs straight and flat next to each other on top of your fists.**
4. **Point your thumbs down toward the ground as much as they can go, flattening your forearms.**

   Congratulations, you've formed a passing platform!

FIGURE 9-1: A fist-in-palm platform.

Photo by Travis Mewhirter

To answer a question you may have: No, it doesn't really matter whether you have your dominant or nondominant hand on top of the other. Players just more commonly wrap the dominant hand overtop because that feels more comfortable to them. Experiment and go with what feels best for you.

Creating a thumb-on-thumb platform

The other technique to make a platform is known as the *thumb-on-thumb*, also referred to as the *seashell* or *clamshell* (see Figure 9-2). To create this platform, follow these steps:

1. **Place both hands flat, palms facing up.**
2. **Gradually bring your thumbs together.**

   Make them flat and parallel on top.
3. **Press your thumbs together lightly.**

   This step brings your palms slightly together, as well.
4. **Point your thumbs down toward the ground and palms up.**

   This step flattens your platform, creating the even surface you want so that you can control your pass.

FIGURE 9-2: A thumb-on-thumb platform.

Photo by Travis Mewhirter

THE . . . GOLFING PLATFORM?

When I (Travis) first began playing beach volleyball at age 24, no one had ever shown me how to form a platform. I knew, of course, that the ball was supposed to hit my forearms and bounce to a target.

Not having a book such as this one in my possession, I stole from my previous best sport: golf. I formed a passing platform that used the interlocking grip I used as a golfer, with my right index finger locked between the ring and pinky fingers on my left hand, and my left hand wrapping over my right thumb.

It was ridiculous, but it — sort of — worked. Sort of.

Over time, and with enough tinkering and experimenting, I gradually shifted, unknowingly, into the seashell platform (which we talk about in the section "Creating a thumb-on-thumb platform" in this chapter). I stopped interlocking my fingers and splayed them out, like a seashell. It's still funky (unconventional), but it does the job — because even though it has some unconventional elements, it still forms a flat and even surface. See what I mean in the photo.

Photo by Steve Gentry

Don't worry about which platform you prefer or if you custom-build your own. Whatever you do, make the flattest, most even surface for your platform. You can use that flat, even surface to make an angle that you can aim at a target. And the ball knows angles.

Focusing on Your Target

In order to be an excellent passer, you need to have the right target in mind for where you want the ball to go — where you want to angle your platform.

Beach volleyball targets

In beach volleyball, the ideal target is an area in the middle of the court, around three feet off the net. This gives your setter enough room off the net so they won't be in danger of running into the net, while being close enough so the set they give you isn't coming over your shoulder as a hitter, which is a far more difficult set to hit. Hitting a ball that is in front of you and that you're able to track it all the way without looking over your shoulder is much easier.

As far as height goes, 10 to 15 feet is ideal, because it gives the setter enough time to get their feet under the ball to set without being too high and imposing to set, be it with their hands or platform.

Indoor volleyball targets

Indoor volleyball's ideal passing target is around 3 feet (0.9m) off the net (like in beach, discussed in the preceding section), although you can err tighter because indoor setters *jump set* (jumping while setting) or *tip set* (using their fingertips to set) more frequently than on the beach, so they can bail themselves out of a tight situation. Indoor passers should aim at the front-right of their side of the court (position 2), where the setter operates.

This target gives the setter the ability to set all of their offensive targets, whether the outside, middle, or right side, and even a back row set or a dump. The ideal height, depending on your offensive system, is about 10 to 15 feet (3–4.5m).

Passing the Ball with Your Platform: The How-To

Passing, one of the most important skills in volleyball, can make or break your team.

Your team may look imposing during warmups, when your hitters can put the ball down anywhere they want. However, if your team can't pass the ball to the setter and keep the ball in system, you're not going to go far as a team.

The following sections break down how to effectively pass by using your platform so that you can practice and improve your passing.

Starting with your feet

You want to put yourself in a position where the ball is in front of you. You can much more easily aim your platform at a target when you have everything in front of you, rather than the ball being overhead or behind you, because it's easier to track.

Get yourself into position by following these steps:

1. **Take a prep step.**

   A *prep step* is similar to what you might do in tennis when waiting to receive a serve. You can also think of this step like the footwork of a boxer, who bounces, small and light on their feet, able to move anywhere or quickly change direction.

2. **While the ball is traveling toward you from the server, stay behind the ball.**

   If you see the ball coming for your chest or over your shoulder, either backpedal, keeping the ball in front of you and on your midline, or open up, dropping your right or left leg back to the end line and allowing you to pass outside of your body.

3. **If you do pass the ball outside of your body, angle your shoulders to aim your platform at your passing target (see Figure 9-3).**

   This quick angle calculation adds a layer of complexity to the pass. Whenever possible, try to pass on the body's midline because it's easier to angle your platform along with your core, but this isn't 100 percent necessary, or 100 percent possible all of the time.

FIGURE 9-3: Passing outside of midline isn't a bad thing! It's a ready to use tool to keep your passing accurate.

primipil/Adobe Stock Photos

Chaim Schalk and Alex Brouwer are two of the best passers of their generation. A pair of Olympians on the beach, Schalk has also competed in six World Championships, while Brouwer has even won one (in 2013) and boasts an Olympic bronze medal in 2016. Both are superior offensive players — thanks, in large part, to almost always being in system, passing to their ideal target.

And both, when asked, offered the same advice when it comes to being an elite passer: "It starts with the feet."

Wait. If you need to calculate angles and properly shape your platforms, how do your feet fit into where your forearms send the ball? Well, your feet and positioning largely determine how you can angle your platform and whether you can remain still upon contact. A hallmark of elite passers is being still — or *quiet*, as many call it — upon contact.

If you put yourself in a position where you can be still, unmoving, when the ball contacts your platform, you produce a consistent pass. If you're still in motion or swinging your arms while passing the ball, you're changing your angles, which produces a wildly inconsistent product. And your setters will be unhappy with you. You don't want unhappy setters.

Taking certain passing steps

You have two basic footwork fundamentals to choose from when passing:

- **Stick step:** Just a step. If the ball is slightly outside of your body, either to the right or the left, you need only a simple step. Keep one foot planted, like you're pivoting in basketball, and step with the other foot to get your platform in the right position to pass the ball — while, of course, angling your shoulders to your target.

  The name *stick step* refers to the fact that you're stepping and sticking, so you're balanced and solid when the ball contacts your platform.

- **Shuffle step:** Say that you're in a scenario where the server has served well outside of your bodyline, and you need more than a step to get there. You can make a shuffle step to your target. Rather than taking multiple individual steps, the shuffle
  - Is far more efficient to get to your position
  - Requires less movement
  - Can get you there faster
  - Keeps space between your legs so that they can stay roughly shoulder-width apart to maintain that nice, steady balance that you need to pass well

A key to the shuffle step, or any movement when passing, is to stay as level as you can, including in your eyeline, throughout the pass. Undulating up and down keeps you off balance and makes it more difficult to pass consistently toward your target.

This phrase can help you remember to get your feet into position first and then worry about the platform: Beat the ball, or the ball beats you.

Beat the ball to its path, and you can form a solid, balanced, even platform. Allow the ball to get where you're going before you do, and you either miss the serve altogether, giving the other team an ace (and a point), or have to make an out-of-system pass to an unhappy setter.

Creating space between your body and platform

When you're passing, in order to maximize your control of the ball, create space between your platform and your body. Ideally, you should be able to fit a volleyball in between your *triceps* (the muscles on the back of your upper arms) and your *core*. If you can't, then you get what volleyball folks call *jammed* — you lose control of your ability to direct the ball to a target because you can't tweak or adjust your platform as easily when it's so close to your body.

REMEMBER

This is why your feet are so important. If you see the ball coming at your chest, either back up or open up, creating the ideal space that you need between your platform and your body so that you can direct the pass.

A viral video hit Instagram in the fall of 2024 that featured young Japanese volleyball players passing volleyballs. A video of volleyball passing, in and of itself, isn't unusual. Japan is a small but mighty powerhouse when it comes to volleyball, both indoors and out. Despite the diminutive frame of many of its players, the Japanese still find ways to thrive, utilizing a magnetic ball control in which they seem to control their passing and setting with a video game controller.

What was unusual about this particular video, and what made it go viral among the volleyball communities, was that these players were passing volleyballs while lying on top of Bosu exercise balls. At first glance, it seems preposterous, an outrageous-looking drill designed for that very purpose: intrigue and a bit of engagement online.

But upon further inspection, what was happening was stressing the importance of creating space between the platform and the body.

Now, we certainly don't recommend you pass while laying on a Bosu ball for hours. But the principle of the video, allowing you to recognize what proper spacing should feel like, allows you to then replicate it when you begin to play or practice.

Holding your finish

A common cue among volleyball coaches, both indoor and out, is to *hold your finish* or *freeze your platform* after contact, meaning you keep your platform still well after the pass is made.

Many newer volleyball players let their platform *break* (meaning their arms separate) immediately after contact, which has an immediate effect on the pass itself. This concept holds true in almost every sport. In golf, players hold their finish. In basketball, the final step of the famed BEEF (balance, eyes, elbow, follow-through) has the player hold their follow-through or finish.

The freeze in your volleyball platform allows you to maintain the angle that you create throughout the entirety of the pass — and the only thing the ball knows is angles (which we talk about in the section "Understanding that the ball knows angles" later in this chapter).

Maintain the platform's angle, even after the ball has left the platform, because

» A consistent angle creates a consistent pass.

» A consistent pass makes for a happy setter.

» A happy setter leads to a happy life.

Connecting Geometry and Volleyball

Did you pay attention in geometry class? We hope you did. We hope that you internalized the Pythagorean Theorem; love doing geometrical translations, reflections, and rotations; and can still use a protractor.

No, no — we're kidding. Mostly.

Volleyball, and particularly passing a volleyball, involves little more than basic geometry. From your middle and high school geometry classes that you may have snoozed through (hey, C's get degrees!), you really only need to know angles, which we discuss in the following sections.

Understanding that the ball knows angles

The ball, as every volleyball coach since time immemorial can tell you, knows angles. And that's it! That's all it knows. A volleyball isn't a thinking being. It doesn't hear your instruction, think better of it, and talk back. It obeys, immediately and perfectly, to whatever you tell it to do by using the angle of your platform.

As Lindsey Knudsen, an All-Conference outside hitter at St. Mary's University who finished her college career with more than 1,000 kills, put it to Travis Mewhirter: "Sacrifice your body for the angle."

Nothing but the angle of the platform matters. Nothing. This angle is almost wholly determined by your shoulders. A common mistake among new volleyball players has them aiming with their wrists, twisting their arms around, or swinging their platform to their target. As we discuss in the section "Holding your finish" earlier in this chapter, do your best to stop moving on contact with the ball.

Angling for serves of all depths

Your angles have to change, of course, depending on where in the court you plan to pass the ball.

Passing short serves

If you're passing a short serve (see Figure 9-4), follow these steps:

1. **Angle your platform more parallel to the ground so that you can get the loft required to pass it more straight up and down.**

   On the beach, if you get served short, you often have to get into a kneeling or lunging position.

2. **Position your inside knee down, with your outside leg still up.**

   The inside knee is the knee closest to the center of the court, while your outside knee is the one closest to the sideline. This positioning keeps your hips and body open to your target.

   WARNING

   If you put your outside knee down, your hips and body are closed to your target, making it difficult for you to angle your platform to where you want the ball to go.

3. **While you pass the short serve, rise with the ball.**

   This movement ensures that you pass with your trunk, rather than swinging your arms, which changes the angle of your platform.

FIGURE 9-4: Passing a short serve.

Photo by Travis Mewhirter

Getting low, and using your trunk, helps you pass the bottom of the ball, angling the pass up so that you don't pass it into or over the net. Sprinting up to the front of the court, lunging to one knee, and rising up is difficult, yes. It's a lot of work, and you won't always be able to execute every step on every short serve, but it's important to do this whenever possible.

Passing a serve aimed at the middle of the court

When you get a serve to the middle of the court, you want to make a roughly 45-degree angle between the ground and your platform (refer to Figure 9-5). Of course, you don't have a protractor available to measure your angles out on the court, so to get a feel for this angle, go out and practice.

Have someone on the opposite side of the net toss balls to you while you're standing in the middle of your side of the net. Experiment with different angles. Eventually, you can find a roughly 45-degree angle and understand what that angle feels like.

FIGURE 9-5: Passing a mid-court serve.

Photo by Travis Mewhirter

Going for a deep-serve pass

When served deep, make sure that you get your body behind the ball and flatten out your platform to give the ball the distance it needs to travel to your passing target (see Figure 9-6).

A golfer has clubs numbered based on their loft, or how high they can hit the ball. A sand wedge is angled at 56 degrees, while a 3-iron (designed to make the ball travel much farther) is typically between 19 and 21 degrees. Drivers, the clubs that can make the ball go the farthest, can have angles as low as 8 degrees, some even lower. The lower the loft, the farther it sends the ball.

Similarly, in volleyball, the farther you are from the net, the less loft you need to get the ball to your passing target. The closer you are to the net, the more loft you need to pick the ball up so that it doesn't shoot over the net.

FIGURE 9-6: Passing a deep serve.

Photo by Travis Mewhirter

Identifying the Passers on Your Team

In beach volleyball, both players on the court have to pass (which applies to any skill in beach). In indoor volleyball, not all players necessarily need to know how to pass.

Anyone playing indoor volleyball must be able to pass, even though you may not be one of your team's primary passers. Indoor teams most generally use these types of serve-receive:

- **Three-person serve-receive:** A team wants its libero, defensive specialist, and back-row outside hitter passing; although who actually does the passing can certainly change based on the serve. It's the opposing team's job to make passing as difficult as possible, and they'll often avoid serving the libero and defensive specialist when they can.

  Opposite hitters, middles, and setters attempt to stay out of the way when their team's in serve-receive so that the libero, defensive specialist, and outsides can pass uninhibited.

The libero takes responsibility of the middle of the court, and the pair of outsides take the left and the right. Depending on your team and the capabilities of the opposite hitter, they can also pass on occasion.

- **Four-person serve-receive:** In the event that the opposing team has a particularly intimidating server, a team can also use this four-person formation. It has the libero in the middle, both outsides, and the opposite or a defensive specialist taking responsibility for passing.

  Although the four-person serve-receive formation adds passers, it also creates more *seams* (spaces between passers) between the passers and can allow for miscommunications. It also ties up more hitters in serve-receive, so fewer hitters are ready to simply attack when the ball is passed.

- **Two-person serve-receive:** If your team has two very strong passers, you sometimes may see this formation. This will often be a libero and a team's best outside hitter serving as the passers. Two people covering a lot of court is difficult, but you can do it when your team has two reliable passers.

In any formation, short serves and serves to the sideline can often force a team's hand to allow the setter or — heaven forbid — the middle to pass. (A middle passing isn't optimal, because they're often a team's worst passers, and when they do pass, they typically won't be a hitting threat).

TIP

Even though everyone needs to know how to pass, if you're an outside hitter, libero, or defensive specialist — or aspire to be one — you have to improve your pass.

Passing a Jump Serve: The How-To

With a *jump serve*, the server tosses the ball and often hits it with pace and sometimes topspin, like they're attacking on offense. So passing a jump serve is a bit like playing defense (refer to Chapter 11 for more specifics).

The goal of a jump serve is to overpower the passer, to make the serve come in so fast that the passer either

- Doesn't have time to react and form a proper platform angle
- Can't absorb the energy of the serve enough to control the ball off the platform

Players use the jump serves far more often in the men's game than the women's (for reasons that we get into in Chapter 8), but every player needs to understand how to pass a jump serve, whether they see those serves often or not.

To pass a jump serve, follow these steps:

1. **Place your feet behind the ball (behind where you anticipate the ball will be after it's served).**

   Keep the ball in front of you while you're passing. The more the ball is in front of you, the more you can control the angle of your platform. (Flip back to the section "Connecting Geometry and Volleyball" earlier in this chapter for discussion of angles.)

2. **If you can, shuffle or step to get the ball on your midline.**

   When you can't reposition, so the ball is outside of your body, ensure that you angle your shoulders to your target.

3. **Crouch low so that you're below the ball when you pass it.**
4. **Contact the bottom of the ball so that it travels up.**

   The speed of a jump serve can often result in an *overpass,* where the passer passes the ball over the net. The lower you get when you pass, the less likely you are to hit an overpass because you angle your platform more vertically than horizontally.

A central difference between jump serves and float serves (which we talk about in the following section) is the speed with which they're coming. Jump serves come in much faster than floats, and so the ball therefore has more energy when it impacts your platform. Oftentimes, if you don't *cushion* the pass properly (meaning you take the energy out of the ball by absorbing it instead of swinging your platform to put even more energy into it), the ball rockets off your platform, creating a high, spinning pass that your teammates find difficult to set.

REMEMBER

Imagine, for a moment, that you're catching an egg. If you swing your hand up to catch the egg, that egg most likely breaks. But if you gently cradle it when it comes into your hands, cushioning it with soft hands while you bring your hands back to your body with the egg, it stays whole. Passing a jump serve is a bit like catching an egg. You want to cushion it, cradle it, and take the energy out of the serve so that you can create an accurate pass.

Passing a Float Serve

Float serves are as unpredictable as a teenager. They drop when you think they'll stay the course, rise when you anticipate a drop, dive to the left on a blink or veer to the right for no discernible reason. They're wolves in sheep's clothing, the devil you thought you knew — but don't know at all, really.

A well-struck float serve is, in the women's game, the deadliest type of serve (refer to Chapter 8 for how you can master the float serve). In the following sections, we discuss ways to remove the threat of the float as best you can by figuring out how to pass it.

You need to add energy to float serves to get the ball to your desired target. That isn't so with jump serves, which we discuss in the previous section.

Going step-by-step through a float serve pass

The sweet sauce of a float serve, the why behind its devastating effectiveness, is its movement. The basic concept behind a float serve involves serving the ball with no spin, thus making it more susceptible to gravity, the wind (if outdoors), and air pockets in the gym (if indoors). With all that movement, your pass must begin with your feet.

Follow these steps to effectively pass a float serve:

1. **Read the direction of the serve.**

   You want to get your feet, body, and platform in the optimal position to pass at that location.

2. **While moving to the location you identify in Step 1, keep your hands apart.**

   Moving with your platform already formed is both inefficient and frequently results in you swinging your arms and platform during the pass contact. (See the section "Holding your finish" earlier in this chapter for why that type of movement is a no-no.)

   TIP

   Brandon Joyner, co-owner of the volleyball instructional company Better at Beach and a former professional indoor and beach player, says on his YouTube Channel, "It's almost going to feel as if you're dancing with the ball."

3. **When you have your feet in the best position possible, put your platform together.**
4. **On contact, encourage the ball, giving it an extra nudge to your target.**

TIP

Floats will mostly be coming in with, at best, medium speed. On contact, you oftentimes have to encourage the ball, giving it an extra nudge to your target.

Getting yourself positioned to pass a float serve

In order to put energy back into a float serve, you need to remember some basic passing principles:

- **Create space between your body and platform.** With that space, you can use your trunk to add that slight encouragement to the ball. If you don't have space between your platform and body, you get jammed and have to absorb the serve, rather than steer it.
- **Pass above your hips, if you can.** The lower you allow the ball to get, the less you can use your legs and core to push the ball to your setter. The higher you can pass a float serve — between hips and sternum if you're using a platform, above the neck for hand passing — the better.
- **Get close.** Oftentimes, players begin their passing position close to the net when playing against a float server to hedge against the drop and unpredictable movement of the float.

Reading a float serve

So how, you might be asking, if 90 percent of the pass is about reading and moving to the spot, can I read a float serve?

You do it. Over, and over, and over, and over again.

There's no hack of this process, no book — sorry! — that you can read that'll tell you how a float serve will move. Being able to figure out how to read a float only comes with repetition after repetition. Go out and pass as many float serves as you can. You'll get a better feel for how they move, though you'll be hard-pressed to find anyone in the world who can explain the exact why to a float serve's movement patterns.

That's why the float is such a devil.

Focusing on Overhead Passing

You probably can't find a greater difference between indoor and beach volleyball than first contact after a serve, and what the sport allows and what it doesn't.

In beach volleyball, an *overhead pass* (a pass over your head) that uses open hands is disallowed. In indoor, however, you can make such a pass without breaking the rules — and an open-handed overhead pass, particularly on a float serve, can give you a huge advantage if you can do it well.

But you may be wondering, "If my platform is so effective, why do I need an overhead pass?" If you're in a position where you can't move back fast enough or open up smooth enough to use your platform, you can often more easily take a small step forward and use your hands for an overhead pass. You don't have to hurry and move quite as much to get into position like you do for a pass that you make by using your platform. You can use your hands for a much more controlled process and, by extension, result.

A deep serve can be radically effective with minimal effort, especially on the beach, if the opposing team struggles with overhead passing. It's an uncomfortable position from which to pass, and if the passers struggle moving their feet, it'll cause the chaos the server wants.

Overhead passing in indoor

As far as technique goes, an overhead pass is remarkably similar to a hand set (see Chapter 8, where we discuss setting with your hands). Just follow these steps (Figure 9-7 shows an indoor overhead pass):

1. **Start from a low to medium position.**
2. **Rise steadily while the ball comes toward you.**
3. **Keep the ball in front of you or just over your head.**

   You can struggle to control anything that gets behind you, and an uncontrolled pass results in either an ace or an unhappy setter (neither of which you want).
4. **Freeze your finish after the ball leaves your hands, holding your arms and hands toward your target.**

   You use this same freezing process in platform passing (discussed in the section "Holding your finish" earlier in this chapter).

FIGURE 9-7: Overhead passing.

von Lieres/Adobe Stock Photos

A critical difference between setting and overhead passing is that you can't double on an overhead pass. On the first contact of indoor volleyball, you can do virtually whatever you want, so long as you don't catch and throw the ball. So, you can make your hands firmer than when you set because you don't need to worry about being whistled for a double contact.

REMEMBER

If overhead passing with your hands seems like a huge advantage, well, that's because it is. Passers have incalculably more control when using their hands to pass a float serve than they do when using their platforms.

Overhead passing on the beach

As a general rule, if you overhead pass your first contact on the beach, something has gone terribly wrong for you (or terribly right for the serving team). If your feet didn't get you in the proper position, you may find yourself with the ball coming over your head. So, you need to use your overhead platform to pass the ball.

Unlike indoor (see the preceding section), you can't use your open hands and double the first contact. Beach volleyball put this rule in place to avoid giving the offense a huge advantage on the beach because the opposing team has four fewer defenders than in indoor.

If you want to overhead pass in beach, your hands and platform need to be connected to each other, adding to the difficulty of controlling the ball. If your hands come apart during the contact, you get whistled for a double. Everything must stay interlocked throughout the pass.

The following sections look at two acceptable options that you have for overhead passes on the beach.

WARNING

These small overhead platforms are very difficult to control. Whenever possible, use your feet to get your forearm platforms on the ball. Consider the taco or tomahawk as a break-glass-in-case-of-emergency platform, and an indicator that you're not using your feet well enough (flip back to the section "Starting with your feet" earlier in this chapter).

The tomahawk

You can form the tomahawk for a beach overhead pass quite easily. However, actually executing a tomahawk pass isn't so simple.

To form the tomahawk platform (see Figure 9-8 to see what it looks like), follow these steps:

1. **Begin with your normal platform.**

   We explain how to set up this platform in the section "Forming a Platform" earlier in this chapter.

2. **Bend your elbows, positioning your hands about a ball's length away from your chest.**
3. **Raise your hands over your head.**

   Have your wrists just above your forehead.

4. **Try to contact the ball on the small, flat platform made by the backs of your palms near your pinky fingers.**

   Because this platform is so firm, you don't need to add any extra energy into the ball; you want to simply allow the ball to contact your platform and bounce off. The energy of the serve plus the solidness of the platform combines for enough force to send the ball to your desired target.

The taco

An acceptable, although difficult, overhead passing technique on the beach is popularly referred to as the taco. Like ordering a taco at an airport, however, you want to use this overhead pass only in a complete and total emergency.

FIGURE 9-8: A tomahawk overhead pass.

Photo by Travis Mewhirter

To form the taco (Figure 9-9 shows what it looks like), follow these steps:

1. **Put your hands together, completely flat.**
2. **Raise your hands just above your forehead, elbows slightly bent.**
3. **Use the back of your palms, extended through your pinky fingers, as your passing platform.**

FIGURE 9-9: A taco overhead pass.

Photo by Travis Mewhirter

Tackling Some Passing Drills

Want to know the best way to figure out how to pass? You pass.

A lot.

There's no substitute for simply passing volleyballs, over and over and over again. The way to improve and figure out things like how to read a float serve, how to absorb the energy of a jump serve, how to move your feet for short serves, and how to open up for deep serves is through trial and error — that means practice and more practice. Here are a couple of our favorite drills.

Rapid fire passing

In this drill, you need two players or more, ideally at least three. One player passes, one player serves, and one stands where the passer's ideal passing target is. Follow these steps:

1. **The server serves ten balls from the endline, standing in front of the passer.**
2. **The passer standing on the opposite side of the net passes those ten balls to the target, who then tosses the ball back to the server.**
3. **The server then moves to the middle of the endline and serves another ten balls.**
4. **The server then moves and serves another ten balls from the angle, or cross-court.**

   Mix in jump serves and float serves, deep serves and short serves. It's as much of a serving drill as it is a passing drill.

You can modify as needed as well. If you want to make it easier, have the server begin at half-court, then three-quarter court, then back to full length. Do ten minutes of this drill at every practice and you'll become proficient in a hurry.

Goldilocks passing

A favorite of the Florida State beach volleyball team, this is a unique drill that teaches you how to manipulate the ball in serve-receive to get it to go wherever you want, virtually on command. Have at least one server and one passer, although ideally you use a multiple of servers for expediency's sake.

Follow these steps:

1. **For one minute, the passer passes as high as they can while still controlling the ball to a target.**
2. **For one minute, the passer then passes as low as they possibly can while still controlling the ball.**
3. **For one minute, the passer passes juuuuuust right.**
4. **Now switch to the left and right.**
5. **For one minute, the passer passes to the left sideline.**
6. **For one minute, the passer passes to the right sideline.**
7. **For one minute, the passer passes juuuuust right.**

Six minutes, a ton of serves, and total and complete control of every type of pass.

IN THIS CHAPTER

» Figuring out the traits of a successful blocker

» Following the process of blocking

» Positioning yourself to block

» Keeping your eye on your opponent

» Becoming a defender when needed

Chapter 10

Pressing the Net to Score: Blocking

Blocking may be one of the most misunderstood skills in the game of volleyball. Casual viewers on television, or those unfamiliar with the game, look at blockers as simpletons with a simple job: To jump and get in the way of the hitter. They're not wrong. The central mission of a blocker *is* to get in the way of the hitter and remove the threat of their optimal, 100-percent attack.

But blocking is a beautiful art, as nuanced as any aspect of volleyball. It's as finely tuned as a handmade watch, with all its tiny dials ticking in the proper order and direction, the engravings precise, those artisanal details making it so valuable and unique.

And size isn't everything when you block. This chapter walks you through the necessities of becoming an effective blocker so that, even if you're only 5 feet 8 inches tall and not exactly explosive, you can get the blocks that your team needs.

Identifying What Makes a Great Blocker

At first blush, you might think the only two traits needed to make a great blocker are to jump high and be tall. Sure, those help, undeniably so. But there are loads of instances where the tallest blockers and the highest jumpers weren't as useful at the net as they should have been, because they didn't possess the traits that truly matter. Here are three traits that we identify to make a great blocker:

- **Disciplined:** Blockers have a job to do, and that's to take away the space they've told the defenders behind them that they'll take. This requires extreme discipline at the net:
  - If your job on the beach is to block the line attack, you absolutely need to make sure the attacker can't *beat you down the line* (hit the ball down the line).
  - If your job is to stop the angle attack, that's your only job, period.

  REMEMBER

  If you're disciplined at the net, and your defender is disciplined behind you — easier to do, by the way, when you're doing your job at the net — then you'll make life so much more difficult for the offense.
- **Patient:** Blockers are, counterintuitively, not really going to block all that many balls. You may, on your best day, block two balls in a set. That means that a lot of balls you won't block — and that's okay! You just need to stay patient, taking advantage of the mistakes the opponent makes when they're undisciplined with their attacks — and you're disciplined with your block.
- **Smart:** Not all blockers are simple cavemen and women who just try to be as big as possible. They're smart, remarkably so. It's your job to read the set and approach from the opponent and determine what type of attack is most likely:
  - If you see that the ball is coming close to the net, it's your job to reach over and surround it.
  - If you see that the ball is drifting off the net, it's your job to adjust accordingly, either pulling off the net in beach volleyball or delaying your jump indoors.

  REMEMBER

  It's all about reading the scenario, seeing what the most likely attack is, and doing your job to prevent that attack from beating you.

Knowing Your Role as a Blocker

If you walked into Florida State University's practices in the late 1980s and looked at the eight freshmen standing there, you probably would have thought, "Which one of these girls might not make it?" And I'm guessing a few people — teammates, maybe even coaches — might have pointed at me, Gabrielle Reece. I was late to the game. Really late.

I didn't get serious about volleyball until my junior year of high school. And when I say I was green, I don't mean inexperienced — I mean brand new. Before going to Florida State on an athletic scholarship, I had played in exactly three club tournaments. Three. That's it. I also came from a very small high school, and my volleyball coach was actually a basketball coach — which probably tells you everything you need to know.

Right before I left for Florida State, my club coach in Tampa, Randy Dagostino, pulled me aside and said, "I really think we should work on your middle blocking steps."

That was polite coach-speak for: "You're about to be exposed."

What I didn't have going for me was experience. What I did have was that I was 6 feet 3 inches and coachable — and, as it turns out, I had a natural middle blocker's mentality.

Being the team's communicator

People always say the setter is the quarterback of the volleyball offense, and that's true. But indoors, the middle blocker is often seen as the quarterback of the defense. From Day 1, I understood that my job wasn't just to jump and hope. It was to read, anticipate, and commit.

I always knew who the biggest offensive threats were. I paid attention to how dynamic the opposing setter was because that told me everything about how honest I needed to stay with the setter and when I could move. Before the other team even served the ball, I was already playing scenarios in my head. If the pass goes here, the percentages say the ball goes there. If their best hitter is front row, the setter is going to try to get her the ball no matter what.

Because of my constant observations and determinations, I talked constantly to my teammates. I let them know who was front row. I pointed. I reinforced the angles that I was taking.

And then I did my absolute best to stay disciplined enough not to move until I actually saw where the ball was going. That's the hard part. Guessing feels powerful. Waiting feels vulnerable. But disciplined blocking is about staying true to your position as long as you physically can — and then moving decisively after you have a clear picture of the play.

If I was playing a team that passed well and had a lineup full of hitters, I sometimes hedged my bets and played the percentages. After I understood where the ball was going, I'd take my eyes off it, move as fast as I could, and get back to the hitter. And here was my rule, always: I took the angle I told my teammates I was going to take. Every time.

I didn't plan my play around being flashy. I wanted to be the most reliable teammate I could be. My job was to take my space first. If I could seal the net and block the ball, great — that's the dream. But my first responsibility was always to close the space that was going to be open. Because that space was mine to take. After I did that, I could freewheel from there.

Blocking the middle ball, I tried to take as much space and as many hard angles as I could. I didn't want to just stop the ball — I wanted to make hitters uncomfortable. To make them hesitate. To make them do something different because I had done my job well.

I admit that if we had one particular hitter who was killing us, I would sometimes fully commit to stopping her — either to stop the bleeding or to try to change the momentum and morale on our side. These are decisions you make as the game goes on.

Blocking on the beach

On the beach (Figure 10-1 shows Gabby blocking), the strategy changes from indoor volleyball, but the mindset doesn't. I started playing beach volleyball four-on-four, which felt similar to indoor. But two-on-two is a different animal:

- **Taking the angle:** My first job was still to take the angle that was my responsibility and then play with the freedom to take away the hard hit.
- **Cleaning up:** I was also always ready to get down as quickly as possible to clean up the little shots around me, so my partner didn't have to kill herself covering the whole court.
- **Hitting in transition:** I put up a hittable ball in transition to my partner, no matter what. That was something I didn't have to navigate indoors, and it's something I really had to work on after I started playing on the beach.

» **Deciding when to block:** I decided when it was best to block based on the other team's dynamic — were they going to shoot us to death, or were they a big, swinging team — and when it was going to be more productive to pull quickly and not get stuck in no man's land.

FIGURE 10-1: Gabby blocking on the beach.

Published with permission from Gabby Reece

Extending the rally

Indoors, another part of my job — and one I took seriously — was covering my hitters. Yes, I was there to block, but I also made it my responsibility to be there if the ball got blocked back so that we had another chance to play it. That attitude alone extends rallies, and it extends careers.

When I say I made a career out of doing two disciplines of volleyball really well — hitting and blocking — I'm not exaggerating. You don't just need to be big to block. Look at someone like Tammy Liley, who stands below 6 feet tall and blocked internationally for Team USA against some of the greatest hitters in the world by staying low, tight, quick-handed, and disciplined.

As a blocker, you don't finish your job by max jumping and taking air. You finish by using your hands in the moment, sealing the net, taking responsibility for your space, and being a constant, intelligent threat. One of the mantras that I committed to indoors was: Close the block first.

Discussing Height: Do You Have to Be Big to Block?

Some of you may be inclined to skip reading this chapter. You may be under the impression that you're too small or don't jump high enough, a pair of easy-to-make mistakes that players all the way up to the professional level frequently make.

We can see why you might think that you have to be tall to play as a blocker. Look at the most successful beach volleyball player of all time, Kerri Walsh Jennings. Nicknamed 6 Feet of Sunshine, Walsh Jennings stands 6 feet 3 inches tall and is the owner of three Olympic Gold Medals and a Bronze. Since 2004, when her indomitable run began, in all but one Olympics, a blocker standing 6 feet 3 inches or taller won the gold medal. (The lone exception, Kira Walkenhorst of Germany, was 6 feet tall.)

So, is height helpful? Supremely so! But we're here to tell you that you are (most likely) not too small, and that you (most likely) do, indeed, jump high enough. Although being tall and jumping high obviously helps you play as an effective blocker, those traits are luxuries, not necessities.

Looking at the stats

When 6-foot-9 Phil Dalhausser did a statistical review of one of his 20-plus seasons as a professional beach volleyball player (a span that included seven Best Blocker in the World awards from the FIVB), he was shocked to realize that he averaged a little less than two blocks per set.

An objective, statistical examination of beach volleyball shows that nobody in the sport averages more than two blocks per set, even the tallest players. In indoor volleyball, the number is even lower: The best blockers on the planet get only about three blocks per match — less than one block per set. (Of course, in individual matches, blockers may have exceptional days and rack up double the expected average.)

Waiting for them to swing low

When Dalhausser reviewed the numbers, he had a thought, after his initial disbelief wore off: You don't have to be all that tall to be an effective blocker. Even the best hitters, he said, make a mistake and *swing low* — barely over the net, or into the top of the net — from time to time. With the women's net standing just 7 feet 4 inches tall, and the men's standing 7 feet 11 inches tall, almost everyone can jump and get their hands over the net.

And if you can do that, you can block the best hitters in the world when they make the mistake of swinging low — which statistically happens on at least two occasions per set, indoors and out.

Need evidence? The 2024 Olympic gold medalist, Jonatan Hellvig, stands 6 feet 3 inches tall — 8 inches shorter than his opponent in the final match, Nils Ehlers. The result? A 21-10, 21-13 victory for Hellvig and his partner, David Ahman, in the most lopsided final in Olympic history.

REMEMBER

Yes, you undeniably have an advantage as a blocker in men's volleyball if you stand tall, like Dalhausser, or in women's volleyball if you're 6 feet 3 inches, like Walsh Jennings. And yes, you definitely have an edge if you can jump 40 inches high, like Hellvig does. But if you don't have these advantages, you can still be an effective blocker. Just focus on the traits we discuss in the section "Identifying What Makes a Great Blocker" earlier in this chapter.

Blocking 101: What You Need to Do

Like any skill, blocking can get complicated. Here, we narrow it down to the main points and tips so that when you're struggling or need a reminder, you can simplify your blocking and refer to this section.

Focusing on penetration

Poll as many blockers as you want, they all give you the same first rule or principle of blocking: You must master *penetration* — getting your hands over the net.

When we asked Brandie Wilkerson, the 2024 Olympic silver medalist and four-time Best Blocker in the World (as awarded by her peers on the Beach Pro Tour — despite standing just 5 feet 10 inches tall) about blocking cues and techniques, one of her first bullet points was: "Penetration, penetration, penetration."

WARNING

The most common mistake blockers make is thinking that the higher they jump and reach up into the air, the more effective they are at the net. Not only is this wrong, in most cases, it's actually harmful because you become an easy target for the offense to hit and use as a tool.

But if you're *pressing* — another way to say *penetrating* — over the net (as shown in Figure 10-2), when you get hit, the ball is more likely to rebound off you and back into the opponent's side of the court — which is what you want. Sometimes, even when you're pressing the ball rebounds off you and out of bounds (called a *tool*). It's inevitable. Your job is to increase the percentages by which you stop the offense.

FIGURE 10-2: Blockers pressing hands over the net.

Ron Alvey/Stocksy/Adobe Stock Photos

Your mindset as a blocker, then, focuses on reaching over the net to penetrate first and foremost.

Encouraging hitters to hit over you

Before your ego as a blocker gets in the way — it will, don't worry, and that's okay — accept the fact that the hitter can hit over top of you, and that you actually want them to. If the hitter hits over you, that means your defender(s) might have enough time to run it down. But if the hitter hits under your block, it's a kill, and the play is over.

In the Czech Republic, indoor national team coach Zdenek Hanik emphasizes this fact to the point that he even allows youth players to hit the net when they're blocking because, he said in a YouTube tutorial video, "the idea of pressing is more important than strict obedience to the rules in the beginning." He wants his players to form the habit and feeling of getting their hands over the net, rather than attempting to go as high as they can.

Here are a few helpful tools and cues to improve your pressing:

- **Antenna string:** Imagine a string connects the antennas together, a foot over the top of the net. As a blocker, your hands can't go high enough to hit the string. Or don't imagine: Many coaches actually tie a string that connects the antennas, and they have their players perform block moves where they work on pressing their hands as far over the net as they can without hitting the string.
- **Bracelets:** Draw circles on the back of your hands or wear bracelets on your wrists. When you jump, try to get that bracelet or circle as far over the net as possible.
- **Getting grabby:** Have a player stand on the opposite side of the net from the blocker, holding an object in either hand. (Beach players frequently use sandals. Or you can use mini balls or cones — or gift cards if you want to throw a real incentive in there.) The blocker needs to jump and either touch or grab the objects and then retract their hands before they hit the net. The player on the other side of the net can take a small step back each time the blocker performs this drill successfully.

TIP

Andy Benesh, a 2024 Olympian and the two-time AVP Blocker of the Year, likes to imagine himself as a wave rather than a wall. A wall is straight up and down, whereas a cresting wave curls. You, as the wave, curl around the top of the net, rather than simply forming a wall that goes straight up and down and gets used and abused by hitters.

Pressing for as long as you can

If an offensive player swings low to the point that they hit the top of the net, you don't need to press particularly far to get the block. Much of your effectiveness as a blocker involves how long you can press over the net. Even on your way down, you want to keep your hands over the net as long as possible in the event that the offense still hits it into those hands.

Pressing over the net for as long as you can also helps your defenders behind you because they can more easily position themselves around you, the blocker, when you provide them with a defensive window around which to dig.

Shaping your hands

As a blocker, the shape of your hands is as important as the length of your press (discussed in the preceding section) because you can press with all your length and might, but if your hands are pointed out of bounds, it isn't going to do you much good, as that's where the ball is going to go. You want the ball going inbounds, on the other side of the court, so your team gets a point with the block, or at least make the opposing team play it again.

REMEMBER

Shape your hands so that the palms or heels of your hands aim at the back middle of the court, or *area six, or zone six* (shown in Figure 10-3).

FIGURE 10-3: When blocking, shape your hands to aim for area six.

Dziurek/Adobe Stock Photos

WARNING

One of the most common mistakes in volleyball is to *hood* (meaning to hook your *inside hand* — hand closer to the middle of the court).

If you're blocking on the right side of the court and the hitter is close to the antenna, you might think that you can form an excellent block if you have your left hand hooded and facing the sideline because it's directly in the way of the oncoming hit.

But if the hitter hits angle, the ball hits you square in the palm — which feels great because it's solid contact and doesn't get through your hands — but that palm faces out of bounds. And the ball, following the angle of your palm, goes directly out of bounds. Easy point for the offense.

If you instead open your left hand a bit, shaping it so that your palm points to the deep middle of the court, that swing is far more likely to go onto the opponent's side of the court.

If the block gets passed or dug (*covered*, in volleyball lingo) by the opposing team, that's fine. You did your main job in eliminating a first ball side out. You're making the offense work. You're reducing their percentages of successful attacks.

WARNING

But when you have hands that aim out of bounds, you become effectively another player — a *tool* in volleyball lingo — helping the offense, not opposing it.

Lining Up the Block

The *lineup*, where we physically stand and jump when blocking, is a critical link in the blocking sequence. What you call determines where you line up (we cover the defensive calls in Chapter 11). The following principles apply to every call:

- **Front the hitter.** If you have your chest aligned with the hitter's chest, and you press with your hands shaped into the court (see the preceding section), you're going to disrupt their attack. That's your main goal: Disrupting their attack. "If you're not going to block the ball," said Andy Benesh, who played indoors at the University of Southern California (USC) and professionally overseas before switching to beach, to co-author Travis Mewhirter, "the best thing you can do is make people feel you. Don't be too far out of the way."

  As a blocker, you primarily want to get in the way. If you front the hitter, you do just that. Here are a couple other ways to think about that concept:

  - Anders Mol, a two-time Olympic medalist (gold in 2021, bronze in 2024) and five-time Best Blocker in the World from his peers on the Beach Pro Tour at just 28 years old, likes to think about his lineup as moving your body in front of the attacker's arm in such a way that the attacker's arm can cut you in half down the middle.

- Think about grabbing the hitter's shoulder with your block, which also reminds you to press over the net (which we talk about in the section "Focusing on penetration" earlier in this chapter).

- **One hand on the ball, one hand on your call.** You can easily remember this cue (which applies primarily to beach) because it rhymes. If you have one hand grabbing the ball, or the hitter's shoulder, you get in the way of their easiest angle of attack. Meanwhile, if you press your other hand into where you're calling your block, be it angle or line, you're covering the ground that you need to, which makes your defenders happy, because they can trust that you'll stay disciplined to your call.
  - **Line block:** Have your inside hand on the ball and your *outside hand* (the hand closest to the sideline) on your call.
  - **Angle block:** Have your outside hand on the ball and your inside hand on your call.

Figure 10-4 shows an example of how you can line up with your hitter and *cut them in half*, reducing the amount of ground your teammate defending the ball has to cover.

FIGURE 10-4: Line up, so you're cutting the hitter in half.

Joe/Adobe Stock Photos

Working on Your Blocking Footwork

Although almost all of the action when you're blocking happens up top of the net — with your hands — it's your feet that do the most important work throughout the blocking process. If a set goes to the left or right of where you think the attacker is going to attack, and you don't move your feet to get in front of the attacker, then you're not going to be of much use as a blocker. But if you're constantly moving your feet to get in front of the hitter, you're going to be a much more capable blocker. The following sections explain what you need to do and remember with your blocking footwork.

Moving your feet in indoor

In indoor footwork, middle blockers have the most ground to cover because they line up in the middle of the court and have little time to put themselves in a useful position while they travel from *pin to pin* (antenna to antenna).

But if you're an outside, opposite, setter, or a middle and don't have to travel far, the easiest bit of footwork is a simple *sidestep* (also called a *shuffle*). Sidestepping keeps your core parallel to the net, making it easier to press your hands into the court and form a disciplined block. Just follow these steps:

1. **If you're moving left, push off to the left with your right foot.**
2. **Step to the left with your left foot.**
3. **Get balanced and square to the hitter.**
4. **Jump.**

If the offense is in system, however, you probably can't get in a perfect position beforehand because you don't know which option the setter will choose to set — opposite, outside, middle, or back-row hitter — and the setter can also choose to attack. If you have little time to cover a lot of ground the *three-step crossover* is the most common way to front the hitter. In a three-step crossover in which you're moving right, follow these steps:

1. **Open and step laterally with your right foot.**
2. **Cross over to the right with your left foot.**
3. **Make a final step to the right with your right foot.**
4. **Jump with your hands pressing into the deep middle of the court.**

   Follow the same sequence, just opposite, when you move to the left.

TIP

The three-step crossover uses virtually the same footwork as an approach and step-close on offense (which you can read about in Chapter 6).

A common mistake on a three-step crossover, or anytime you travel a bit of distance across the *plane of the net* (the vertical space above the net), involves you drifting while you jump and block. This drift gives your defenders a difficult window to dig behind you, and it makes your block weaker and easier for the attackers to tool because your angle constantly changes and it's hard to shape your hands and body back into the court. You want to land exactly where you started your jump (or as close as you can get). Imagine landing in your footprints (on the beach, discussed in the following section, you don't have to imagine — you can aim for your actual footprints in the sand).

Working on your beach footwork

In beach volleyball, you only ever have to worry about one hitter, which radically simplifies your footwork. Just follow these general steps:

1. **As soon as you see which player you served, position yourself in between the hitter and the setter.**

   This spacing allows you to track a set that goes outside, as well as inside. If you stick with the setter too long, you're late to the hitter. If you front the hitter too early, you risk being late or out of position if they get set too far inside or outside, or if they run a back set.

2. **While the set goes up, sidestep to your lineup.**

   We talk about sidestepping earlier in this chapter. See the section "Lining Up the Block" earlier in this chapter to figure out where you need to go.

You need the three-step crossover (discussed in the preceding section) for indoor because you face such a fast offense and such a big court. On the beach, you may need to cross over on occasion. But you need only sidestepping on at least 95 percent of occasions.

TIP

Make your sidestep small, light, and quick. Try to keep it around 2 feet per step. Going small and light allows to cut down on drift and stay balanced, while also making it easier to jump when it's time to rise up for the block.

A cue from Brandie Wilkerson, the four-time Beach Pro Tour Blocker of the Year, perfectly sums this concept up: "I try and think small in my movements but act big in my finish."

Setting Up Your Eye Sequence

Spend any time around blockers, and you hear the jargony phrase *eye sequence* used repeatedly, which essentially boils down to this: What are you looking at?

You base everything you do in blocking, from where you line up (see the section "Lining Up the Block" earlier in this chapter) to when you actually jump (discussed in the following section) based on what's happening in front of you:

1. **After the hitter passes, check in on them to gather information.**

   Are they moving inside to outside, outside to inside? Did they dive and therefore begin their approach on the ground? In indoor, doing so practically takes that hitter out of the play. On the beach, it drastically changes their approach angle and what options they have to hit.

2. **Check in on the setter.**

   Can the setter attack, dump, or option? If they can potentially do any of these moves, you need to maintain a distance from them that allows you to make a play. In indoor, the setter leaning back slightly can indicate that they plan to execute a back set. If the ball is well in front of the setter, a set in front is most likely. Take note.

3. **Lock in on the hitter's nose or forehead.**

   This focus allows you to see virtually everything you need to know in your peripheral vision: Where the hitter is looking, where their hips are pointing, and the angle of their approach.

As the hitter approaches, knowing where they have their hips pointing, shoulders angled, and arms moving toward all provide major indicators of the hitter's 100 percent best attack. And as a blocker — and in defense, as a whole — you want to impede upon that 100 percent attack. To reiterate: You're supposed to lose as a defense. You simply want to decrease the offense's scoring percentages. When you take away the offense's 100 percent attack and make them revert to a slightly less optimal option, you've done your job.

Note the speed of the attacker's approach. This is less important indoors than on the beach, because indoor volleyball features far more swings than shots. Beach volleyball, meanwhile, has a much higher percentage of off-speed attacks. Remember the following:

- **Slowing down:** A shot or off-speed attack is likely coming, so you can wait, or delay, your block, as the attack will be slower and higher than a hit would be.
- **Speeding up:** Jump either early or with the attacker so that your hands are pressed over the net before the ball beats you there.

REMEMBER

We never once mention the ball in our discussion of eye sequence because the ball can do nothing without the setter, the hitter, or someone contacting it. You just need to pay attention to the players.

Timing Your Block

Perhaps the most contentious, and most disagreed-upon, principle of blocking involves when to time the jump of a block. The following sections examine the different schools of thought.

Jumping after the hitter

The conventional wisdom says that blockers should jump slightly after the hitter. Other schools of thought recommend jumping when the attacker pulls their elbow back in their arm swing.

There's a lot of benefit — and evidence — to the theory that jumping late is better, as it allows you to:

- **Stay hidden.** Blocking slightly after the hitter jumps allows you to hide from the hitter, who can't see you very well when you're still on the ground; and therefore they don't know exactly where you're positioned and where the defense is positioned behind you. This factor is especially important on the beach, a game built more on deception than indoor's pure power game.
- **Get hang time.** Jumping a beat after the hitter allows you to hang in the air for a bit longer so that you can swat a tip or an off-speed shot.

Jumping before or with the hitter

Olympian Andy Benesh believes that adhering to the advice in the preceding section and jumping after the hitter means that most blockers jump too late to effectively block:

- The attack goes by where you should have already been positioned.
- You get tooled by the hitter because you haven't fully formed your block and press yet; you're still going up in your jump.

David Lee, one of the best middle blockers in the world who has a pair of Olympic medals to prove it (gold in 2008, bronze in 2016), encourages blockers to jump with the hitter.

Jumping with the hitter, or even slightly before their jump, allows you to fully form your block, pressing over the net early, providing your defender with the information that they need to know where you're blocking and what space you're taking, and therefore what space they can move into to more effectively defend. Jumping early ensures that you're never late on the block.

WARNING

But if you jump too early, you give up your positioning, allowing the offensive player to know where you are — and therefore where you're not. And the whole point of offensive volleyball, as Olympic gold medalist Kent Steffes likes to say, is to "hit it where they ain't." (We talk about offense in Chapter 6.) Go too early, and you become a billboard for where you are and where you ain't.

Finding your jump timing

Like all things in sports, and life, you don't have one right answer, despite what many passionate disciples in proper timing would have you believe.

You need to base your timing largely on factors such as

- Your athleticism
- What kind of blocker you are
- What type of defense you're attempting to run
- The type of opponent you're playing

Size also plays a part in timing your jump:

- **Smaller blockers:** Tend to rely on being sneaky and difficult for the attacker to see; generally want to go a beat later because their greatest strength is not being seen. This comes with the tradeoff of sometimes being late.
- **Bigger blockers:** Can afford to go a touch earlier because who are they fooling, anyway? Anybody can see the 6-foot-9-inch Andy Benesh, the 6-foot-9-inch Phil Dalhausser, and the 6-foot-8-inch David Lee. But because you can't avoid being seen, you sometimes expose what defense you're running.

Funneling to your defender

Blockers often have egos the size of the typical blocker's unusually large frame. They want to get blocks. When they get them, they're happy. When they don't, they leave matches frustrated, even if they win those matches.

Easily the biggest misconception about what makes for an impactful blocker is that, well, they block. It's even in the name of the position: A *blocker* is supposed to get blocks, right? Yes — and also no, not really.

REMEMBER

A blocker is one part of a greater whole that makes up the defense of the team. To give you what might seem like a strange measuring stick with which to measure the effectiveness of a blocker, consider this: How many digs and touches is the defender getting behind their blocker?

If the best blockers in the world are expected to block less than two balls per set (which you can read more about in the section "Discussing Height: Do You Have to Be Big to Block?" earlier in this chapter), that means the majority of your impact at the net involves creating a funnel for your defenders to dig attacks behind you (see Figure 10-5). Do they get all the credit for those digs that you're making so easy for them? Sure. But who cares about the credit when you're winning?

FIGURE 10-5: Often your job as a blocker is to allow your defender to make a dig.

Microgen/Adobe Stock Photos

Here are three simple blocking priorities to stop more attacks and win more matches:

- **No. 1:** Line up in front of the hitter and stay disciplined to your call, impeding upon the attack we're supposed to stop.
- **No. 2:** Block as many balls as you can, while remaining patient and understanding that these will be few and far between.
- **No. 3:** Make your defenders' lives easier.

Do this, and you'll stop the offense. Stop the offense, and you win matches. Win matches, and everyone's happy.

One of Olympic-medalist Brandie Wilkerson's pillars as a blocker is trust:

- Trust in the play that you're running on defense.
- Trust in your intuition on what you read from the hitter.
- Trust in your teammate who's behind you on defense.

Blockers can easily fall into the trap of trying to block everything. Do that, however, and you block nothing — and your defender is lost behind you. Trust your play. Trust your defender. Funnel for the win.

Getting the Lowdown on Pull Digging

In beach volleyball, if you have the set far off the net or the hitter shows some indication that they're not going to hit the ball, blockers often pull off the net and, instead of blocking, play defense. Volleyball terminology calls this move *pull digging* or *peel digging* because you either pull or peel off the net. They are, we want to clarify, the same thing, and the terms are used interchangeably.

Pull digging is an art form, and one you see primarily in women's beach volleyball (Figure 10-6 shows what pull digging looks like) — although you can find a number of excellent pull diggers on the men's side. Because men hit more often and with more velocity than typical female players, male blockers generally choose a wiser (and safer) play, staying at the net.

The following sections give you the ins and outs of pull digging in case you want to incorporate it into your game.

FIGURE 10-6: Pull digging.

Photo by Travis Mewhirter

Recognizing when to pull

The most important aspect of pull digging is recognizing when to pull — you're waiting to see the set from the opposing team.

The following can help you identify when to pull:

- **Always expect perfection.** As a blocker, assume that, even after a horrendous pass, the setter will set a perfect ball.
- **Wait to pull dig.** After you see that the set is far off the net or the hitter is going to struggle to make an explosive approach to hit it, then — and only then — can you pull off the net.

WARNING

New players often pull off the net before they see the set. Many get back in defense as soon as they recognize that the pass is out of system. But this move is a mistake because a decent setter (or just a lucky one) can still set the ball close enough to the net to bring their hitter back into a good position to hit the ball. Oftentimes, a setter can even set over the net, and if you pulled early, you can't get back to the net in time, meaning the ball touches the ground on your side of the court, giving a point to the other team.

Getting your pull-digging footwork down

The most important aspect when moving your feet is staying balanced when the opposing hitter contacts the ball. You have a number of generally accepted ways to pull off the net. The most common is very similar to the footwork of a middle blocker, the three-step crossover (see the section "Moving your feet in indoor" earlier in this chapter).

Say that you're blocking on the left side of the net and you recognize that the set is bad and you should pull. Follow these steps to perform an open-crossover-hop sequence:

1. **Open up by dropping your right foot back.**
2. **Cross over your right foot with your left foot.**
3. **Perform a small hop.**
4. **Land in an athletic, balanced, defensive position, able to move in any direction.**

   Square up toward your hitter, with your body angled slightly into the court.

Because the ball knows angles (which we discuss earlier in this chapter), if you're angled into the court, your dig more likely winds up in the middle of the court where your partner can set it.

Following the preceding steps should leave you positioned a little more than halfway into the court, around 15 feet (4.5 meters) or so, which allows you to

- Dig a hard-driven attack that the opposition hits at you.
- Chase any deep shot that they hit over you.
- Move forward to dig a short shot in front of you.

Throughout this move, your eyes never leave the hitter. The hitter controls everything about the play. Their body gives you an abundance of information about the potential attacks that are incoming and allow you to react accordingly.

The open up-crossover-hop footwork sequence is the most common, but backpedaling into the court is also regularly used. Many players *backpedal*, meaning they move backward, parallel with the net the whole way, which works well enough. But if you use the backpedal, you can't get back into the court as quickly as you can if you use the crossover footwork. Backpedaling does, however, keep you square to the court, with your eyes on the hitter at all times.

Keeping your hands up

Your hands should always be up when you're blocking, somewhere in between your chest and shoulders and about as wide as your shoulders. Have your hands high and ready for a deep attack. If you have your hands down, you don't have time to react to a quick swing.

REMEMBER

You transition to pull digging because the attacker is — or should be — off the net, which means they likely won't hit a sharp swing into the front half of the court, and any shot into that area should be loopy enough to give you time to chase it down. When pull digging, you play primarily for a deep swing or shot, and having your hands high allows you to dig that deep swing much more easily than if you have your hands down (and it prevents you getting hit in the face with the ball, which you want to avoid, too).

THE MASTER OF PULL DIGGING

In the late stages of a tournament in Rio de Janeiro, Brazil, in 2025, Kyle Friend was going through his usual prep as a commentator for Volleyball TV, parsing through each team's results and seeing whether any significant stats jumped out at him. One in particular gave him pause, to the point that he had to double- and triple-check.

Carol Salgado, the 38-year-old who has played in more events than anyone in the history of the sport, was in the top five in digs, accumulating more, even, than her own partner, Rebecca Cavalcanti.

If you simply passed Salgado on the beach, without any prior knowledge of her, this would make sense. She stands 5 feet 10 inches tall and has wiry, twitchy muscles, the type that makes a human move exceptionally fast and change direction as quick as a hiccup. She could very well be a phenomenal defensive beach volleyball player.

What made Friend pause, however — and double- and triple-check — was that Salgado plays as a blocker. Her position doesn't lend itself to a high volume of digs. Yet there she was, piling them up in numbers that most defenders would get.

Adding Some Blocking Drills to Practice

Here you actually get to work on and become better at blocking. We detail two of our favorite drills for blockers, both of which can be used indoors and on the beach.

Dunk blocks

With this drill, we break the rules: You're allowed to net. In fact, we encourage you to net, even, as you work on pressing as far over the net as you can. Follow these steps:

1. **Have a coach or partner stand on one side of the net with a ball; you, the blocker, are on the other side.**
2. **The partner tosses a ball slightly above the net and on their side of the net.**
3. **You shuffle to the toss, jump, press over the net, and dunk or slam the ball with both hands down to the ground.**
4. **Repeat and see how far the partner can toss the ball on the other side of the net for you to dunk.**

Do this for a few minutes per day as a warmup, and you'll be pressing over the net big time.

Blocker versus hitter

Nothing is fancy about this drill. You need three people — one to be the setter, one to be the hitter, and one to be the blocker — and a ball. Do the following:

1. **Mark off a section of the blocker's side of the court that would be their job to make sure the hitter can't attack there with a swing.**
2. **Have a setter set a hitter, and the hitter must attack at that section of the court with the intent to beat the blocker.**
3. **Go through all of the various blocks: line block on the left, line on the right, angle on the left, angle on the right.**

   Keep score and make it a game. If the hitter successfully beats the blocker into the scoring area, it's a point. If the hitter hits it off the blocker and out of bounds, it's a point. If the blocker blocks the ball, it's a point for the blocker. If the blocker is able to tip the ball and set it as they would in a game, it's a point for the blocker.

The beautiful part of this drill is that it's as useful for the hitter as it is the blocker, so it's something of a multivitamin, with multiple benefits.

IN THIS CHAPTER

» Figuring out what makes a great defensive player

» Getting defensive practice by yourself

» Introducing the defense basics

» Keeping your defense working, whether on the beach or indoors

» Putting defense into practice with drills

Chapter 11

Playing Reverse Dodgeball: Defense

Offense gets so much of the credit. The leader in kills will get the limelight, the hitter with an excellent success rate the accolades — but defense? That's the unsung hero of volleyball, the true test of a team's greatness.

That's what this chapter covers: How to stop the opposing team's offense, both on the beach and indoors.

This chapter (or book, for that matter) doesn't pretend to offer a get-elite-quick guide to becoming a masterful defensive volleyball player. Here, we simply give you the fundamentals and basics that can help you build a good foundation for success as a defensive player.

Following the instructions in this chapter can't guarantee anything, instead simply making some results more likely to occur than others. Defensively, your main goal involves increasing your chances or percentages of making a play, of keeping the proverbial balloon off the floor — in other words, not allowing the opponent to score.

Recognizing What Traits a Good Defensive Player Exhibits

The list of what useful traits qualify to make a good defensive player great could go on for quite some time. If you incorporate the following three into your game, you'll be well ahead of the curve:

- **Dogged:** You don't need to overly complicate defense in volleyball, both indoors and out: Just go get the ball. What makes a great defensive player often comes down to little more than a desire and a willingness to lay out on the sand or hardwood to keep the ball from hitting the floor. It's as much about doggedness as it is about platform technique. After all, scoring against a team that simply doesn't let the ball hit the ground is frustrating.

  Be that dogged individual.
- **Intelligent:** Positioning yourself in the optimal spots on the court is more than half the battle. If you can identify a hitter's *tendencies* — where they like to hit the ball — and place yourself there, you're going to make your life as a defensive player that much easier, and their lives on offense that much more difficult. Make sure you're taking in as much information as you can and ask yourself these types of questions:
  - Where do the hitters like to hit?
  - What do they do after they get blocked?
  - How do they respond after getting dug?

  TIP

  Take in that information and adjust accordingly, and suddenly you'll be making digs with little effort.
- **Patient:** Understanding the offense's goal — which obviously is to score — and that you're at a disadvantage when you're on defense is an important part of volleyball. When the offense scores, that isn't necessarily a problem — it's a useful data point you can then use to figure out how the other team likes to score. For example, if the offense tends to, say, hit to a certain area of the court again and again, your defense can be patient and then adapt to better defend those tendencies. Patience allows you to become a more intelligent defender, making the right plays exactly when the right play is needed.

Getting Defense Practice against a Wall

One of the best ways to improve your defense is simple: Practice. Increase the number of repetitions, also known as *reps*, and you can do that by yourself if you have a wall that you can hit against. Follow these basic steps:

1. **Find a wall.**

   Any flat surface where you can bounce a ball back to you without breaking or denting something works.

2. **Pick a spot on said wall.**

   Choose a spot as your passing target on the wall.

3. **Pass to that spot until your forearms are pink and sensitive.**

   After you've passed to a certain target for, say, 25 accurate reps, take a break. And then . . .

4. **Pick another wall spot.**

   Focus on a spot that requires a different angle and a different height than the spot you choose in Step 2.

5. **Repeat Steps 3 and 4.**

   Repeat these steps again, and again, and again until you're a passing machine.

A wall is the most readily-available and consistent partner you'll have. You can pass, hit, and set all day against a wall and it'll never get bored (see Figure 11-1).

FIGURE 11-1: Travis Mewhirter working on one-handed passes against the wall.

Photo by Travis Mewhirter

By doing it over and over again — by doing more reps — you're going to get a feel for how the platform works — its various angles and touch required for certain heights. Keep messing around: pass sideways from the right, sideways from the left. Pass in a flat line, pass with a loopy trajectory. Make a game out of it. Just pass.

You can increase the difficulty of the preceding steps — and practice a wider range of skills — by tossing the ball to yourself, hitting it against the wall, and defending a hit, called *digging,* or passing your hit. Pass or dig by using your forearms (called your *platform*) or your hands, by using one arm or two, and by using your platform together and separate. Experiment and tinker.

All of this passing, even against an inanimate object, where you know with certainty how it's going to come off the wall, can help you in more ways than you can imagine.

Erik Shoji, a two-time Olympic bronze medalist (in 2016 and 2024) and twice named the Best *Libero* in the world, started this way (we discuss him more in Appendix B). He was a 10-year-old kid off to the side in gyms across Hawai'i. As the son of the legendary coach Dave Shoji, who worked with the University of Hawai'i volleyball team for four decades and won more than 1,000 matches, Erik found a wall, hit a volleyball against it, and was getting reps before he even hit the court.

Those reps turned him into one of the best volleyball passers and diggers that the world has ever seen. Of course, you can point to his genetics, family, and upbringing in one of the most volleyball-mad states in the United States. Yet to say that those factors separate Erik from everyone else who attempts to stand in the way of a 75-mile-per-hour hit does a tremendous disservice to the time and effort he put in to craft his unique set of skills.

"My athletic ability wouldn't push me this far," he said on the SANDCAST podcast. "It's a special set of skills I've developed that for me are more important than my athletic ability."

When Erik coaches camps and clinics, or he does a private lesson on the side (somehow, he finds the time, despite competing professionally roughly 50 weeks out of the year), he has to deal with the exasperation known to many high-level athletes when they try to teach something that they can do instinctually after so much time.

"It's just reps. I've been doing it for a long time, but it's seeing these fast-paced balls coming in your direction — over, and over, and over — and there's a certain amount of coordination that volleyball needs," he said. "I'll be coaching, and they're like 'I'm missing the ball!' You just have to see the ball at a certain point to get it on your platform. I do believe I have a certain amount of hand-eye coordination that helps me with my skills. It's a combination of that plus reps. It doesn't get easier, but you develop a certain technique and an ability to see it early."

We agree with him. To be a better defensive player, pass the ball off a gym wall. Just when you think you're done, give ten more minutes to the wall.

INTRODUCING THE DEFENSIVE SPECIALIST: THE LIBERO

Almost since its inception, one of the FIVB's central missions has been to increase the number of rallies in volleyball, be it indoors or beach, while still maintaining the integrity of the game. As the sport grew . . . and grew . . . and grew, and the hitters were increasingly taller and more offensively efficient, the rallies began decreasing.

An experimental solution was proposed by the FIVB in 1998, creating a new defensive specialist position, with its own set of rules, called the libero. In fact, other governing bodies, including USAV, NCAA, and NFHS, have adopted the libero in their rule codes.

This wasn't entirely groundbreaking. Already, teams were informally doing this, substituting smaller defensive specialists when the front row attackers rotated into the back row. Introducing the libero position just formalized it, in a way. Here are a few roles specific to the libero:

- The libero can't rotate into the front row, block, attempt to block, or attack the ball above the height of the net. The libero can't set the ball using fingertip action in front of the 10-foot line to any teammate who then subsequently attacks the ball above the height of the net.
- The libero can replace any back-row player without it counting as a substitution.
- If the libero sets the ball using fingertip action from behind the 10-foot line, the attacker can attack the ball at any height.
- The position even comes with a different colored jersey to identify which player is playing as the libero.
- The libero can serve in NCAA and NAIA women's, NAIA men's, NFHS, and USAV matches. The libero can't serve in NCAA men's matches or in FIVB matches.

(continued)

(continued)

What began as an experiment to create more defense has been widely adopted, and liberos not only serve as the defensive nucleus of the team but also tend to be one of the on-court emotional leaders. The following figure shows Emma Halter, the University of Texas libero in a 2023 match versus Stanford.

ZUMA Press/Alamy Stock Photo

A high-level libero can be devastating to the opposition's best hitters, able to frustrate them by digging balls that most any player wouldn't or couldn't. It's a position that comes with no small deal of power, and also tremendous responsibility. The libero is in charge of the defense and plays a mighty role in serve-receive and passing. Any slip in either the defense or passing, and the accountability is on the libero.

Recognizing the Basics to Playing Defense: The How-To

Here we get into the physical side of playing defense — simple tips and cues that put you in a position to make accurate defensive plays — and a lot of them.

Misty May-Treanor is the greatest defensive player in the history of beach volleyball, a woman who has three Olympic gold medals and has received the FIVB Best Defensive Player in the world award three times. The following sections walk you through May-Treanor's tips on playing defense.

Getting low and passing the bottom of the ball

When it comes to defense, if May-Treanor tells you to jump, the correct response is: "How high?"

She wouldn't, of course, tell you to jump because jumping is exactly what you shouldn't do on defense. May-Treanor's first principle of defense is, in actuality, the exact opposite: Get low. Then a little lower.

Make your positioning in defense athletic:

- Feet shoulder-width apart or a touch wider
- Weight evenly distributed across your feet
- Body low enough to dig a hard-driven ball in an upward trajectory but still able to move quickly out of that position if you need to run down a shot or a deflection off the blocker

When you finish your dig, think low to high (as Figure 11-2 shows). You don't need to stand up after the dig, but if you can go from low to higher, you can do a more up-and-down dig that is easier to set.

You may compare the techniques of digging a ball and passing a ball, and for good reason: The two skills have a lot of similarities. Many of the principles remain the same. A key difference, however, is that on defense, your main goal is to simply keep the ball from touching the floor — to get the ball up. Ideally, the up ball goes directly to your setter, but the main objective is to keep the other team from scoring. You can most easily get the ball up by passing the bottom of the ball.

REMEMBER

If you contact the bottom of the ball, the ball travels up instead of out, which keeps the dig controlled on your side of the net and gives your setter enough time to make a play (set another hitter, dump the ball, or attack the ball).

FIGURE 11-2: An example of dig in a low position.

master1305/Adobe Stock Photos

Being still

Like when you pass a jump serve or you dig a hard-driven attack, focus on removing the energy from the ball. The most common mistake, both in passing and digging, involves swinging your arms or moving your feet when you make contact with the ball.

TIP

When the ball contacts your platform, stay steady, unmoving, and stopped on contact, which allows the ball to simply hit you, letting the angle that you form with your platform do the rest of the work.

"A lot of people swing their arms," May-Treanor told the *New York Times* in 2008. "You shouldn't do that. You're not trying to hit the ball. You're deflecting the ball. It supplies the momentum. You supply the direction and control."

How to do that? "Position yourself as the ball approaches with your feet shoulder-width apart. Thrust the heels of your hands together, wrists touching. I press my elbows together, but the shape of some people's arms won't allow that. Lock out your shoulders. Your arms should be a steady, unmoving platform."

Focus on being steady and unmoving.

Focusing on your hips

REMEMBER

The angle of your hips simply helps the ball know the angle of your platform. In defense, you want to position your hips square (aligned) toward the hitter. Your hips tell the ball where you want it to go.

Your body positioning in defense is more important than in passing a serve. When you're in defense, you often don't have time to consciously react, and sometimes your body — chest, shoulders, elbows, the occasional head — can become your platform. For this reason, and especially indoors, you want your hips square toward the hitter because that's the direction the ball is most likely coming from.

You're playing "reverse dodgeball," as 2008 gold-medalist *libero* Rich Lambourne describes defense.

If you're square toward the hitter and get hit — ideally, with your platform, but you just want to keep the ball off the floor — the ball travels back toward the hitter. If you follow the advice in the section "Getting low and passing the bottom of the ball" earlier in this chapter, the ball also travels up and stays on your side of the net, making for an easy ball for your setter to set.

Keeping your hands ready

As your opponent gets ready to attack the ball, make sure that you keep your hands apart for as long as possible, rather than creating your platform too early, for the following reasons:

- **Avoiding platform swings:** Keeping your hands apart prevents you from swinging your platform (because you want to be still, unmoving on contact with the ball, as we discuss in the section "Being still" earlier in this chapter).
- **Reacting with one hand:** Doing so allows you to make one-handed reaction plays when you need to (which is quite a bit). If your hands come together too early and your opponent hits a hard-driven ball, you have to swing your platform, which makes it harder to control the ball, or break the platform and then try to stab the ball with one hand. Keeping your hands apart for as long as possible allows you to cover far more ground and react more instinctively. When you can, use both arms of your platform to dig a ball, but you just can't every single time.

Becoming an overcooked spaghetti noodle

Mike Dodd is one of the rare men who played at the highest levels of indoor and beach volleyball at the same time. Few controlled the ball better than Dodd on either surface, and he remains, to this day, one of the best defensive players to ever live on the beach.

His secret? He became, as he describes it so wonderfully, an "overcooked spaghetti noodle."

When you watch Dodd play volleyball, you see a man as relaxed as a piña colada–sipping vacationer sitting in a beach chair in Cancun. His posture — arms hanging loosely in front of him, expression almost bored — doesn't suggest that he's about to get blasted with a 50-mile-per-hour spike.

That's the point. You need to stay relaxed on defense so that you can make a smooth reaction. Dodd's cue to himself was to feel like he was an overcooked spaghetti noodle, all loose and bendy, taking the shape of whatever holds it.

HERE'S WHAT A FEW DEFENDERS DO

When you want to learn how to play defense, keep the ball from hitting the floor, and frustrate your opponent, what better way than look at what some of the sport's best defenders do. Consider the following:

- Rich Lambourne, a Gold Medalist winning libero on the 2008 U.S. men's indoor team, wiggled his fingers as the opponent was rising to hit. This both kept him relaxed and kept his hands apart to prevent swinging his platform.
- Nick Lucena, the two-time Olympian, visualized his hands as paddles, for the same reason Lambourne wiggled his fingers: It relaxed him, and it kept his hands separate from one another.
- Taylor Crabb, recipient of numerous AVP Defensive Player of the Year Awards, as well as his Olympic appearance and AVP titles, played with this mindset.

  "Three out of the four balls, you're not going to get," he told the McKibbin Brothers in a YouTube tutorial, "but you should get that fourth ball. How do you make that the easiest to get? As a defender, it's frustrating because you think you should get every ball."

  But you can't. On the beach, the best offensive teams score 65 percent of the time or more. In indoors, the average range is between 50 and 65 percent, with the best also eclipsing that 65 percent threshold. You have to remember, then, that when you play on defense, you're expected to fail.

Observing what the offense is doing

When playing defense, you have to pay attention to what your opponent is doing. Watch your opponent's approach speed and position yourself accordingly:

Approach speed

Consider how slowly or quickly the hitter's approach speed is. The following explains how to defend a slow and a fast approach:

- **Slow approach:** Indicates the opponent plans to attack with a *tip* or a *shot* (two off-speed attacks). If you notice a slow approach, stay light on your feet and ready to run down the ball.
- **Fast, explosive approach:** Indicates your opponent plans a more powerful hit. If you notice a more explosive approach, prepare for a hard-driven attack by being stable and balanced and ready to react to the swing.

Arm swing

After you note the approach, take a look at their arm swing:

- **Slow or careful:** You'll likely face an off-speed attack. Be prepared to move to run down a shot or off-speed attack.
- **Fast:** Prepare for a hard-driven attack. Remember to stay loose and prepare to react to a swing.

Hitter position, not ball position

A key to both beach and indoor volleyball defense involves watching the hitter — not the ball. The ball can't do anything on its own. It simply takes and follows orders from the hitter.

Nick Lucena, arguably the best beach volleyball defender on the planet from 2010 to 2020, told me (co-author Travis) — the two coach together at Florida State — to "watch the strike zone: where the hitter is actually going to contact the ball."

TIP

To figure out where and how the hitter is actually going to hit the ball, answer these questions:

- **Where does the hitter have their shoulders positioned?** You generally want to have your hips aimed square at the hitter's shoulders.

» **Where is the ball in relation to the hitter?** Assess the ball position in relation to the hitter's dominant shoulder when the hitter makes contact affects the type of attack:

- **In front of the hitter:** It's likely to be a powerful attack because all of the hitter's energy can go forward into the ball.
- **Behind the hitter's head:** They can't summon as much power, so you probably have an off-speed attack to defend.

THE DEFENSIVE MINDSET: YOU DON'T KNOW TILL YOU GO

People frequently asked Zana Muno throughout her volleyball career for defensive tips, and for good reason. She played four years indoor at University of California, Los Angeles (UCLA), where she graduated fourth in career digs at 1,607 and set the record for digs in a single match with 38. On the beach for the UCLA Bruins, she finished 73–15 and won two NCAA National Championships.

Her first season as a professional on the AVP Tour saw her win the Breakthrough Player of the Year and Rookie of the Year, where she averaged more digs per set than any other player on tour. See the following photo that shows Muno digging a ball on the beach.

Photo by Mark Rigney

"It's not very methodical to me. It's all instinctual," she said on the *SANDCAST* podcast in 2022. "Why would I let it drop if I can try my hardest to not let it drop?"

Her coach, Patty Dodd — an AVP champion herself and wife of Mike Dodd, see Appendix B — said something to her as a junior that she still remembers: "'You don't know till you go.' I surprise myself all the time."

That, in a nutshell, is the mindset every defender, be it beach or indoor, should have: Just go. Didn't get the shot or swing you expected? Just go. The shot got tipped off the block and redirected? Just go. It looks too perfect to make a play on? Just go. Surprise yourself.

REMEMBER

This sequence will happen quickly, and the best way to improve at reading the hitter is to simply do it over, and over, and over again. You can begin to pick up on this information on a subconscious level, reading without even knowing you're reading.

Knowing What You're Giving Up

Eventually, you have to dig a human being who is actually attempting to score — they're trying to either hit it where you're not or hit it so hard you have little chance of making a play on the ball. The first general rule to digging as many volleyballs as you can, both indoors and on the beach, is understand what you're not going to dig.

TIP

Try to dig everything, you dig nothing. Put yourself in a position where if someone hits it where you're supposed to be standing, you'll be able to make a play; and pick a shot — one shot — to run down.

So, how do you know what you're supposed to be digging and what your blocker is supposed to be blocking?

When playing beach, you and your teammate don't have enough time in between most points to discuss defensive strategy, so blockers use numbered sign language behind their back (see Figure 11-3) to communicate to their defender the defensive play they're going to run. In the following sections, we cover the five most basic defenses — anything beyond that gets too complicated and is more custom-fit for each partnership.

FIGURE 11-3: Blockers use signals to communicate with defenders.

vallejo123/Adobe Stock Photos

Using a basic one defense

When a blocker signals a one (by displaying one finger), they're calling for the most common, and most basic, defensive play in beach volleyball:

- **Blocker:** This player blocks the offense's attack *down the line* (straight in front of the attacker) to ensure that the offensive player can't swing down the line. And if the attacker hits a shot over the blocker, the blocker wants to make the attacker go so high that it gives the defender enough time to go run it down and make a play.
- **Defender:** The defender stays in the angle or the *cross*-court attack of the offensive player, ready to dig a hard-driven swing into the angle while being light enough on their feet to run down either a cut shot into the angle or a line shot overtop the blocker, known as a *high line.*

Here's what you defend and give up in this defense (see Figure 11-4):

- **Defending:** A hard-driven swing into the angle, and either — but not both — a loopy high line shot or a cut shot.
- **Giving up:** A perfect high line shot, a perfect cut shot, and either an imperfect (too high, too far from the lines) high line or cut shot.

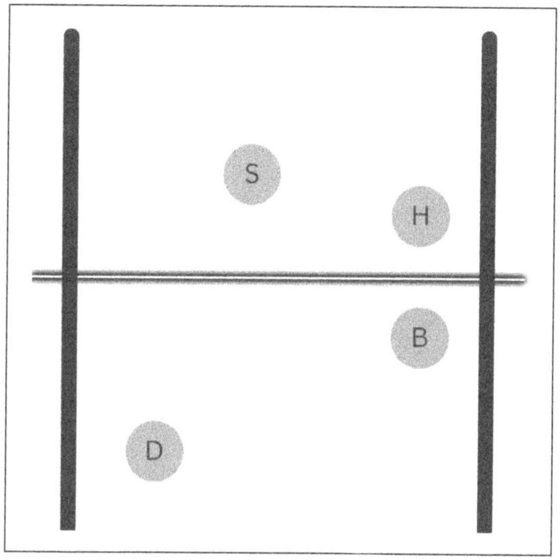

FIGURE 11-4: Lining up for a line block.

In Figure 11-4, in the far court, S is the setter and H is the hitter. In the near court, B is the blocker and D is the defensive player/digger. The blocker's position blocking the line forces the hitter to attack cross-court toward the defensive player.

Sometimes the hitter will attack over the blocker down the line. The hope here is that the blocker forces the attacker to put a lot of height on the shot, giving the defender enough time to chase it down and make a dig.

Flipping things around

This defense is the reverse of a one (see the preceding section). The blocker raises two fingers to signal this formation:

- **Blocker:** Obstructs the angle or cross attack of the offensive player
- **Defender:** Defends and takes away the line

The two call is a little less common than the one call, although you see it far more frequently at higher levels of the game. A one is simpler and allows for the defender to chase down shots with a little more ease. Here's what you defend and give up in this defense:

- **Defending:** A line swing, a high line shot, and a loopy shot into the angle
- **Giving up:** A cut shot or a perfect high shot into the deep corner of the angle

Going from two to three

When the blocker signals a three defense (by raising three fingers), the play gets tricky.

The setup of this play looks exactly like a two (discussed in the preceding section), with the blocker in the angle and the defender in the line. At the last second, however, when the offensive player begins looking upwards at the set, therefore losing vision of all else in front of them, the blocker and defender switch: The defender begins moving into the angle, while the blocker jumps back into the line.

These plays are called *dive plays* or *bait-and-switches* because blocker and defender dive into the area that they previously left open in an attempt to bait the hitter into hitting the ball there.

With this defense (see Figure 11-5), you leave some shots covered and some exposed:

- **Defending:** A loopy shot into the angle and maybe an angle swing if you're coordinated enough to dig on the move
- **Giving up:** An angle swing (unless you can react well while on the move) and a high line shot over the blocker

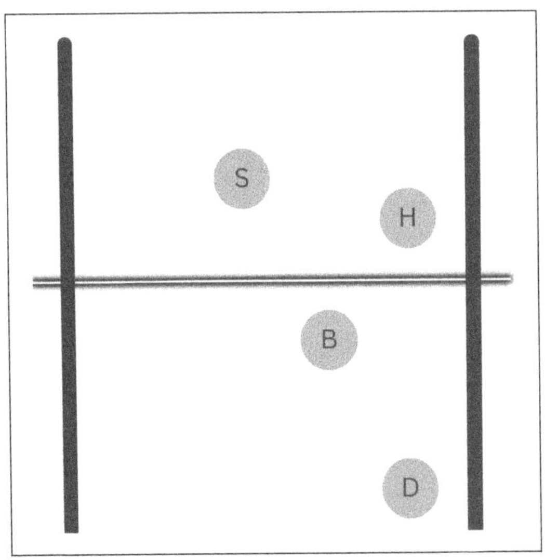

FIGURE 11-5: Lining up for an angle block.

Going from one to four

The setup of a four defense (signaled by raising four fingers) looks exactly like a one (see the section "Using a basic one defense," earlier in this chapter), with the blocker in the line and the defender in the angle. At the last second, when the offensive player begins looking up to find the set, the blocker and defender switch. The defender moves into the line, and the blocker jumps into the angle.

Here's what you get and give up with this defense:

- **Defending:** A loopy shot into the line
- **Giving up:** A line swing and a shot into the angle over the blocker

Digging Indoor versus on the Beach — Focus on the Percentages

Many of the principles of playing defense apply to both indoor and beach volleyball. Of course, you have the central difference that indoor has three times as many players on the court, and therefore far less court to cover for each player, than on the beach.

The plays that we mention in the section "Knowing What You're Giving Up" earlier in this chapter deal with beach volleyball plays because defense in beach volleyball relies much more on *reads* (predicting what the opponents will do), *jukes* and *fakes* (starting in one place, ending in another) than indoor volleyball, which instead focuses on designated positioning based on the defensive scheme that your team designs.

Understanding what swings to give up applies to indoor as well.

REMEMBER

Volleyball players have a saying: Perfect works. If the offense hits a perfect shot or swing, you can't successfully defend against it — it's just going to work. As a defensive player, you want to dig the imperfect hits, the sloppy ones, the mistakes. If the opposing team doesn't make a mistake in an entire set or match, then good for them.

"It's all percentages," Erik Shoji said on SANDCAST. "We're lining up on what we're digging and what we see. How well can we dig this ball?"

THE TODD ROGERS RULE OF LINES

Todd Rogers, the 2008 Olympic gold medalist and four-time FIVB Best Defensive Player, had a rule that we call the *Todd Rogers Rule of Lines:* If any ball came within a foot of hitting the line, he accepted it as a shot that he shouldn't expect himself to dig. He waited for mistakes and made plays on those. He'd still try to dig those shots, of course, but if they scored, he'd tip his cap and move onto the next play, understanding that he wasn't going to dig them all.

It worked out pretty well for him: Fifty-four AVP wins, 24 gold medals on the World Tour, and more than $2 million in prize money. And he was playing against the best players on the planet!

You probably don't have to worry about competing against players of that caliber. Your opponents will make mistakes — plenty of them. Focus on digging the mistakes — forget the rest.

He has humbly accepted that if he reads that a hitter is planning to attack into the low seam between his blockers, he's going to give it up — because he won't be able to dig such a powerful swing, even if he's in the right location.

"Am I going to dig it from someone hitting it 15 feet away?" he said. "I might read that, but I'll stay a little bit deeper so if it's off the hand or he hits it a little bit deeper with less pace, I have a better chance at digging that ball."

Adding Defense Drills to Practice

Now is the time for the fun stuff — playing defense. Here we detail a few of our favorite drills to get you digging more balls in no time.

Dig like Nuss

Kristen Nuss has been voted by her peers on the Beach Pro Tour as the Best Defensive Player three consecutive years — as many years as she has been eligible. (Refer to Appendix B where we include her in our list of the best beach defenders.) There's a drill she loves to do that we simply call "Dig like Nuss," and this can work for indoor or beach volleyball.

You need two tennis balls, two volleyballs, and a partner.

Here's what to do:

1. **Your partner stands on one side of the net, while you, the defensive player, are in a defensive position in the cross-court.**
2. **Your partner holds a tennis ball in each hand above their head.**

   They can toss a ball either into the high line or the cut shot.
3. **Your job as the defender is to react to the toss and catch the tennis ball before it hits the ground.**
4. **Do this for a few repetitions and then switch to volleyballs.**

   Instead of catching the ball, dig it, targeting the center of the court, about three feet off the net.

Do this drill for a few minutes every day — it makes for a wonderful warmup — and you'll be digging, maybe not like Nuss, but vastly improved in no time.

Blind defense

Defense is all about reacting.

Playing blind defense trains your defensive reactions to simply see the ball and either go get it or react to a swing. You only really need two players to do this drill, which makes it easy to do, and you can do it anywhere. A volleyball court is optional.

Here's what you do:

1. **One player stands at the net with their back turned, while their partner, the hitter, slaps the ball.**

   The slap serves as an audio cue for the defender to quickly turn and react while the hitter either hits a tip or off-speed shot or hits a hard-driven swing for the defender to dig.
2. **Do ten reps and switch.**

3 Creating Your Volleyball Body

IN THIS PART . . .

Move like a volleyball player by exercising like one.

Discover the best lifts and mobility exercises to maximize your ability on the court.

Explore how to extend your volleyball years while playing and feeling better.

IN THIS CHAPTER

» Hitting the gym for peak volleyball physique

» Getting into shape without doing damage

» Designing your workouts around your menstrual cycle

Chapter 12

Building a Body That Can Handle the Game

Volleyball is explosive. But what most people miss is this: It's not the jump that breaks people. It's the landing and the change of direction and doing it over and over again.

We both spent a lot of our careers chasing strength — jumping higher, hitting harder, doing more. The sexy stuff. And all of that matters, it does. But what we didn't always pay attention to was how we moved and how we actually felt. And that's the part that eventually catches up with you. Knee pain, shoulder pain, back pain — it adds up.

Volleyball is decidedly less fun when you're in pain, and you wind up practicing less, playing less, and enjoying it less. You get worse, which makes it even less fun. It's a downward spiral, and it's one that you can prevent (or at least delay) by establishing a proper weightlifting program.

We wish that we understood this simple fact earlier in our careers: Strength is only as good as the positions that you can control.

This chapter doesn't focus on how to look like an athlete. It explains how to move like one — and protect yourself in the process. Don't feel like you have to do everything. You just need to do the right things — consistently.

That's what this chapter is about. We want to help you fend off those body pains and make you stronger so that you can play this game longer. We provide some essential exercises that can build strength and protect our body from all the repetitive motions. We also include some important information geared toward women about training and your menstrual cycle.

Getting Stronger with Weightlifting: Why It's Key to Playing Volleyball

Weightlifting for volleyball is always one of those strange paradoxes in sports. Take a look at your average volleyball player: They don't have a whole lot of mass. You might even wonder whether volleyball players ever lift anything above their waists at all. But you'd be wrong if you assumed they don't.

The ideal build for a volleyball player is drastically different than, say, a football player. In volleyball, you want to develop your arms into livewires that you can use to whip into a volleyball, not meaty clubs that you use to push around a defensive lineman or tackle a bulldog of a running back. And because you're optimizing for different skills and functions in volleyball versus football, you have a drastically different weight program than a football player.

An upper-body weightlifting program for volleyball aims to increase strength, yes, but the primary focus is health and maintenance so that you can prevent damage from the overuse of swinging overhead repeatedly in an explosive manner, as well as developing strength through the movement pattern. Volleyball doesn't have you pick up or push heavy things and then put them somewhere else. You need to be lithe and lean, limber and quick, strong and fast.

Imagine how a panther moves, so smooth and flowy, yet so dangerously explosive, able to pounce in the span of a blink. That's how you want to move on the court (or beach).

TIP

Before starting any workout or strength program, especially if you have any existing injuries or health concerns, consult with your doctor or qualified healthcare professional (even a certified strength coach). The goal is always to build strength safely and progressively.

Elevating Your Game with Specific Exercises

If you want to get stronger so that you can play longer with more explosiveness, then the exercises in the following sections can give you a great start.

TIP

We strongly encourage — especially young athletes — to stick with lower load squats unless you're supervised by a coach.

REMEMBER

If you strip everything down, weightlifting for volleyball comes down to needing

- Strength in your knees, ankles, and hips
- The ability to control your body on one leg

That combination gives you a higher vertical, better durability, and confidence when a play breaks down.

Back and front squat

Although the back and front squat are two distinctly different lifts that each have their own range of benefits, they both fall under the squat lift pattern. Both squats are incredible, compound lifts that get all the muscles in your legs firing. You can't find a better exercise for strength-building in your legs, and both front and back squats can improve your vertical jump, your speed, and the power produced by your lower body.

Follow these steps to execute a back squat:

1. **Set a barbell at shoulder height on a rack.**

   You can adjust the height as needed to rest the bar on your shoulders.

2. **Step under the barbell and position yourself so that it rests on your shoulders.**

   Specifically, you want it on your upper trapezius muscles (upper traps), which distributes the load from your lower back muscles to support the weight.

3. **Place your hands on the barbell a few inches from your shoulders on either side depending on what feels most comfortable.**

4. **Position your feet roughly shoulder-width apart and angle your toes slightly out.**

REMEMBER

Form and body position are essential before you begin.

5. **Stand up to lift the barbell off of the rack.**

Figure 12-1 shows Steps 1–5.

FIGURE 12-1: Starting a back squat.

Photo by Travis Mewhirter

6. **Inhale, brace your core, and squat until your thighs are parallel to the floor (see Figure 12-2).**

Imagine you're sitting in a chair. Keep your knees tracking over your toes and your chest vertical.

7. **Drive through your feet to stand up.**

REMEMBER

Even though you feel your toes and whole feet working, you should feel the main load in your glutes, quads, hamstrings, and heels. This position keeps you in a safer position when generating force.

8. **Exhale when you reach the top.**
9. **Repeat Steps 6 through 8 for three to four sets of three to five reps.**

FIGURE 12-2: Squatting in a back squat.

Photo by Travis Mewhirter

To do a front squat, you use the exact same motion as the back squat described in the preceding list, only with a different bar position and balance (see Figure 12-3):

- **Position:** On your front shoulders, near your collarbone.
- **Balance:** Most people cross their arms and use the hands to lightly stabilize bar, or some athletes if they have the mobility won't cross their arms and hold the bar with a *reverse grip* (palms up with fingers around the bar and elbows straight out) and push their elbows out in front to hold bar in place.

REMEMBER

Keep the weight stable and push your back as you lower your body. You want to avoid the weight rolling forward as you lower down because it's not great for your lower back or for training goals of being explosive.

When you rise back up in a front squat, drive your heels into the floor. Do the same number of sets and reps as back squats (three to four sets of three to five reps).

FIGURE 12-3: A front squat.

Photos by Travis Mewhirter

Pull-up

Consider the pull-up the gold standard for an upper-body focused exercise for volleyball — and for life, really. This exercise can turn your shoulders to steel, help protect more of the spine from overuse injuries, and keep your arm swing live and explosive. Although many volleyball players or viewers might assume that an arm swing predominantly uses the muscles of your chest (pectoral muscles) and front of the shoulder (the deltoids), the upper back actually provides the power. The muscles in your upper back and the back of your shoulder (rear delts) act as the slingshot, pulling, pulling, pulling the arm back — and then releasing it into a hellacious swing.

If you can do only one upper-body exercise, let it be the pull-up. Follow these steps:

1. **Grab the pull-up bar with your palms facing away from you, about shoulder width apart.**

2. **Pull yourself up, focusing on using your upper back to pull your body up.**

   You want to get your chin over the bar.

3. **Slowly lower yourself until your arms are fully extended again.**
4. **Repeat Steps 2 and 3 until you just can't pull yourself up anymore.**

You can change your grip, placing your hands farther apart or closer together. You can also have your palms facing you, which makes the motion a *chin-up*, but don't let the verbiage confuse you. Pull-ups and chin-ups are both phenomenal exercises:

- » **Pull-ups:** They focus on upper back strength, scapular control, and shoulder stability.
- » **Chin-ups:** They also work elbow flexion and the bicep. They're often easier for most athletes.

Pull-ups are difficult, and not everyone can do them. If you can't complete a pull-up, worry not. Follow these steps for a simple modification, called an *isometric pull-up:*

1. **Place a chair or stool underneath the pull-up bar.**
2. **Stand on the chair and grab the bar with your chin above it.**
3. **After you have a firm grip, remove your feet from the chair and hold yourself in that position as long as you can.**
4. **Lower yourself slowly, resisting throughout.**

   Resisting not only gets you stronger but also protects you during the exercise because you aren't using gravity or allowing your muscle to shut off on the descent.

5. **Repeat Steps 2 through 4.**

   Start slow. Set a goal of 2 to 5 in the beginning for 4 sets. You can always increase reps as you become stronger. You'll be shocked how quickly these isometric pull-ups can increase your strength.

Shoulder taps

You can file shoulder taps under "exercises that won't make you sexy but should be done anyway." In fact, this exercise is one of the best moves for helping your knees with landing and for long-term protection of your knees and hips.

That tap, done repeatedly throughout the weeks of your season, will save you untold amounts of unnecessary pain.

Follow these steps to do shoulder taps:

1. **Get into a plank position with both arms fully extended (see Figure 12-4).**

   Make sure your head, scapula, and lower back are all level.

FIGURE 12-4: Start in a plank position.

Photo by Travis Mewhirter

2. **Lift one hand off the floor and slowly move your arm until you can tap the other shoulder (refer to Figure 12-5a).**

   Brace your core during this movement to keep your body still.

3. **Lower your arm back down and place your hand on the floor.**
4. **Repeat Steps 2 and 3 with the other hand (see Figure 12-5b).**
5. **Repeat Steps 2 to 4 for 20 or so reps.**

Single-leg Romanian deadlift

A *Romanian deadlift* (RDL) is where balance meets power. Volleyball is rarely symmetrical, and a single-leg RDL routine builds strength and control in each leg independently, while also strengthening your *posterior chain* — your glutes and hamstrings (the muscles of your butt and the backs of your thighs).

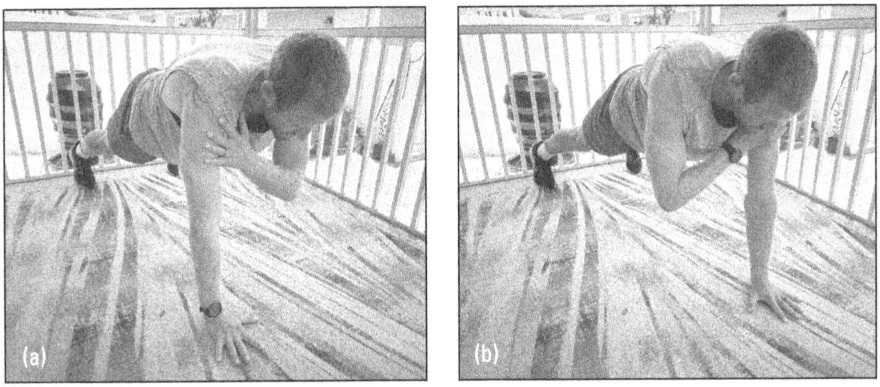

FIGURE 12-5: Tap the right and left shoulders.

Photos by Travis Mewhirter

If your hips do their job effectively, your knees don't have to compensate. This kind of stability builds confidence.

To do single-leg RDLs, follow these steps:

1. **Stand on one leg (see Figure 12-6a).**

   Have your balance spread evenly across the entire foot.

2. **Hinge at your waist, keeping your leg as straight as you can.**

   You want a slight flex at the knee.

3. **Slowly lower your upper body to the ground so that your chest is parallel to the floor (refer to Figure 12-6b).**

   Reach your hand opposite the leg you're standing on and try to touch the ground, although you may not be able to touch. Most importantly, make sure your body stays level and your head doesn't go below parallel (in other words, lower than the glutes).

   Lower yourself down with your glutes and hips and not by bending the back and by using your spine or lower back.

4. **Using your hamstrings and glutes, slowly raise yourself back up to a standing position.**
5. **Repeat Steps 2 through 4.**
6. **Switch the leg you're standing on.**
7. **Repeat Steps 2 through 5 and do 3 sets of 10 reps.**

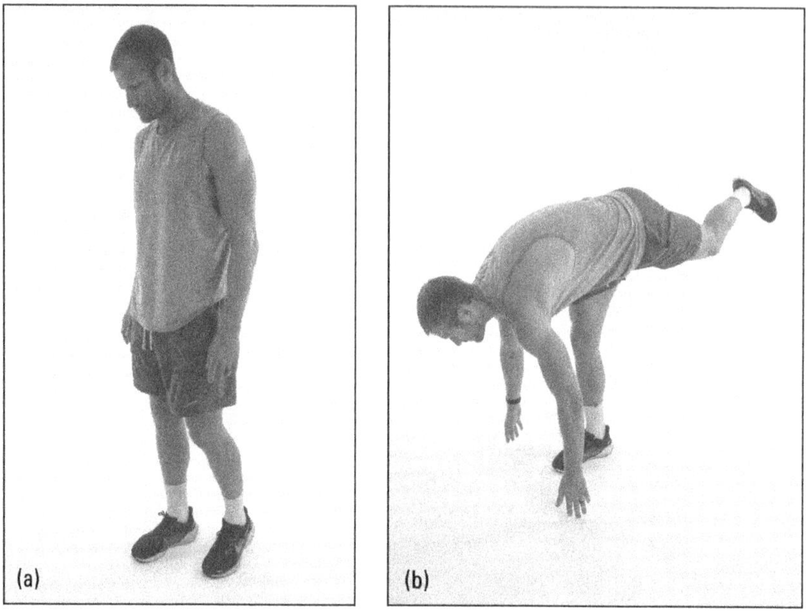

FIGURE 12-6: Single-leg Romanian deadlift.

Photos by Travis Mewhirter

If you want to add weight to this exercise, hold a dumbbell in the opposite hand of the leg you're standing on.

TIP

You might lose your balance while doing single-leg RDLs, and that's fine. You're training strength through balance with this exercise. Pick a spot on the ground to fix your focus on, which makes staying stable easier.

Sled push

Doing a sled push is simple, honest work. No tricks here. This exercise builds acceleration, leg drive, and conditioning — without beating up your joints.

WARNING

If a sled push feels easy, you're not doing it right. Trust us — this exercise ain't easy.

To do this exercise, you simply push a weighted sled across whatever surface you have available. A lot of gyms have a sled and a turf or grass area on which you can push it. Load the sled up with an amount of weight that feels comfortable and then push. Make sure to drive your legs with an activated upper body so you protect your back, ensuring that your foot is balanced and the origin of your power. Doing sled pushes can get you running faster and jumping higher before you take your first water break (okay, maybe not that fast — but you get the point).

Split squat

A split squat is your knee insurance policy. This exercise is one of the most important ones that you can do if you want your knees to last and you want to have strength in all of those weird, deep positions where volleyball actually happens. In other words: The split squat helps you build knees that can handle real movement.

To do this exercise, follow these steps:

1. **Get into a split squat or lunge position with your hands by your sides.**

   You can hold dumbbells if you want to add weight to the lift; otherwise, you can use body weight only.

2. **Slowly descend and let your front knee travel forward over your toes.**
3. **Keep your back leg long so that you open up the hip.**

   You might even feel a slight tug or pull at your hip while you stretch that front knee over your toes — and that's okay!

   WARNING

   Don't do it if it's painful.

4. **Keep your upper body straight and vertical while you descend.**

   A straight spine is important. Really focus on your using legs, hips, and glutes to control the down.

5. **Drive up from stable feet using your legs, glutes, and hips to generate force.**

   You don't want to use movement from the lower back/spine to push the weight up. Go slow and controlled throughout the entire movement.

If you need assistance with your split squats, don't hesitate. You can use a spotter, or if you're newer to this exercise, start with kettlebells or dumbbells so the weight is below you.

Step-through lunges

Think of step-through lunges as exercises that use real-world movement, where strength and coordination meet. You're not just building muscle — you're teaching your body how to move through space. That movement control matters when you're transitioning from defense to attack or reacting under pressure.

Follow these steps to do step-through lunges:

1. **Stand with both feet roughly shoulder width apart (see Figure 12-7a).**
2. **Lunge backwards.**

   Stop when your knee gets roughly 1 inch (2.5 cm) from the ground (see Figure 12-7b).
3. **Pause briefly at the bottom of your lunge.**
4. **Using your glutes, lift yourself up.**
5. **Continue without pausing into a forward lunge.**
6. **Using your glutes, power yourself back up to a standing position.**
7. **Repeat Steps 2 through 6 at least 20 times for both sides.**

FIGURE 12-7: A step-through lunge.

Photos by Travis Mewhirter

TIP

While you build strength, you can add weight by holding a dumbbell in each hand.

Tibialis raises

The missing link of your Average Joe's workouts involves the front of the lower leg. Most athletes train their calves. Almost no one trains the front of the lower leg. That's a mistake.

This exercise, called *tibialis raises,* builds strength where you need it (in the tibialis muscles) for deceleration and landing. It helps reduce stress on your knees and gives you more control when your foot hits the ground. It's simple, but it pays off quickly.

Follow these steps to do tibialis raises (think of them like reverse calf raises):

1. **Stand with your back against a wall (see Figure 12-8a).**
2. **Using your ankles to flex, raise your toes as far as you can off the ground (refer to Figure 12-8b).**

   You should feel the muscles surrounding your shins strain with the weight of your foot.
3. **Slowly lower your toes back to the ground.**
4. **Repeat Steps 2 and 3 with 4 sets of 10 to 20 reps.**

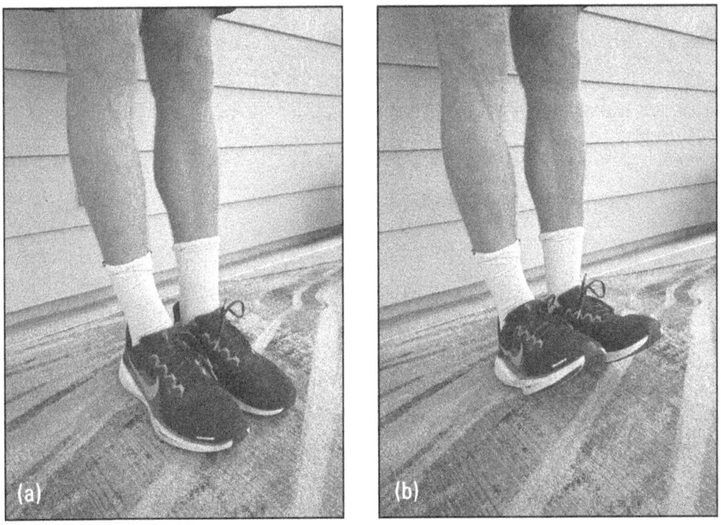

FIGURE 12-8: Tibialis raise.

Photos by Travis Mewhirter

Trap bar deadlift

This move called the *trap bar deadlift* is the Holy Grail of volleyball training, the most all-encompassing lift that a volleyball player could ask for. From the front of the thighs (the quadriceps) to the bum (the gluteal muscles) to the lower back — not to mention hand and grip strength — it hits them all.

And you can do the exercise because you lift the load from below you, not above, and you don't put strain on your shoulders or back.

The motion itself mimics the exact motion that a blocker performs on a block jump, and directly transfers to your vertical leap, whether on a step-close while you rise to hit a ball, a jump-serve from the end line, or going up for a block. The exercise emphasizes explosiveness overall but doesn't build a ton of strength.

REMEMBER

Heavier, slower lifts increase your strength, but they don't necessarily make you more explosive. Lighter, faster lifts, such as the trap bar deadlift, both increase strength and improve your explosiveness and speed.

REMEMBER

The key benefit of keeping the load below protects the athlete's spine and puts them in a position to have correct form. They'll also be working on grip strength, which is great for hitting the ball.

To do this exercise, follow these steps:

1. **Stand in the middle of a trap bar.**

   The handles are on the sides to start the lift. Your feet are shoulder-width apart, and you make sure to lift from legs and glutes and brace midsection to protect the spine. Keep the spine as straight as possible and inhale on the upward or the concentric part of the move.

2. **Squat down and hinge slightly at the hips, keeping your back flat.**
3. **Grab the trap bar handles.**

   Your back stays flat, and the hinge occurs at the hips and glutes.

4. **Drive yourself up explosively by pushing the floor away.**

   REMEMBER

   Keep your core tight and hips lower than your shoulders. The more you can keep the load over your hips, the safer it is. When your head goes forward, the load will shift forward as well and put more load on the lower back versus the hips, glutes, hamstrings, and quads.

5. **After you straighten up, lower the bar slowly.**

   Go slow enough that it takes you 3 to 5 seconds to return the bar to the ground.

6. **Repeat Steps 3 through 5.**

   Do 3 to 4 sets of 5 to 6 reps with moderate weight. Rest about 2 to 3 minutes between sets.

For a modification on the trap bar deadlift, you can do a trap bar jump, in which you put only a little weight on the bar — if any additional weight at all — and jump while holding the bar. The weight needs to be very light and the jump is a forceful movement out of the seated squat. Try to land softly and then get organized again before the next rep. Make sure you're using the correct form.

The trap bar deadlift is such a complete exercise because you can modify it depending on where you are in of your volleyball season:

» **Off-season and preseason:** To build strength, load up the weight to the point that you can perform only three to five reps. Going heavy on the weights builds up a base of strength that can help you remain strong throughout the course of a season.

» **During the season:** Lighten up the weights and make it your goal to move as quickly and explosively as possible with your lifts, while still remaining controlled and safe. You can do the same three to five reps that you do in the off- and preseason, only now move the bar much, much quicker during each rep. Don't lift too heavy during the season.

Walking backward

You can build durability, as well as strength in your *quadriceps* (quads; the muscles on the front of your thighs), patellar tendon, and all the muscles that support the knee, without risking the damage that oftentimes comes with lifting weights, by simple backward walking.

It's simple, and it works. Over time, this exercise can help your legs still feel strong late in a match, not just early. Furthermore, this exercise is great for supporting the knees while jumping and more importantly landing.

If you want to add weight to the exercise, tether a sled or a weight around your waist with a weight belt and drag the tether while you walk backward (called reverse sled drags). Simple but mighty.

Training Hard without Always Paying the Price

We wish more athletes understood that you don't always have to take impact to build explosiveness. Co-author Gabby Reece and her husband, surfer Laird Hamilton, have leaned on for many years. As we discuss here, find other environment or modalities that improve your game but don't crush your body. Sand and water are great environments to get stronger and improve with less impact to your joints.

Getting wet

If you have access to water — whether a pool or the ocean — use it. When you train in water, you can train power and speed in explosive jumps, lateral movements, and even approach work without having to absorb the punishment on the way down. Training in water gives you a way to keep working on that explosiveness without constantly beating up your joints.

TIP

If you don't have access to water to reduce or totally remove the impact of landing, include *box jumps* because box jumping is a controlled environment activity that helps build up your strength to handle jumping and landing that translates to real game situations. Box jumping allows you to control your form.

Moving in all kinds of ways

Take the opportunities to improve your performance without always repeating the exact same stress that your sport already demands. If you only ever stack the same load in the same way, eventually, something gives.

Train smart. Mix up what you do. Diversity in training is important for all athletes, not just volleyball players, for strength, balance, flexibility, and explosiveness.

And give your body a chance to rest without always having to recover from the damage of playing your sport or training hard, either in the gym or during practice.

Training around Your Menstrual Cycle

Female athletes have a unique physiology. Understanding your cycle can help optimize training, recovery, and long-term performance. The times to know when it's best to work on technique versus strength.

Physiologist Dr. Stacy Sims says, "Your body isn't inconsistent — it's responsive. If you understand that, you can train smarter."

By planning your workouts around your menstrual cycle, you're not working around your body — you're working with it.

Menstruation (Days 1–5)

During this time you have lower hormone levels, which can actually be a good time for strength work — if you feel up for it.

TIP

Listen to your body and notice if you feel good or need to dial your training back a bit.

Estrogen and progesterone are at their lowest levels during menstruation. As their period starts a lot of women feel stronger, more energetic, and more recovered.

Follicular phase (Days 6–14)

During the follicular phase of your menstrual cycle your body produces more estrogen. This is a great window to push strength, power, skill development, and higher intensity workouts. See if you can go a little more during this phase.

Ovulation

You may feel strong and explosive while you're ovulating. Athletes often feel strong, explosive, and powerful. Just be mindful — you may have slight reduction in your joint stability during ovulation.

TIP

Pay attention to quality of movement and recovery.

Luteal phase (Days 15–28)

During the luteal phase, your body has to work a little harder to recover. As your body prepares for its next cycle, be mindful of hydration, recovery, and sleep. Notice how you feel after hard training. Now may be a good time to focus on flexibility, consistency, technique, and slightly lower intensity.

IN THIS CHAPTER

» Keeping your body moving without pain

» Getting your hips and legs loose

» Stretching your spine

» Opening your upper body

Chapter 13

Mobility: Owning the Positions, Staying in the Game

The mobility that we talk about in this chapter doesn't focus on being flexible. You can leave that for the hot yoga classes and folks who simply want to be stretchy and bendy. *Mobility,* rather, is about strength, having access to the positions your sport demands — and being able to move through them without your body having to compensate.

When you lose mobility, something else takes over. When something else takes over, you'll hear the word "overcompensating" in conversation more than you'd like.

When your body starts overcompensating for something, pain shows up. And when you have pain, you have less fun. When you have less fun, you do less playing. That's the opposite of what you want. You want more play, more fun, and more access to strength in all of the strange positions this sport puts you in.

This chapter explains what mobility ultimately gives you: a greater freedom of movement. A greater freedom to play. In this chapter, we walk you through several different exercises that can improve your mobility and keep you on the court or the sand.

Appreciating Mobility: The Way to Keep You Playing

Don't start working on your mobility after things start hurting. Use it to keep yourself moving well so that things don't hurt.

If you can't get into a position, your body will find a way around to do what you're trying to do. And that workaround usually comes at a cost.

We — Gabby Reece and Travis Mewhirter — paid the price of those workarounds so that you don't have to. What we have in the following sections is the closest thing to an antidote that we can provide, the multivitamin of mobility that can get you feeling strong in a variety of positions and able to harness strength that you didn't realize you had. You needed only to unlock it with the right practice, exercises, and knowledge.

You don't need more exercises. You need to do the right ones — consistently.

Mobility gets you into the position. Strength lets you own it. And if you maintain both mobility and strength long enough, you not only play better, but you can also keep playing longer.

Focusing On Lower Body Mobility

The following sections detail some specific stretching and exercises that can improve your lower body mobility and increase your strength.

Deep squat hold

Never lose this position. If you have children or had youngsters in the house in the past, you no doubt looked upon them with awe and envy. The hip mobility!

Goodness! How do they squat all the way down, diapers brushing the floor, moving as if their joints and muscles were made of rubber and magic?

In essence, you want to get back to that pose with the *deep squat hold,* otherwise known as a *campfire squat.* You just sit at the bottom of a squat. Heels down. Chest tall. Breathe. Squat as low as you can with your heels on the ground and settle in. Stay in the squat for 30 seconds, a minute, two minutes (see Figure 13-1).

FIGURE 13-1: A deep squat hold.

Photo by Travis Mewhirter

Squatting like this restores range in your hips, ankles, and knees, and directly improves how you load into movement — you put force into the ground to create an explosive movement. Boring? Infinitely so. Effective? You have no idea how much.

This stretch is especially important for mobility if you sit at a desk all day. And if you're on a team that travels a lot, you need to do this stretch.

Do this stretch several times throughout the day. Scroll on Instagram. Read a book. Meditate. Doesn't matter. Whatever helps you stay in that squat can help your hips, ankles, and knees stay functional and healthy, and therefore help you stay in the game.

Couch stretch

The couch stretch is the hip unlock that your knees didn't know they needed. Pretty much every volleyball player who has seen a masseuse or been worked on by an athletic trainer has heard the same refrain, over and over and over again: "Your hips are tight."

We know, okay? WE KNOW!

What some might not realize is that tight hips create stress downstream. Those cranky knees that send jolts of pain every time you walk up the stairs? That tightness probably doesn't come from your knees at all, but your hips. Open up the hips, and your knees will be forever grateful.

The couch stretch is a simple one: Kneel with one shin against a wall or couch and position the other foot forward in a lunge. Hold for one or two minutes per side (refer to Figure 13-2).

FIGURE 13-2: A couch stretch.

Photo by Travis Mewhirter

Your hips (and knees!) will thank you.

90-90 hip stretch

Few stretches hit the hips better — in a good way, promise — than 90-90 hip stretches. Follow these steps:

1. **Sit on the floor with one leg bent in front of you at 90 degrees and the other leg also at 90 degrees behind you (see Figure 13-3a).**

   Keep your chest upright.

2. **Hinge forward to stretch the front hip.**

   Drive your chest toward the ground without forcing it and keep your back flat.

3. **After you go as far as you can while remaining balanced, slowly return to the top.**

   Even though you're in a stable position, you want to distribute the stretch evenly into the hip and groin. You don't want to force the stretch. Come back up until you're back upright with the top of your head facing the ceiling.

4. **Without leaning backward or sliding, lift your back knee off the ground and rotate your chest so your legs are reversed.**

   The leg that was at your back is now at your front and vice versa (see Figure 13-3b).

5. **Repeat Steps 2 and 3 to stretch the other hip.**
6. **Repeat Steps 2 through 5 eight times.**

   Voila! You have some happy hips.

FIGURE 13-3: A 90-90 hip stretch.

Photos by Travis Mewhirter

Frog rocks

Although the couch stretch and 90-90 hip stretch (see the preceding sections) stretch the hips individually, frog rocks stretch them both at the same time. Follow these steps to do frog rocks:

1. **Start on your hands and knees.**
2. **Widen your knees as far as possible.**

   You may be able to go quite wide, or you may be a little more limited. Widen your knees as far as you can without breaking form as in Figure 13-4a.

3. **Align your ankles with your knees.**
4. **Rock your hips backward toward your heels until you can't go any farther (see Figure 13-4b).**

   REMEMBER Your goal: You want to feel a nice stretch but not like you're tearing or ripping your muscles in the stretch.

5. **Sit in that position for a few seconds.**
6. **Slowly rock forward to your starting position.**
7. **Repeat Steps 4 to 6.**

   Do 10 to 15 reps or repeat for about a minute and a half.

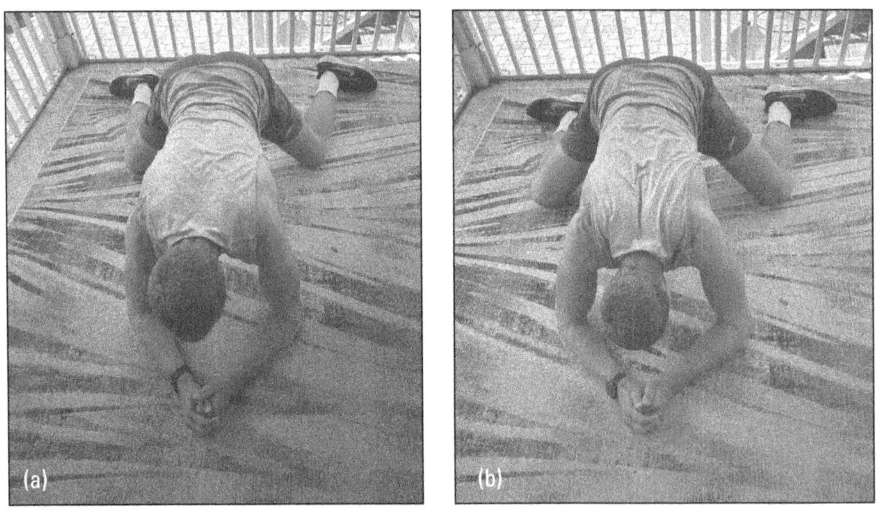

FIGURE 13-4: A frog rocks stretch.

Photos by Travis Mewhirter

Reducing Tightness

These exercises loosen your back and stretch your spine.

The world's greatest stretch

It's really called *the world's greatest stretch*, by the way, we aren't just commentating. Athletes around the world know this stretch, and they recognize and acknowledge the name. How often can you call something in this hyper-polarized age *the world's greatest*, and everyone just agrees? That's how effective this stretch is.

It's not actually a stretch at all, but a series or flow of movements that stretches everything you need to stretch as a volleyball player — and human being:

- **Ankle mobility:** Which directly impacts your ability to jump and land. If your ankles are stiff, something else has to compensate, and overcompensation acts as the thief of all joy in your muscles and joints.
- **Thoracic spine and rotation:** Incredibly important when it comes to an arm swing. You want your upper back to rotate and create the whippy motion of your arm swing, taking much of the load off your shoulders.
- **Hamstrings:** These giant muscles on the backs of your legs are responsible for your speed and changes of direction.

If you do only one exercise for mobility, do this one. Just follow these steps:

1. **Start in a push-up position with your hands lined up with your shoulders.**

   Maintain a straight, engaged body. Maintain form or even use something to elevate your upper body like a step or block if you can't do it with your hands on the floor.

2. **Step your right foot forward to the outside of your right hand.**

   Keep your back left leg straight and your hips low. You might feel a tug in your left hip — that's fine! That's good! It means you're properly stretching your hip.

   REMEMBER Make sure that while you get into this lunge position, you move your knee over your toe, working your ankle mobility.

3. **Slowly, in a controlled manner, lower your right elbow toward the ground, near your left thumb.**

   This step creates a deeper hip stretch.

4. **Lift your right hand off the ground and twist your torso to the right.**

5. **Raise your right arm toward the ceiling and turn your head to follow that arm.**

   This part of the stretch hits your *thoracic rotation,* which allows for better rotation of your spine.

6. **Bring your right hand back down to the floor.**
7. **Step back to the plank position.**
8. **Repeat Steps 2 through 6 on the opposite side.**

   You move your left foot forward instead of your right, and so on.

9. **Repeat Steps 2 through 8 ten times.**

Crab reach

Want to cure a whole lot of that tightness and terrible posture that you get from sitting at a desk all day? Go no further than the crab reach, dear reader, by following these steps:

1. **Sit on your butt with your knees bent and your feet flat and about as wide as your hips (see Figure 13-5a).**
2. **Place your palms on the floor behind you.**

   Place your palms under the shoulder joint. You may prefer having fingers away from body. Some people are mobile enough to have their fingers facing their feet. You don't want to have discomfort in the wrist.

3. **Lift your hips so that you're in the tabletop position.**
4. **Reach one arm over your chest and behind you.**

   For an advanced move, shift to the balls of your feet to create space to arch.

5. **Rotate your torso, squeezing your glutes to lift your hips.**

   Doing so provides stability so the load doesn't go to your lower spine.

6. **Look toward the bottom hand (refer to Figure 13-5b).**
7. **Hold this position for 1 to 2 seconds.**
8. **Return your torso and arm to the position in Step 3.**
9. **Repeat Steps 4 through 8 for the other side.**
10. **Repeat Steps 4 through 9 for six to eight reps.**

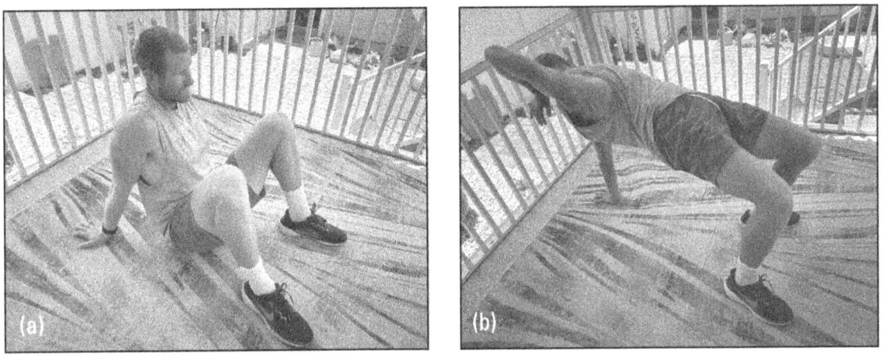

FIGURE 13-5: A crab reach stretch.

Photos by Travis Mewhirter

Exploring Upper Body Stretches

Here are a couple of stretches to incorporate into your workout to loosen your chest and shoulders.

Big rainbows

Your shoulders and chest inevitably get tight while the season progresses and you use your hitting shoulder a lot for all of those sets that you hit the ball. Big rainbow stretches can provide the antidote. Just follow these steps:

1. **Lay on your right side, with your left leg kicked over your right.**
2. **Place your right arm straight out in front of you.**
3. **Put your left hand on top of your right (see Figure 13-6a).**
4. **Slowly trace a rainbow over your head (refer to Figure 13-6b) and behind you with your left arm (refer to Figure 13-6c).**

   Keep your fingertips on the ground, until your arms form a straight line, making a semicircular rainbow with your hand.
5. **Trace back to the starting position.**
6. **Repeat Steps 4 and 5 eight times.**
7. **Turn over to lay on your left side.**
8. **Repeat Steps 2 through 6 for the left side.**

Do this stretch once or twice a day to help your shoulders and chest retain their mobility no matter how many sets you're hitting in a season.

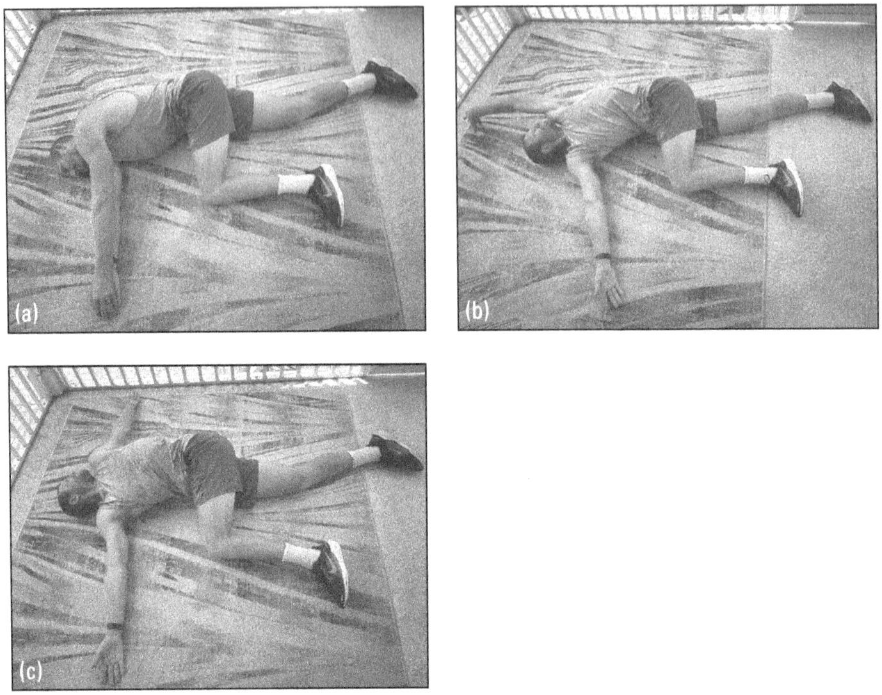

FIGURE 13-6: Start of the rainbow stretch (a), trace a rainbow (b), and finish behind you (c).

Photos by Travis Mewhirter

Shoulder rotations

Protect your arm swing for the long term. I (Gabby) wish I had done more consistent work to protect my shoulder. You need more than strength from your shoulder — you also need control, positioning, and endurance.

Use very light weights, bands, or light cables to work through controlled ranges of motion. Follow these steps to perform external shoulder rotation stretches:

1. **Secure a light-resistance band to a sturdy, anchored point at roughly waist or elbow height.**

   Bands can be secured by someone or clipped to something. Anchor the band at waist height or elbow height.

2. **Stand sideways to the anchor point.**
3. **Grab the band with your outer hand.**

   Your *outer hand* is the hand furthest from the anchor. Your other arm can just hang normally at your side.

4. **Bend your outer elbow of your working arm to 90 degrees and tuck it firmly against your outer side.**

   Your arm starts straight out and then rotates away from the front to the side with the hand while the elbow stays fixed at your waist, touching your torso.

5. **Rotate your outer forearm away from your body, stretching the band, while keeping your elbow tucked at your side.**

   Move only your forearm; your upper arm should stay tight to your torso.

6. **Using control, slowly return your hand toward your body until you return to the starting position.**

   Put both hands out in front of you with elbows locked by your side. One has the weight going toward the body and one has the weight opening the arm away from the body.

7. **Repeat Steps 4 through 6 at 8 to 12 reps, 3 to 4 sets.**

   You may want to do this motion as a warm-up. If so, do fewer reps so maybe less so as not to fatigue your shoulder before playing.

8. **Turn around so that your other arm is now your outer arm.**
9. **Repeat Steps 4 through 6 the same number of times.**

For internal rotations, you have the same setup and positioning as the external rotations in the preceding list, you simply work the other arm on each side. Follow these steps:

1. **Secure a resistance band to an anchor point and stand sideways to that anchor point.**
2. **Grip the band by using the hand closest to it.**
3. **Form a 90-degree angle with your elbow and between your forearm and body.**
4. **Move far enough from the anchor to create slight tension with the band.**
5. **Slowly pull the band inward across your stomach.**

   Rotate your shoulder inward while keeping your elbow firmly against your ribs.

6. **Briefly pause at the end of the range of motion.**
7. **Using control, slowly return your arm to the starting position in Step 3.**

8. **Repeat Steps 5 through 7.**
9. **Turn around so that your other arm is now your inner arm.**
10. **Repeat Steps 4 through 8.**

These rotations don't have you doing serious weightlifting. Instead, they focus on building durability and control in small, important muscles. Over time, this work can keep your arm swing strong without breaking down your shoulder.

The one thing I (Gabby) did right in my career — thanks to my trainer T.R. Goodman — was take care of my shoulders by doing these exercises. This routine wasn't flashy, and it didn't involve using heavy weights — but it kept me playing longer than I probably deserved.

4 The Part of Tens

IN THIS PART . . .

Understand the ten commandments of volleyball and why they're so important if you want to be a good player.

Discover the ten places that we recommend for beach volleyball.

Dive into ten of our volleyball hopes and predictions.

IN THIS CHAPTER

» Keeping track of the simple details

» Focusing on teamwork

» Recognizing the critical importance of fun

Chapter 14 Volleyball's Ten Commandments

Combined, we (your authors Gabby Reece and Travis Mewhirter) have multiple decades of experience in the world of volleyball, both indoors and out. Between playing at the highest level, coaching, commentating, writing, and hosting our own respective podcasts, we've had the chance to inspect the minds and habits of many of the greatest volleyball players who ever lived.

What follows in this chapter are ten of the most oft-shared insights, distilled into what we call the Ten Commandments of Volleyball.

Are we the volleyball equivalent of Moses, who trudged up the slopes of Mount Sinai to hear God's wisdom and inscribe the original Ten Commandments? Not quite. These commandments don't carry such weight. But if you master only ten points about volleyball, these are the most important ones.

The Ball Knows Angles

Regardless of where you begin reading this book, these four words — *the ball knows angles* — are the recurring motif in these pages, and in gyms and on beaches around the world. From passing to setting to blocking and defense, every single skill in the sport of volleyball revolves around the concept that the ball goes only where your angle tells it to go:

- Where is your *platform* (the flat, solid surface players create with their forearms to either pass or bump-set) angled when you pass and set — skills you can find out more about in Part 2?
- How are your hands shaped and angled when you block (see Chapter 10)?
- Where are your body and platform facing when you make a dig (refer to Chapter 11)?
- Where is your core facing when you set (see Chapter 9)?

The ball knows angles. Angle yourself, and your platform, accordingly.

Make Fun the Name of the Game

"If it's not fun, why are you doing it?" Delaney Mewhirter, a National Champion at Pepperdine University and a longtime professional beach volleyball player, both on the Association of Volleyball Professionals (AVP) and World Tour (also the wife of your author Travis), asked this important question. She made her first professional main draw when she was a teenager and would go on to win a handful of medals for the United States. Even as a professional whose livelihood depended on her ability to win, she operated under this simple ethos.

This perspective applies to every player at all levels. If you're reading this book, you aren't playing professional volleyball, be it indoors or out. If you're reading this because your son or daughter, niece or nephew, or grandson or granddaughter plays, maybe they'll play professionally, maybe not. Regardless, it all boils down to one central facet:

It comes down to fun. It's that simple.

REMEMBER

Volleyball should be fun. And fun, we should note, looks different for everyone:

- For some people, fun is goofy and giggly, slapping the ball around. It looks like a backyard barbeque game, drinks in hand and few to no rules. This is wonderful. Enjoy it.
- For others, fun looks like the small improvements you see while you practice and compete. Seeing yourself improve is also wonderful and immensely rewarding.

Matt Fuerbringer, a longtime professional indoor and beach volleyball player, who has also coached both versions of the sport from juniors all the way up to the National Team level — and whose daughter, Charlie, currently stars at Wisconsin — defined fun as well as anyone we have seen in the sport of volleyball.

"You got to make it fun," he said on a 2021 episode of the SANDCAST podcast (`https://sandcastvolleyball.com`). "There's a grind to it, always a grind to it, but if you can make it fun to learn that skill, it makes it a little better to do. That's the fun [stuff], when you're in it. I tell my kids all the time that when you go home, and you tell your parents that practice was ok, then you didn't have a good practice. But if you went home, and you tell a story about something you did at practice because you were so locked in, and you're on that — when I say have fun, I'm not saying laugh. I'm not telling you smile after you get blocked. What I'm telling you is respect that guy that blocked you and be so focused and so locked in that you go back at it, and you're not beating yourself up. Focus would be more fun to me than laughing. Respect that focus. Respect all that work that it takes to be great and enjoy that."

Keep the Balloon off the Floor

At the end of the day, volleyball is one of the simplest games in the world: Just keep the ball from hitting the floor or sand.

It boils down to nothing more than just a giant game of keep the balloon off the floor. If nothing else, remember this: If you keep the ball off the floor, you're going to win.

If you think you can't chase down your opponent's shot — just try and keep it from hitting the floor. Nothing gets into an opponent's head more than touching everything they hit. Even if you don't make the dig or play, that's okay! Getting a touch plants that seed of doubt that they have to hit it even more perfect the next time — and when they try to be more perfect, the result is often an error on them and a point for you.

So if you think you can't go save your teammate's errant pass — sprint as if your life depended upon it and see if you can't extend the play for one beat longer.

If you think the serve is too short, or too deep, or too fast to get a platform on before it hits the sand, see if that assumption is true.

Just keep the balloon off the floor.

The Team That Doesn't Beat Itself Is a Good Team

Successful teams, both indoors and on the beach, have a common denominator: The teams that win make fewer errors than teams that don't win. It's a statistical fact. If you can manage the risk-reward ratio better when serving and hitting than the team across the net from you, you're going to win more often than not.

If you're hitting from off the net, or out of system, you may feel tempted to attempt the hero, high-risk, highlight swing or shot. And sure, you might make that swing or shot a small percentage of the time — and it looks and feels awesome when you do, especially when you get all of those likes and comments and shares on social media.

But the boring play, the smart play, is the winning play.

Let the other team make the hero shots — and miss most of them. Let the other team beat themselves. As for you? You're going to be smart because you're reading this book. You're not going to beat yourself.

Trust Your Teammates

Every person on the court has a role, and those roles fall into systems. When you perform your role as well as you can, you allow your teammates to do their roles to the best of their abilities. But when you don't trust your teammates and try to do too much, that's when systems break down — and that's when you beat yourselves (see the preceding section).

Trust your teammates:

- If you're an opposite hitter and your libero or defensive specialist is supposed to pass for you, you need to trust them to do just that.
- If you're a blocker on the beach and your job is to take away the hitter's line attack, you need to trust your defender to cover the angle.
- If you're a libero and your setter can get to the out-of-system pass, you need to trust them to get there and make the right set.

Chapter 2 explains in detail what these different positions are. When you trust your teammates, your team's system hums like the well-oiled machine you want it to be. When that trust breaks down, you not only begin to beat yourselves, but you also stop having fun (see the section "Make Fun the Name of the Game" earlier in this chapter), and all of your commandments begin to fall apart.

Communicate, Communicate, Communicate

Trust (mentioned in the preceding section) begins with communication. When everyone is on the same page about who does what and where and when, you can more easily trust one another to do your jobs and play your roles.

When something breaks down, communicate about it:

- When your setter or partner doesn't put the set where you want or need it, communicate that to them. If you don't, they likely won't realize they're missing your window and just keep on missing.
- When a hitter keeps hitting low-percentage swings that aren't scoring, let them know an area of the court that might be open or any other potential solution.

And when someone does something awesome, let them know! Communicate it to them. Communication is everything.

Have a Purpose with Every Touch

Volleyball players, like all athletes, can easily succumb to laziness: going through the motions on a pass or set, not approaching aggressively, not finishing the touch with the care they need.

It happens.

But because you're reading this book, you won't let such a thing happen. You know that every touch has a purpose, and you must have a purpose with every touch.

Your passing can become mindless while you attempt to get the ball on your platform without a specific target in mind. You can get apathetic with your setting while you attempt to hit a general area, rather than exactly where your hitter wants it. Your attacking can become rote and routine, with minimal thinking involved — just swing hard . . . somewhere. Your serving can devolve into simply hitting the ball over the net, without a destination in mind.

REMEMBER

Each touch of the ball must have a specific purpose:

- When you're passing, pick a small target and focus on nailing it.
- When you're setting, shoot for your hitter's perfect window. (Chapter 7 explains what your hitter's perfect window is and shows you how.)
- When you attack, find the swing or shot that has the highest percentages of scoring and hit that specific shot.
- When you serve, think about not only where you want to serve, but also how you plan to get the ball to that exact location on the court.

Aim every touch at improving upon the one before it — *bettering the ball,* in volleyball lingo.

Pick the smallest possible target on the court. It could be a shadow, a line, a smudge — anything — and hit that target. It'll reduce the range of possibilities for where your serve or pass or set or attack will wind up if you strike the ball imperfectly, keeping every touch that much more accurate.

Be Precise with Your Passing

The pass is everything.

In fact, passing is the skill that unlocks all the others. It's the one skill that makes it difficult for other teams to beat you, and even more difficult for you to beat yourself. Passing makes everything else about this sport feel easier, and when all the other skills feel easier, winning, too, feels easier — and winning is fun.

You and your teammates can do virtually nothing without passing:

- Even if you're the best hitter in the world, it doesn't matter if you and your team can't pass because without a good pass, there is unlikely to be a good set, and without a good set, hitting becomes exponentially more difficult.
- You can be the greatest server in history, but your team will never be serving if you can't pass and consistently score.

» If you have the stiffest defensive volleyball team the world has ever seen, you render that defense moot if you never actually play defense because you and your team can't pass.

As we say in the section "Make Fun the Name of the Game" earlier in this chapter, fun is important. Make passing fun, in part by being precise with it. Chapter 9 gives you more details about passing.

Keep the Ball in Front of You

To be precise with your play, including passing (see the preceding section), keep the ball in front of you.

When you have it in front of you, you can more easily control your angle; and the section "The Ball Knows Angles" earlier in this chapter talks about this relationship. However, this commandment to keep the ball in front of you goes beyond passing and into every skill:

» When you set, you want your energy going back to front, which you can do only when the ball is in front of you.

» When you serve and attack, you can summon the most power and accuracy when the ball is slightly in front of your shoulders.

» When you block — well, if the ball isn't in front of you, that means it's behind you, and you missed the block.

Play Smarter, Not Harder

Kent Steffes is famous for a long list of things when it comes to volleyball, including winning nearly 50 percent of the tournaments he played (making him statistically the most dominant beach volleyball player of all time), winning an Olympic gold medal in 1996, writing a book on the explosion in popularity of beach volleyball in the 1990s, and producing a homemade documentary as a visual representation of that book. He also has a prolific Facebook blog that talks about all things volleyball. That's just scratching the surface.

He has said over, and over, and over again, "Volleyball is a simple game: Hit it where they ain't."

He's not wrong.

Just like the commandment in the section "Keep the Balloon Off the Floor" earlier in this chapter, this advice is simple: You can always, always, always find a space on the court where the defense isn't. Hit it there.

Of course, simple doesn't mean easy. But if the game ever feels out of control, or you're too much in your head, simplify. Hit it where they ain't.

IN THIS CHAPTER

» Finding the best California beach volleyball beaches

» Playing beach volleyball across the Americas

» Going around the world for beach volleyball

Chapter 15 Ten Best Places to Play Beach Volleyball

A cursory internet search tells you that the world contains upwards of 100,000 beaches. Australia has as many as 10,000 all on its own.

You can find a lot of beaches out there. That gives you a lot of places to play beach volleyball.

To help you narrow down your bucket list of places that you absolutely need to play, this chapter gives you our ten favorite places in the world to play or watch beach volleyball.

Manhattan Beach, California

The Olympics hold the beach volleyball tournament that every player wants to win. But the Olympics happen only every four years. The sport — and its players and fans — needs a tournament in between those four years that is the Wimbledon, the U.S. Open, the Super Bowl, the World Series of beach volleyball.

That tournament is the Manhattan Beach Open (see Figure 15-1).

FIGURE 15-1: The Manhattan Beach Open.

Photo by Ed Chan

Manhattan is the most storied event in beach volleyball, one first held in 1960. The location, California's South Bay, provides obvious allure as it is the very personification of a Beach Boys song, where the summers are endless and the cares are few. We can offer only one reasonable argument for a better place to play: Rio de Janeiro, Brazil (we discuss Rio in the following section).

But the history and legacy of the event make it truly spectacular. The winners have their names engraved on a plaque that's cemented onto the Manhattan Beach Pier. Outside of an Olympic gold medal, you can receive no better prize in beach volleyball.

REMEMBER

If you're not a professional, worry not: Manhattan Beach has nets as far as the eye can see, ready for you to play pickup in one of beach volleyball's most storied locations.

Rio de Janeiro, Brazil

Rio de Janeiro has a legacy that nearly rivals that of Manhattan Beach, California (see the preceding section). Rio hosted the inaugural beach volleyball World Championships in 1987. It quickly became the richest hotbed for talent outside of the United States, and Brazil has since pumped out future gold medalist after future gold medalist, making for a tremendous rivalry between the United States and Brazil. At one point, beach volleyball even surpassed soccer as Brazil's most popular sport.

In 2016, Rio hosted the Olympic Games, where the hometown heroes of Alison Cerutti and Bruno Oscar Schmidt won men's beach volleyball gold, in front of a stadium packed with 20,000 screaming, singing, dancing Brazilians.

Beach volleyball is Brazil. Brazil is beach volleyball.

Hermosa Beach, California

Literally and metaphorically nudging up to Manhattan Beach (discussed in the section "Manhattan Beach, California" earlier in this chapter) you can find the aptly named Hermosa Beach — *hermosa* means *beautiful in Spanish*. It remains one of the most active beaches in terms of people regularly playing beach volleyball on it. It hosted its first professional event in 1970, ten years after the inaugural Manhattan Beach Open, and has hosted one of the biggest tournaments in the world nearly every year since.

Hermosa Beach has produced more top-shelf talent than virtually any other city on the planet and is the location of U.S.A. Volleyball's training headquarters. The nets stretch for miles and miles, making Hermosa one of the easiest places to find a game of pickup to enjoy the beautiful deep sand year-round.

Huntington Beach, California

Co-author Travis Mewhirter cut his teeth as a professional in Huntington Beach, California. More of a down-to-earth, blue-collar coastal town, Huntington Beach is traditionally more open to casual games of pickup and generally more friendly for beginners than the professional hotbeds of Manhattan Beach (see the section "Manhattan Beach, California," earlier in this chapter) and Hermosa Beach (which we talk about in the preceding section). Look for multiple nets on every block where you can play pickup. Huntington also typically hosts a professional event of substantial magnitude on an annual basis.

Gstaad, Switzerland

The most epic event on the beach volleyball calendar is the annual tournament held in Gstaad, Switzerland. Tucked into the Swiss Alps, this tournament (and its majestic views) can take your breath away, over and over again (see Figure 15-2). Now, can you drop in and play a casual volleyball game here? No. But is it one of the best places in the world to play, if you can? Absolutely.

FIGURE 15-2: Beach volleyball in Gstaad, Switzerland.

Volleyball World

Every professional player has this tournament on their bucket list; and attending this tournament, held on July 4 weekend every year, should be on yours.

Oak Street Beach, Chicago, Illinois

Not too many people, at first blush, would put *Chicago* and *beach volleyball* together. But Chicago has, perhaps surprisingly, one of the most vibrant volleyball cultures in the United States. Oak Street Beach, located on the shores of Lake Michigan, hosts an annual tournament on Labor Day Weekend. The stands are perpetually packed, filled to the brim with knowledgeable, excited fans. But even when no professional event is happening in town, you will typically find both Oak Street

Beach and North Avenue Beach (just a few blocks down the lake) filled during the summer months with leagues and pickup games.

Kits Beach, Vancouver, Canada

What a stunner Kits Beach is. With the mountains and Pacific Ocean providing the backdrop, Kits provides a marvelous location to play beach volleyball and hosts one of the best annual tournaments on the calendar: the Vancouver Open. You can't ask for a more fun, open, and relaxed culture — a vibey beach town for the vibey beach player.

Manly Beach, Sydney, Australia

You may have heard of Manly Beach when you tuned into the 2000 Olympic Games and watched Kerri Pottharst (we talk about her in Chapter 2) and Natalie Cook win a gold medal at home in Australia. Or maybe this is your first time hearing of it. Either way, it's a place you don't want to forget.

Australia decided to host its Olympic Games on Manly Beach for a reason — it's one of the best beaches in the world. It ticks all the boxes you'd want: stunning views, soft sand, the sound of waves providing the soundtrack — waves you can surf in between matches. And not just for the pros, either. Manly boasts a robust pickup volleyball scene, and anyone can easily find a net and play some ball.

Marseille, France

Marseille is a hub of French sports, and the city, which overlooks the Mediterranean Sea, is forever humming with folks playing something — soccer (football to non-Americans), sailing, or any kind of outdoor sport, as well as people just running and moving outside. It established itself as a bona fide top location on the beach volleyball map when it hosted the World Championships in 1999, and it has become a must-play or see location since.

WARNING

The place is windy — routinely one of the windiest places on the World Tour calendar. But it's also worth it. Go see for yourself.

Clearwater, Florida

With its sugar-white sand that seems lifted straight out of a postcard, Clearwater, Florida offers the finest place to play beach volleyball on the East Coast. The town is wonderful, and the sand is beyond incredible. And the best part? The sand never gets hot! Because it's white, it doesn't absorb heat, so you can play all day long, no matter the weather, without worrying about burning your feet. A plethora of bars and shops line the walkway near the Pier, making it the ideal spot to throw down a beach chair and play volleyball until the sun goes down.

IN THIS CHAPTER

» Increasing the popularity of all forms of volleyball

» Getting the United States back into the volleyball game

» Giving volleyball the admiration it deserves

Chapter 16
Ten Wishes for Volleyball's Future

What does the future have in store for indoor and beach volleyball? Your guess is as good as ours. Both sports are currently experiencing an explosion in popularity, with new records being set on an annual basis in terms of the number of individuals playing and spectators watching in person and on TV. Will that translate to other success? Bigger TV contracts? Mainstream recognition? Viable professional avenues? Time will tell.

This chapter discusses ten of our hopes and, in some cases, optimistic predictions of what the future of volleyball has in store.

Women's NCAA Volleyball Will Surpass Basketball in Popularity

In 2016, volleyball surpassed basketball as the most popular high school (and club) sport for girls, with both categories booming. From 2013–2023, club participation surged more than 40 percent for girls and 50 percent for boys, and there are now more than 1,300 volleyball clubs in the United States. Since then, the gap has only widened, especially when counting the number of girls who added beach volleyball during the summer months.

Interest among fans has followed: A record 1.7 million people viewed the 2023 NCAA Volleyball Championship finals. In-person attendance has also grown. The University of Nebraska women's volleyball team hosted a match on the university's football field and sold more than 92,000 tickets, becoming the largest in-person audience for a women's sporting event, of any sport, in history (see Figure 16-1).

FIGURE 16-1: The University of Nebraska set an in-person attendance record on the university's football field.

The University of Nebraska Athletic Department

The average viewership during the 2025 NCAA Championship flew up 13 percent, with 666,000 viewers per match. And during the 2025 season, spectators broke several attendance records across the country. The explosive, and wildly entertaining, rise of volleyball as a women's college sports draw is a rocket ship on a one-way course: up.

Someone Will Figure Out Professional U.S. Indoor Volleyball

Businessmen and women have taken note of the sweeping popularity of women's NCAA Volleyball. As we write this book, three professional volleyball leagues exist in the United States: LOVB, MLV, Athletes Unlimited (all women's leagues, by the way). None of them are doing particularly well from any measurable metric — finances, attendance, viewership — with the exception of a few franchises. By the time you're reading this book, only two leagues may remain, maybe even one. But given the explosion in popularity of NCAA women's volleyball, we see it as a matter of when, not if, the United States will have a thriving indoor volleyball league. Refer to Chapter 5 for more about watching volleyball.

Someone Will Figure Out Professional U.S. Beach Volleyball

At one point, in the mid-1990s, professional beach volleyball had television numbers that rivaled that of Major League Baseball (MLB) and the Professional Golfers' Association (PGA) Tour. However, since then, viewership has plummeted. As we write this book, you can combine all the views from the entire beach volleyball season, and that number doesn't measure up to just a single decent draw of a midseason MLB game.

Beach volleyball took a precipitous fall. But as long as money continues to pour into sports by the billions (the MLB's San Diego Padres sold for $3.9 billion as we write this), you inevitably find people who will take a chance on beach volleyball as a potential *buy-low opportunity*. With the proper investment and strategy, someone might just figure out a way to make beach volleyball a viable professional sport again.

The United States Will Host a Yearly Major International Beach Event

As we discuss in Chapter 1, volleyball was founded in the United States by William G. Morgan. It's a bummer for the sport that the United States is now a nation struggling to sustain a professional league indoors and failing to host an annual international tournament on the beach. Prior to Newport Beach stepping in to host an international event in 2025, the United States hadn't hosted an international event since 2018 — a seven-year gap that left American players constantly punching their passport to play professionally. Prior to that seven-year gap, however, the United States almost always held a major international event, dating to the very founding of the Fédération Internationale de Volleyball (FIVB). We hope that U.S. professional volleyball gets back to that point.

Major International Leagues Will Experience a Boom

Given the dearth of legitimate professional options to play indoor volleyball in the United States (at the time of this writing, anyway), the best players frequently compete for clubs overseas, with the golden standard being Italy's SuperLega, Brazil's Superliga, or Turkey's Sultanlar Ligi. Like the Premier League for soccer (or football, depending on your parlance), the SuperLega might see a boom in visibility while the sport grows in popularity.

Volleyball Will Lose the "Girl-Sport" Stigma

If you ask male volleyball players how they got into the game, regardless of whether they play beach or indoor volleyball, a staggeringly high percentage of the answers sound something like, "My sister played volleyball, and I was dragged to the gym for her games and practices and eventually began to like it."

Volleyball in the United States has long been, and continues to be, considered a girls' sport. We hope, more than predict, that this perception will change. While we write this book, there are only 34 NCAA Division I men's volleyball teams, compared to 347 for women. Although the exact numbers vary, around 95,000 boys play high school volleyball in the United States, compared to almost 500,000 girls. One day, when boys and men have more opportunities to play, we hope that stigma changes.

People in Charge Will Stop Messing with the Rules

Writing the rules and regulations chapter (Chapter 2) was a challenge for us, and one we laughed at a few times. If the rate of rules changes keeps pace, that chapter may already be outdated by the time you're reading it. Here are a few examples:

- *Double contacts* are legal, until they aren't — until they are again.
- *Libero* rules are constantly in flux.
- The Association of Volleyball Professionals (AVP) even messed with the format of the sport in 2024, truncating matches to three sets with scores of 15-15-15, rather than the traditional 21-21-15.

Perhaps — we hope — soon, the rules will be the rules, and only minor tweaks that don't change the essence of the sport itself will be made. Chapter 2 examines the different rules codes in greater detail.

Beach Volleyball Will Ditch Its Reputation as a Backyard Sport

Although sports fans view indoor volleyball as a credible sport of genuine athleticism, they often view beach volleyball more akin to cornhole or beer pong — a backyard sport that's fun to play at parties with a drink in hand or nearby. But the more people watch and play the game, the more they understand the athleticism and physicality required to play it. That requirement doesn't mean that the sporting world must take beach volleyball seriously, but we hope to see the sport respected a bit more, rather than just being dismissed as a BBQ sport.

Volleyball Will Become More than an Olympic Sport

For many people, volleyball comes into the collective consciousness only once every four years, during the Summer Olympic Games, whether beach or indoor. The challenge that the various indoor leagues, the AVP, and the Beach Pro Tour faces is making the jump from a blip every four years into the mainstream like any other major sport.

We think it will do just that.

Volleyball Will Remain the Highlight of Every Summer Olympics

We think that volleyball can stay in its place of power when it comes to the Summer Olympics. Can we have our cake and eat it, too? Maybe. Or maybe we're hoping for too much. Even though we want volleyball to cross into the mainstream (which we talk about in the preceding section), we love seeing the sport get its flowers during the Olympic Games as the most popular sport every four years at the Summer Olympics. The hardest tickets to come by during the 2024 Paris Olympics? Beach volleyball, played at the foot of the Eiffel Tower.

5 Appendixes

IN THIS PART . . .

Familiarize yourself with important volleyball terms and lingo in the glossary.

Discover the GOATs — the greatest of all time — players for both indoor and beach volleyball.

Appendix A

Glossary: Volleyball Lingo

Like any sport, both indoor and beach volleyball have their own specific languages, jargon, slang, and terminology. This glossary gives you a basic list of most of the terms that you might hear at any given volleyball tournament — but, of course, volleyball lingo will continue expanding and changing while new generations bring their own flavor and verbiage to the table.

3-meter line: Line on the court that separates the front and back rows.

4-2: An offensive system in indoor volleyball that uses four hitters and two setters (the setters set from the front row).

5-1: A player rotation system that has five hitters and one setter who plays all rotations.

6-2: A player rotation system that has six hitters and two setters (the setters set only from the back row).

10-foot line: See *3-meter line.*

ace: A serve that results directly in a point.

approach: The footwork used before jumping to attack.

attack: An attempt to score by the offense.

attack line: See *3-meter line.*

back row: Players positioned behind the attack line, closest to the endline.

bic: A lower, quicker set to a back row hitter.

block: A defensive play at the net to stop or deflect an attack.

block touch: Contact by the blocker before the ball goes out or is dug.

blocker: A player who primarily challenges the attacked ball at the net.

bump: A pass made with the forearms.

bump set: A set made with your platform rather than your hands.

carry: Illegal prolonged contact with the ball.

chicken wing: Awkward arm dig, often accidental (but used as a reaction more often than you might think).

cobra: Using fingertips pressed together to push the ball.

collective block: When two or three front-row players coordinate to block an attacker together.

cut shot: A sharp-angled shot across the court.

defender: A player who covers shots and hard-driven balls. See *shot* and *hard-driven.*

defensive specialist: A back-row defensive player.

dig: A defensive save of a hard-driven attack.

double: Illegal contact, where the player mishandles the ball by using two or more contacts, instead of one; most common on sets and overhead digs.

double block: When two players execute a block.

dump: When the setter sends the ball over on the team's second contact.

fake: When the defender makes a slight move in one direction to mislead the attacker about where the defender will actually play defense.

float serve: A serve that has little to no spin and moves unpredictably.

foot fault: Stepping on or over the service line while serving, resulting in a point for the opposing team.

four hits: Violation that occurs when a team contacts the ball more than three times.

free ball: A ball sent easily over the net, rather than an attack.

front row: Players near the net and in front of the attack line.

hard-driven: A powerful attack from the offense with velocity and power, often referred to as a *spike* or *hit.*

hand set: A set made with the hands positioned above the forehead.

high hands: An attack that is aimed to hit the fingers of the blocker and score a point for the offense.

high line: A looping shot to the sideline over a blocker.

hit: Sending the ball forcefully over the net.

house: A slang term for a *stuff block.*

jammed: When there's little space between your body and platform when making a pass.

joust: When two players contact the ball simultaneously at the net.

juke: See *fake.*

jumbo: A high, safe shot to the deep corner (which makes the shape of the tail of a jumbo shrimp).

jump serve: A high-speed serve that the server hits, most often with *topspin,* while jumping.

left-side hitter: A player who attacks from the left side, plays defense, and blocks; the star of the show.

lift: See *carry.*

line shot: An attack that goes down the sideline.

kill: An attack that results immediately in a point.

libero: A type of defensive specialist who wears a different color jersey and plays only back row.

middle blocker: A position that specializes in quick blocking and attacks.

net violation: Touching the net during play.

on-one: Attacking on the first contact of the play. Occasionally, this happens in serve-receive, when the passer sees an opening to score. More often, it's in defense, when the defender makes a dig with the intent to score.

open: When a passer drops a leg back to turn or angle their body to create a better platform angle to their target.

opposite hitter: A player who attacks from the right side and often blocks the outside hitter of the other team.

option: Attacking on the second contact, rather than setting your teammate.

out of rotation: A fault called when players aren't in the correct rotational order when the ball is served.

outside hitter: See *left-side hitter.*

overpass: A pass on the served ball that goes over the net and to the opposing team.

pancake: A one-handed defensive save where the other hand lays flat on the floor.

pass: The first contact after a serve, usually (hopefully!) toward the setter.

passing window: The ideal space in front of the passer where the ball should be contacted for a controlled pass.

peel: When the blocker fakes a block, then drops back to defend; occurs in beach, not indoor volleyball.

pin: The two outside hitting positions near the antennas on the net.

plane: An imaginary area that extends straight up from the net.

platform: The flat, solid surface players create with their forearms to either pass or bump-set a volleyball.

pokey: Attack by using the knuckles; beach volleyball's legal alternative to a tip.

pull: See *peel.*

quick: A fast, low set, usually delivered close to the net, to an attacker who is already approaching or jumping before or just as the setter contacts the ball.

rally: A sequence of play from the serve until the point is finished.

rally scoring: Every rally results in a point, regardless of which team served, as compared to side-out scoring where a team could score only when it served.

read: Identifying either what movement the ball will take on a serve, or identifying what attack is coming from the opponents.

right-side hitter: See *opposite hitter.*

roll shot: A soft, controlled topspin attack.

roof: A strong block that prevents an opponent's attack from crossing the net.

rotation: The clockwise movement of players when a team wins the serve.

scoop: A dig made below the waist by using open hands (like you're scooping something).

seam: The gap between players.

serve: The action that starts a rally by putting the ball into play.

service line: The back line on the court, behind which the server must stand when making a serve.

set: The second contact (after the first contact, a pass), which places the ball for an attacker.

setter: The player who runs the offense and sets up attacks.

shank: A badly misdirected pass.

shot: An off-speed attack, typically high and loopy over a blocker.

side out: When the receiving team wins the rally and gains the serve.

side-out scoring: The original method of scoring, in which only the serving team can earn a point.

soft block: Redirecting the ball to the defender (or, on the beach, to yourself); doesn't qualify as one of your three countable touches in indoor but does on the beach.

solo block: A block by one player.

spike: See *hit.*

step close: The final two steps of the approach.

stuff block: A block that sends the ball straight down on the attacker's side. See *roof.*

swing: See *hit.*

swipe: An attacking technique where a hitter intentionally contacts the ball so it brushes or deflects off a blocker's hands and then goes out of bounds, earning a point.

tip: A soft, controlled attack placed over or around the block; legal in indoor volleyball, but not beach.

tomahawk: Overhead dig that uses interlocked fists or open hands.

tooling the block: Hitting the ball off the block to score; also called a *tool.*

topspin: Forward rotation on the ball.

transition: When the defense digs a ball and now becomes the offense in a volleyball rally.

triple block: When three players execute a block.

zone serve: Serving the ball to a certain area on the court.

Appendix B

The Volleyball GOAT Pasture

This appendix identifies some of the greatest of all times (GOATs) in indoor and beach volleyball. However, how do you take a sport that's been around since the 1800s and whittle the greatest in every category down to just the top five?

To come up with this list, we read a lot. We watched a lot. We asked a lot of folks around both sports.

We didn't create this appendix as an objective list of who the greatest volleyball players of all time are in their respective categories. Consider it an ode, a subjective nod, to the five in each — offense, defense, serving, blocking, and setting — that we simply couldn't ignore. We start with beach men, then women, before delving into the indoor world. All lists are in alphabetical order, not, we must be clear, order of what we deem the greatest to the least. That matter is for you to decide. We probably made plenty of wrong decisions, and of course, we inevitably have snubbed some amazing players (none intentionally).

But to us, personally, this appendix offers the best of the best — the GOATs who reside in volleyball's GOAT Pasture.

Top Offensive Players

We first focus on offense — the most formidable players when the ball is in their hands, the surest bets to get a kill when a kill was needed.

Male beach offensive players

Here are five of the top male beach volleyball offensive players:

- **Phil Dalhausser:** Voted Best Offensive Player in the World five times by his peers on the FIVB and Beach Pro Tour, across a career that included four Olympic Games and a gold medal for the United States in 2008, Dalhausser forever changed the sport of beach volleyball — altering the way players block, the way offenses are run, and the aggressive manner in which players must serve. Standing 6 feet 9 inches tall, his peers dubbed him The Thin Beast, and a beast he was. He was so good at so many positions that he also appears in the sections "Male beach setters," "Male beach blockers," and "Male beach servers" later in this appendix.
- **Karch Kiraly:** You can find Kiraly's name in many places in this book, including Chapter 3, where we talk about those who were able to enjoy success both indoors and out (he has won gold medals on the beach and indoors, and as a coach indoors as well). This American player was, at the same time, both brilliantly surgical and unbelievably powerful, a rare combination. The winner of the first beach volleyball Olympic gold medal in 1996, Kiraly won his first professional tournament in 1979 and his last in 2005. He also played as a powerhouse in indoor volleyball (see the section "Male indoor offensive players" later in this appendix), as well as on defense (he appears in the section "Male beach defensive players" later in this appendix).
- **Anders Mol:** In his late 20s and still in his prime at the time of this writing, this Norwegian (see Figure B-1) has been voted by his peers on the Beach Pro Tour (FIVB) Best Offensive Player in the World five times by 2025 and owns two Olympic medals, including Norway's first gold in 2021, as well as a World Championship in 2022. We also recognize him in the sections "Male beach setters" and "Male beach blockers" later in this appendix.
- **Emanuel Rego:** Of the five partnerships that have won the most tournaments in the history of beach volleyball, Rego is a member of three. Nobody won quite like the Brazilian Rego, a three-time World Champion, five-time Olympian, and three-time Olympic medalist; he also appears in the section "Male beach defensive players" later in this appendix.

FIGURE B-1: Anders Mol.

Photo by Mark Rigney

- **Ricardo Santos:** Nicknamed The Wall for his prowess at the net as a blocker (he appears in our list in the section "Male beach blockers" later in this appendix), he was also an unstoppable force when he had the ball in his hands. Thrice voted the FIVB's Best Offensive Player, Santos is a four-time Olympian and three-time Olympic medalist for his native Brazil.

Female beach offensive players

Here are five of the top female beach volleyball offensive players:

- **Duda Lisboa:** Nicknamed Duda, this Brazilian's precocity is unmatched in the sport of beach volleyball. Her peers voted her both the Most Outstanding Player in the World and Best Offensive Player at the age of 18. Like Anders Mol (discussed in the preceding section), she's still very much in her prime while we write this book, and she already has a pair of Olympic appearances and a gold medal to her name. She also appears in the section "Female beach servers" later in this appendix.
- **Misty May-Treanor:** American May-Treanor operated with a precision that might never be seen again in the world of beach volleyball, cutting opponents up so effectively with her shots and placement that she and Walsh Jennings (also in this list) won 112 straight matches and 19 consecutive tournaments — records that we think it's safe to say will never be broken. She was voted Best Offensive Player

by her peers three times in her career. She also appears in the sections "Female beach setters" and "Female beach defensive players" later in this appendix.

- **April Ross:** When Ross won the 2021 Olympic gold medal for the United States in Tokyo, she became the first female to win Olympic beach medals of every color, adding to her silver in London (2012) and bronze in Rio de Janeiro (2016). Both powerful and brilliant, Ross used a combination of intelligence and sheer force to win more than 70 tournaments throughout her career. You can also find her in the sections "Female beach setters" and "Female beach servers" later in this appendix.
- **Ana Patricia Silva Ramos:** A 6-foot-4-inch *unicorn* (a sports term describing extremely rare athletes who blend together skills not often seen blended together), Ana Patricia was voted Best Offensive Player for the first time by her peers in 2023, where the runner-up was her own Brazilian partner: Duda Lisboa (who's also in this list). The following year, she was runner-up, falling a few votes shy of . . . Duda Lisboa, her partner. That's how dominant these two are offensively. We also recognize Ana Patricia in the section "Female beach blockers" later in this appendix.
- **Kerri Walsh Jennings:** The mostly undisputed GOAT of the sport of beach volleyball, regardless of gender, Walsh Jennings (see Figure B-2) won three consecutive Olympic gold medals for the United States with Misty May-Treanor and added a bronze in 2016 with April Ross. Nicknamed Six Feet of Sunshine, Walsh Jennings was twice voted Best Offensive Player and four times voted Best Hitter. Flip to the section "Female beach blockers" later in this appendix for more of her prowess.

FIGURE B-2: Kerri Walsh Jennings.

Martin Rickett/Alamy Stock Photo

Male indoor offensive players

Here are five of the top male indoor volleyball offensive players:

- **Gilberto Amauri de Godoy Filho:** Known as Giba, this Brazilian (at 6 feet 4 inches) wasn't the tallest man to ever grace a volleyball court, but his creativity remains unmatched in the world of volleyball. That creativity led to his Olympic gold medal in 2004 and three appearances in the finals of the World Championships. We also include him in the section "Male indoor servers" later in this appendix.
- **Karch Kiraly:** Before he won an Olympic gold medal for the United States on the beach in 1996 (see the section "Male beach offensive players" earlier in this appendix), he did so twice indoors, in 1984 and 1988. And he also made our list in the sections "Male beach offensive players" earlier in this appendix and "Male beach defensive players" later in this appendix. He was, simply, deadly with a ball in his hands, regardless of the surface he played on.
- **Wilfredo Leon:** How good is Leon? He made his first appearance on the Cuban National Team at the age of 14. Since then, he's (see Figure B-3) lived up to the considerable hype, winning a silver medal at the World Championships in 2010 before defecting to Poland, with whom he won an Olympic silver medal in 2024. We also include him in the section "Male indoor servers" later in this appendix.

FIGURE B-3: Wilfredo Leon.

SOPA Images/Alamy Stock Photo

» **Maxim Mikhaylov:** The only player on this list who wasn't an outside hitter, Mikhaylov, as an opposite, powered Russia to an Olympic gold medal in 2012 and a silver in 2021. Rarely making errors, Mikhaylov was the cornerstone of a Russian program that dominated throughout the 2010s. You can find him in the section "Male indoor servers" later in this appendix, as well.

» **Earvin N'Gapeth:** N'Gapeth boasts a game made for the current social media world, mixing flash and creativity with raw power and swings that make you wonder how in the world he came up with such a thing. The outside hitter led France to consecutive Olympic gold medals in 2021 and 2024 and a European Championship in 2015.

Female indoor offensive players

Here are five of the top female indoor volleyball offensive players:

» **Tijana Bošković:** A lefty powerhouse, Bošković (see Figure B-4) can boast, at the age of 28, to being a two-time Olympic medalist for Serbia (a silver in 2016 and a bronze in 2020) and a two-time World Champion. For both World Championships, she was also named MVP. She has five European Championships medals, two of which (in 2017 and 2019) are gold. We also include her in the section "Female indoor servers" later in this appendix.

FIGURE B-4: Tijana Bošković.

René Nijhuis/Alamy Stock Photos

- **Mireya Luis:** The smallest player on this list, Luis, who stood just 5 feet 9 inches, boasted a 40-inch vertical that led her to become arguably the most electrifying player of all time. She's also a three-time Olympic gold medalist for Cuba (in 1992, 1996, and 2000).
- **Lang Ping:** This Chinese player earned the nickname Iron Hammer, which should tell you almost everything you need to know about her power as a hitter. A gold medalist at the 1984 Olympic Games, Ping later dispensed her knowledge of the game as a coach, leading the United States to a silver medal at the 2002 World Championship and China to a 2016 Olympic gold medal, becoming the first person to win an indoor Olympic gold as both a player and a coach.
- **Zhu Ting:** Standing 6 feet 4 inches tall, Ting was positively unstoppable at her peak, and indeed, her teams could rarely be stopped. She was named the MVP of the 2016 Olympic Games in Rio after winning gold for China; and she received gold medals in the 2015 and 2019 World Cups in which, again, she was named MVP. We also include her in the sections "Female indoor blockers" and "Female indoor servers" later in this appendix.
- **Kim Yeon-koung:** Unlike many of the players in this list, the South Korean Yeon-koung didn't hail from a country known for its volleyball prowess. She therefore had to carry much of the burden — and carry it she did. (We also talk about her in the section "Female indoor servers" later in this appendix.) Yeon-koung was so dominant, in fact, that she won the MVP and scoring title of the 2012 Olympics — and didn't even medal, finishing fourth. She'd finish fourth again in Tokyo in 2020 and again lead the tournament in points scored. But she did lay claim to a gold medal at the 2014 Asian Games and the 2015 Asian Championship.

Top Setters

The setters are the quarterbacks, the CEOs, the point guards of the offense. Everything goes through them, as they are the ones who ultimately decide who gets set — and they're the ones, in the end, who are responsible for the success of their hitters. In beach volleyball, there is no specific "setter" — that responsibility falls on both players, as whoever doesn't pass the ball is the one who is setting.

Male beach setters

Here are five of the top male beach volleyball setters:

- **Adrian Carambula:** If you can ever describe a player in beach volleyball as a streetballer, Carambula is it. Standing just 6 feet tall — small by volleyball standards — this Uruguayan (who plays for Italy) introduced a creativity to the game that beach volleyball had never before seen, using his hands to set a variety of tempos, locations, and offensive routes that have since become vogue.

- **Phil Dalhausser:** When he began playing internationally in 2004, this American (see Figure B-5) was not only one of the biggest men on Tour, but also the rare man of his size who could hand set. Because of this versatility, he could succeed with whomever he was partnered, be it Rogers (2008 Olympic gold medal; see the section "Male beach defensive players" later in this chapter), Sean Rosenthal (Number 1 team in the world in 2013), Nick Lucena (Number 1 team in the world in 2017), and Trevor Crabb (Association of Volleyball Professionals [AVP] League Champion in 2025). We include him in the section "Male beach offensive players" earlier in this appendix, as well as the sections "Male beach blockers" and "Male beach servers" later in this appendix.

FIGURE B-5: Phil Dalhausser.

Photo by Ed Chan

- **Bartosz Łosiak:** Like Carambula (also in this list), Łosiak is a pioneer of the modern creative offense. When he and Piotr Kantor came on the scene in 2014, they drove defenses mad with a blurry-fast offense that required pinpoint setting precision with both hands and platform. A three-time Olympian for Poland, Łosiak will go down as one of the best hand setters to ever live.

» **Anders Mol:** The next in the generation of blockers revolutionizing the sport, behind Randy Stoklos and Dalhausser (also in this list). The best blocker on the planet is rarely also one of the world's best setters, but the Norwegian Mol is exactly that (he also appears in the section "Male beach blockers" later in this appendix). It helps to explain why, from 2018 to 2025, Mol and fellow countryman Christian Sørum won more than 30 events, including a World Championship (in 2022) and an Olympic gold medal (in 2021). Mol also appears in the section "Male beach offensive players" earlier in this chapter.

» **Randy Stoklos:** Played in an era that had the tightest standards for what defined a clean or legal set — and he was almost never called for a foul. One of the all-time winningest players in the sport, this American revolutionized the game as one of the first big men who could hand set, changing offenses forever. He also appears in the section "Male beach blockers" later in this appendix.

Female beach setters

Here are five of the top female beach volleyball setters:

» **Kelly Cheng:** Like Jordyn Poulter (whom we talk about in the section "Female indoor setters" later in this appendix), Cheng is young to be on this list, just 30 years old. But she has already established herself as an all-time great. She won four straight National Championships at the University of Southern California (USC), played in the youngest team in U.S. history to qualify for an Olympic Games for the United States (in 2021 in Tokyo with Sarah Sponcil), won a World Championship in 2023 (with Sara Hughes), and has won virtually every big tournament there is to win, other than an Olympic gold. She has great creativity as a setter, both with hands and platform, and even a jump set here and there.

» **Melissa Humaña-Paredes:** She reset the Canadian record books, both with Sarah Pavan (with whom she won the 2019 World Championship) and Brandie Wilkerson (with whom she won Canada's first female Olympic medal in beach volleyball, a silver in Paris in 2024). (You can read more about both of these Canadian players in the section "Female beach blockers" later in this appendix.) Like Larissa Maestrini, Humaña-Paredes uses her hands almost exclusively, which puts her partners in a position for offensive success, because hand setters tend to be more accurate and can set a wide variety of tempos and locations.

» **Larissa Maestrini:** Prior to this Brazilian coming on the scene, you rarely saw a female hand set. Larissa is one of the finest hand setters in beach volleyball history, the singular player who broke down a barrier and introduced a new generation of female hand setters to the game. We also recognize her in the section "Female beach defensive players" later in this appendix.

- **Misty May-Treanor:** Although she didn't hand set, we would make a ghastly error if we didn't include her on this list. May-Treanor won three straight Olympic gold medals alongside Walsh Jennings (who appears in the section "Female beach offensive players" earlier in this chapter). May-Treanor's perfect location and tempo with her bump setting is a huge reason why they had so much success. May-Treanor is arguably the best bump setter of all time. We also include her in the sections "Female beach offensive players" earlier in this appendix and "Female beach defensive players" later in this appendix.
- **April Ross:** An exclusive bump setter who clearly had no issue with it (similar to Misty May-Treanor, also in this list) and the only female player to win an Olympic medal of every color — silver in 2012, bronze in 2016, and gold in 2021 — for the United States. She enjoyed success with players of all sizes and skillsets, and nobody ever had trouble scoring on her setting. We also include her in the sections "Female beach offensive players" earlier in this appendix and "Female beach servers" later in this appendix.

Male indoor setters

Here are five of the top male indoor volleyball setters of all time:

- **Lloy Ball:** Longevity is a hallmark of athletes who make any all-time list, and no setter had more of it than Ball. The first and only American male to set in four separate Olympics, he led the United States to a gold medal at the Beijing Games in 2008 — the same year that the Americans won the FIVB World League, at which Ball was named both MVP and Best Setter. In 2015, Ball was elected to the International Volleyball Hall of Fame.
- **Micah Christenson:** One of those freaky athletes who could have gone professional in any number of sports, whether volleyball, golf, or basketball. He (see Figure B-6) landed on volleyball, utilizing that extreme athleticism and ambidexterity to act as an offensive threat at all times, a dangerous server, and a setter so precise and dynamic that the United States didn't take a step back after the retirement of Ball (also in this list). Christenson has helped the United States to a 2014 FIVB World League title, as well as a 2015 FIVB World Cup, to go along with a pair of bronze medals at the 2016 Rio Olympic Games and Paris in 2024.
- **Ricardo Garcia:** A six-time FIVB World League champion (2001, 2003, 2004, 2005, 2006, and 2007), a two-time World Champion (2002 and 2006) and a two-time Brazilian Olympic medalist (gold in Athens in 2004 and silver in London in 2012), Garcia (who goes by the nickname Ricardinho) will go down as one of the all-time most-decorated setters, and one of its all-time greats.

FIGURE B-6: Micah Christenson.

IPA/Alamy Stock Photo

- **Nikola Grbic:** Nikola and his brother, Vladimir, pioneered the golden generation of Serbian volleyball, winning a bronze medal at the 1996 Olympic Games in Atlanta and a gold four years later in Sydney. Many fans and players regard that 2000 team as one of the greatest of all time, in large part thanks to the setting of Grbic, who played his club career nearly exclusively in Italy's Serie A1, considered the top league in the world.
- **Bruno Rezende:** Athletes in Olympic sports such as volleyball are generally remembered for their performances on the sport's biggest stage, the Olympics. Bruninho, as he's nicknamed, shined on that stage, winning gold for Brazil at home in Rio in 2016 and setting Brazil to silvers in 2008 and 2012. He bowed out after yet another Olympic appearance in 2024, where Brazil finished fifth, capping a remarkable career.

Female indoor setters

Here are five of the top female indoor volleyball setters of all time:

- **Alisha Glass Childress:** If you win a World Championship, are named MVP of that World Championship, and get chosen as the Best Setter of said World Championship (which Glass did in 2014), well, that's a convincing metric to land you on a list such as this one. Glass also helped the Americans win a bronze medal at the 2016 Olympic Games in Rio and is widely considered the best American setter of the 2010 era.

- **Eleonora Lo Bianco:** Lo Bianco's game had no holes — none. Because of her all-around abilities, she served as the longtime captain of the Italian National Team (one of the strongest federations in the world), won a World Championship in 2002 (Italy's only World Championship as of this writing), and went to a remarkable five Olympic Games. Few players enjoyed more success over such a long period of time as Bianco, nicknamed Leo.
- **Maja Ognjenović:** One of the most decorated setters of all-time. This Serbian was a World Champion in 2018 who also boasts a pair of Olympic medals — silver in Rio in 2016 and bronze in Tokyo in 2021. She eclipsed 300 matches played for Serbia, a wild number that speaks to her generational longevity in the sport.
- **Jordyn Poulter:** Only 28 at the time of this writing, Poulter (see Figure B-7) already belongs on this list. She set the United States to its first gold medal at the 2021 Tokyo Olympic Games and helped the Americans return to the finals again in Paris in 2024, eventually winning a silver medal. These Olympic successes, along with two Volleyball Nations League (VNL) titles, land her in our GOAT Pasture at such a precocious age.

FIGURE B-7: Jordyn Poulter.

LiveMedia/Alamy Stock Photo

- **Hélia Rogério de Souza:** The world may never see sustained success like de Souza, nicknamed Fofão, experienced in her career. For nearly two decades, she was the setter on the feared Brazilian National Team, winning three Olympic medals — bronze in 1996 and 2000, and gold in 2008 — for the country that has the deepest pool of volleyball talent.

Top Blockers

Blockers are the wall, the first line of defense, the men and women at the net attempting to stop an attack before it even crosses onto their side of the court. They can single-handedly change a match, altering everything an opponent wants to do with a single block. They make lives easier for the defensive players behind them, forming funnels behind which they can dig. They are the unsung heroes of the volleyball world.

Male beach blockers

Here are five of the top male beach volleyball blockers of all time:

- **Alison Cerutti:** Nicknamed The Mammoth, this Brazilian used his enormous frame to punch his ticket to three Olympic Games and win medals in two of them: silver in 2012 and gold in 2016. Twice, he was voted Best Blocker by his peers on the FIVB and Beach Pro Tour, and likely would have won far more had it not been for Dalhausser (also in this list).
- **Phil Dalhausser:** When this American, nicknamed The Thin Beast, broke into the professional ranks, he forever changed the way the game was played. Standing 6 feet 9 inches tall, he had the coordination, quickness, and speed (ability to chase down a ball) of a man much smaller, able to make moves at the net that the world had never before seen from such a giant. His peers on the FIVB and Beach Pro Tour voted him Best Blocker in the World a record seven times, a skill that helped him win an Olympic gold medal in 2008. We also included him in the top five in the sections "Male beach offensive players" and "Male beach setters" earlier in this appendix, and "Male beach servers" later in this appendix.
- **Anders Mol:** Even the great Dalhausser considers Mol the greatest blocker ever in the sport of beach volleyball. This Norwegian picked up where Dalhausser left off and evolved the skill of blocking even further, making radically athletic moves that continue to leave hitters perplexed. At just 28 years old, Mol has been voted Best Blocker in the World five times by his peers on the FIVB and Beach Pro Tour, has already won a pair of Olympic medals — gold in 2021 and bronze in 2024 — and is on a fast track to being the unquestioned greatest blocker, if not greatest player, of men's beach volleyball. He also made the list in the sections "Male beach offensive players" and "Male beach setters" earlier in this appendix.
- **Ricardo Santos:** Nicknamed The Wall because nothing ever got past Ricardo, this giant Brazilian will go down as one of the most decorated beach volleyball players of all time, regardless of gender. (You can find him in the section "Male beach offensive players" earlier in this appendix.) His blocking is a central

reason why he went to four Olympic Games and came away with three medals: silver in 2000, gold in 2004, and bronze in 2008.

- **Randy Stoklos:** The original unicorn in beach volleyball, American Stoklos combined size — 6 feet 4 inches — with mobility and athleticism to be a force at the net. (We also have him in the section "Male beach setters" earlier in this appendix.) His blocking, as well as his exceptional setting, allowed him to become beach volleyball's first million-dollar man. He'd go on to win 122 tournaments, a trio of MVP awards, and a Hall of Fame nod in 1999 as one of the best.

Female beach blockers

Here are five of the top female beach volleyball blockers of all time:

- **Juliana Felisberta:** Not only one of the best blockers of all-time, but one of the best players, period, in all of women's beach volleyball. This Brazilian was dominant at the net without an overly dominant height, standing 5 feet 10 inches, yet possessing such a tremendous presence that she was twice voted Blocker of the Year and thrice the MVP by her peers on the FIVB and Beach Pro Tour. Winner of 48 professional events, Felisberta also won an Olympic bronze medal in 2012 alongside her longtime partner, Maestrini (who pops up in our list in the section "Female beach setters" earlier in this appendix).
- **Sarah Pavan:** The 6-foot-5-inch Pavan played a major part in filling out the Canadian beach volleyball record books when she made the switch from indoor to beach volleyball. Thrice named the Blocker of the Year by her peers on the FIVB and Beach Pro Tour, Pavan was also the first Canadian to win a World Championship (in 2019), first to be named Team of the Year (also in 2019) on the FIVB, and first to win a Commonwealth Games gold medal (2018). She received all these accolades with her partner, Humaña-Paredes, who appears in the section "Female beach setters" earlier in this appendix. She retired as a two-time Olympian and one of the best to ever tend the net.
- **Ana Patricia Silva Ramos:** We honestly don't know whether this Brazilian player is better at the net or off it, pull digging when she pulls off the net to play defense. Her 6-foot-4-inch frame doesn't immediately suggest she'd be one of the best pull diggers of all time because players with her height generally stay at the net to block. Yet she most certainly qualifies for this list (as well as the section "Female beach offensive players" earlier in this appendix): a two-time Olympian, winning gold in 2024 and World Champion in 2022, who utilized her wild coordination and athleticism to be an enormous problem for opposing hitters.
- **Kerri Walsh Jennings:** This American, nicknamed Six Feet of Sunshine, is the most decorated player of all time thanks, in large part, to an incredible seven Blocker of the Year awards on the FIVB and Beach Pro Tour. Defense is said

to win championships, and Walsh Jennings' work at the net helped her to four Olympic medals — golds in 2004, 2008, and 2012, and bronze in 2016 — and the most wins of any player — men or women — of all time. Not to ignore her offensive skills, she also appears in the section "Female beach offensive players" earlier in this appendix.

- **Brandie Wilkerson:** The shortest member on our list of all-time great blockers, this 5-foot-10-inch Canadian (see Figure B-8) more than atones for her lack of notable height with an astonishing vertical leap and an athleticism that the women's game had never seen prior to her arrival. She's a mix of perfect fundamentals with instinctual, can't-teach-that volleyball IQ that allows her to make reads and moves that offensive players can't see coming. At the time of writing, she's a four-time Blocker of the Year on the FIVB and Beach Pro Tour (and counting).

FIGURE B-8: Brandie Wilkerson.

Image of sport/Alamy Stock Photo

Male indoor blockers

Here are five of the top male indoor volleyball blockers of all time:

- **Andrea Giani:** A relatively diminutive man (compared to some other players on this list), standing just 6 feet 5 inches tall, is on this list because — aside from his astounding vertical — he virtually wrote the book on blocking. His Italian teams won silver in the 1996 Olympics and bronze in 2000, leaning on

Giani's brilliance to turn their defense into a wall. In 2016, as an assistant, he coached Germany to an Olympic silver medal, and while serving as the head coach for Slovenia, he won a European Championship silver medal.

» **David Lee:** Talk about middle blockers in the United States, and David Lee's name will immediately arise, and for good reason. The 6-foot-8-inch chiseled rock of a man formed the foundation of a U.S. team that would make a scintillating run through the 2008 Olympic Games, ultimately winning a gold medal. If he wasn't such a genuinely nice guy, you could easily call Lee a bully. On the court, he certainly filled that role, and opposing teams had no answers for him.

» **Srećko Lisinac:** Blockers can get hot — but Lisinac just operated hot on a nearly nightly basis. It wasn't particularly unusual for Lisinac to rip off two or three blocks in a row, and his streaky nature — in a good way — helped Serbia win an Olympic bronze medal in 2016. One especially telling trait of a dominant blocker involves how the team responds when that player no longer stands in the front row. The Serbian Olympic team simply wasn't the same when it didn't have Lisinac in the front.

» **Dmitriy Muserskiy:** Standing 7 feet 2 inches tall, Muserskiy (refer to Figure B-9) didn't leave a whole lot of room to go around him — and he certainly didn't leave much room to go over him, either. He's most remembered for the 2012 Olympic final against Brazil. Down 0–2, Muserskiy moved from middle to opposite, and Brazil's hitters froze. The move provided the impetus for Russia to complete a wildly improbable comeback to win the gold medal and make Muserskiy the tallest Olympic gold medalist of all time.

FIGURE B-9: Dmitriy Muserskiy.

NurPhoto/Alamy Stock Photo

- **Robertlandy Simon:** This natural, instinctual, and fundamental blocker, a 6-foot-10-inch Cuban, turned his federation from a contender to a perennial winner. Perhaps most significantly, Simon defied the nature of sports in that he never really had an off rotation, much less an off match. This consistency kept Cuba more than relevant, and landed Simon plaudits from many as the best middle blocker in the world when he dominated the Serie A and SuperLega in Italy.

Female indoor blockers

Here are five of the top female indoor volleyball blockers of all time:

- **Foluke Akinradewo:** Was she the most physically imposing of the bunch? No. Standing 6-foot 4-inches tall, Foluke atoned for any perceived lack of height with an athleticism and explosiveness that helped her lead the United States to an Olympic silver medal in 2012, bronze in 2016, and silver in 2021. Over more than a decade, she regularly finished in the top five in blocks per set, tremendous longevity for a middle.
- **Regla Torres:** In the same way that the National Basketball Association (NBA) had Michael Jordan as the linchpin to the Chicago Bulls' three-peat era, Torres was the blocking foundation for Cuba during its golden era, in which it won Olympic gold medals in 1992, 1996, and 2000. It was Torres who set the standard for what it means to be in control at the net, and she had no problem going one-on-one against the best hitters in the world.
- **Thaísa Daher de Menezes:** When Regla Torres (also in this list) retired, Menezes took the title as best blocker in the world, serving as the cornerstone for Brazil while it claimed Olympic gold medals in 2008 and 2012, and a silver in 2016. The 6-foot-6-inch middle was also as clutch as they come, repeatedly coming up huge in the biggest moments, often late in sets and matches.
- **Yekaterina Gamova:** We can't think of anyone more imposing at the net than Gamova, a 6-foot-8-inch tower of an opposite who led Russia to two Olympic medals — silvers in 2004 and 2008 — and another two appearances in 2012 and 2016. That type of sustained success in the rapidly evolving game of volleyball is nearly impossible to come by, and yet Gamova did it, perpetually changing hitters' angles, as well as their shot and swing selection.
- **Zhu Ting:** You may feel surprised to see an outside hitter make this list but make no mistake: Ting belongs on it. The 6-foot-6-inch star led China in blocks per set on the way to an Olympic gold medal in 2016 and was again clutch at the net in a silver medal-winning performance in 2021. You can't easily find a

hitter who can score and block at such an elite level, and Ting will go down as one of the best two-way stars in volleyball. She also appears in the sections "Female indoor offensive players" earlier in this appendix and "Female indoor servers" later in this appendix.

Top Defensive Players

Welcome to the second line of, ahem, defense in volleyball: The players behind the blockers, the ones digging the hard-driven swings or chasing down shots, the ones making opposing hitters' lives as miserable as possible.

Male beach defensive players

Here are five of the top male beach volleyball defensive players of all time:

- **Karch Kiraly:** Who's Number 1 on that all-time wins list? Karch Kiraly, a triple-black-belt when it comes to the sport of volleyball. (We talk about him in offensive roles in the section "Top Offensive Players" earlier in this appendix.) The American who won a pair of Olympic gold medals indoors won another on the beach and then added a gold medal as a coach when he led the U.S. women to the mountaintop in 2021. As a player, it was his control and tenacity on defense (see Figure B-10) that provided the foundation for his ubiquitous success, amounting to 148 career wins and more than $3 million in prize money.

FIGURE B-10: Karch Kiraly.

ZUMA/Alamy Stock Photo

- **Emanuel Rego:** One of the smoothest athletes in any sport, on any surface, this Brazilian is a five-time Olympian and three-time World Champion. He's second to none in his defensive prowess, able to make any blocker in front of him successful and any opposing player against him maddeningly frustrated. His offense is just as strong, and he also appears in the list in the section "Male beach offensive players" earlier in this appendix.
- **Todd Rogers:** Where Bruno Schmidt (who appears in this list) was all magic and pixie dust, Rogers, called The Professor, was all smarts and patience. Somehow, someway, he always seemed to just know where you were going to hit the ball. It's one thing to be there, of course, and another thing entirely to make and finish the play. For years and years, he made the plays, winning four Defensive Player of the Year nods on the World Tour, another four on the AVP, an Olympic gold medal, and a unanimous selection in the Hall of Fame.
- **Bruno Schmidt:** He was called The Magician during his dazzling run from 2010 to 2016, a stretch that included an Olympic gold medal for Brazil, four Defensive Player of the Year awards from his peers on the FIVB and Beach Pro Tour, and 13 gold medals on the World Tour. The nickname fit because Schmidt could simply do things that seemed like magic to the rest of the mere mortals on the World Tour.
- **Sinjin Smith:** Sinjin's place in beach volleyball is singular: He is, bar none, the most influential individual in the sport. He pushed the sport into the Olympic Games in 1996 (taking great personal risk to do so); helped found the Association of Volleyball Professionals (AVP), the premier U.S. pro beach volleyball tour; built the sport into a rollicking success in the 1980s and '90s — and he's one of the best defensive players of all time. The AVP voted him Best Defensive Player three times (it would have been more if the voting had begun earlier). He had a skillset that led him to winning 139 tournaments, second all time (behind Kiraly).

Female beach defensive players

Here are five of the top female beach volleyball defensive players of all time:

- **Shelda Bede:** One of the original Brazilian bad-asses, the first in a long line of greats to come. In five straight seasons (1997–2001), her peers on the FIVB and Beach Pro Tour awarded her Team of the Year alongside Adriana Behar (whom you can read about in the section "Other Important and

Influential Figures in the Volleyball World" later in this appendix) and then she added another with Behar in 2004, and a seventh with Ana Paula Connelly Henkel (2008; we talk about Connelly Henkel in the section "Female beach servers" later in this appendix). The best part? Bede stood just 5 feet 5 inches, a mighty mouse if the sport has ever seen one, using her size to her advantage — more quickness, more speed, easier change of direction.

- **Laura Ludwig:** In many respects, Ludwig changed how defensive players viewed their role, turning her digs and platform into not just a frustrating nuisance for the offense, but an actual offensive weapon for her. Ludwig pioneered the over-on-one attack, becoming so adapt at sending digs over the net for points that the move became known as, simply, The Ludwig. It led her to an Olympic gold medal for Germany and a pair of Best Defensive Player in the World nods from her peers on the FIVB and Beach Pro Tour. We also include her in the section "Female beach servers" later in this appendix.
- **Larissa Maestrini:** Maestrini won at least one tournament in all 13 seasons of her professional career, highlighted by an eight-win deluge in 2009. What made her so successful? Many skills and factors, but few bigger than her defensive grit and IQ. She was as hard to score on as anyone in the world, a feisty and spunky Brazilian who took the torch from Bede (also in this list) and carried it high for more than a decade. She also appears in the section "Female beach setters" earlier in this appendix.
- **Misty May-Treanor:** The sport may never see another defensive player the likes of her. A consummate winner, May-Treanor won three Olympic gold medals, was named Defensive Player of the Year as many times by her peers on the FIVB and Beach Pro Tour, and collected a cool 199 career victories. We also include her in the sections "Female beach offensive players" and "Female beach setters" earlier in this appendix. To see a career like that again would be akin to witnessing lightning strike not just twice, but 1,000 times.
- **Kristen Nuss:** It might seem premature to put this 5-foot-6-inch American dynamo (refer to Figure B-11) on this list, seeing as she's just 28 years old at the time of this writing. But Nuss, in just three years as a professional, has made her presence felt, winning Defensive Player of the Year thrice on the World Tour and twice on the AVP. Meanwhile, she's collected a pair of World Championship medals — bronze in 2023 and silver in 2025 — and has piled up 20 career victories in a short amount of time.

FIGURE B-11: Kristen Nuss.

Photo by Mark Rigney

Male indoor defensive players

Here are five of the top male indoor volleyball defensive players of all time:

- **Fabio Balaso:** The Italian libero doesn't have an Olympic medal, but he has something that holds nearly as much weight: a World Championship victory. What makes him elite enough to belong on this list? He's . . . boring. A hallmark of elite athletes is that they make the difficult look easy and the easy look mundane. Balaso is a technician, making the most difficult plays look like a Sunday stroll to the café for another shot of espresso.
- **Sergio Dustra Santos:** The longtime Brazilian libero, nicknamed Serginho, anchored a defensive unit that made four consecutive Olympic finals, collecting two gold medals (in 2004 and 2016) and a pair of silvers (in 2008 and 2012). He essentially redefined what it meant to be a libero, showing the outsized impact such a diminutive player can make in a sport otherwise made for giants.
- **Jenio Grebennikov:** Does anybody dig a hard-driven hit better than Grebennikov? Hard to say. He doesn't just keep balls off the floor — he puts them right into his setter's hands, a huge reason why France won an Olympic gold medal in 2000. Just as good as his hard-driven defense is his uncanny ability to keep a pancake dig alive, making for one highlight reel after the next.

- **Erik Shoji:** One of the most consistent, reliable players that the United States has ever had, Shoji (see Figure B-12) may also hold the title of best passer in the world. These things, of course, are impossible to objectively state, but with a pair of Olympic medals — bronze in 2016 and 2021 — Shoji has been the linchpin of the U.S. defense for nearly two decades.

FIGURE B-12: Erik Shoji

Volleyball World

- **Paweł Zatorski:** Zatorski is in rarefied air as one of the only liberos to have won multiple World Championships, which he did with Poland in 2018 and 2022. While he doesn't have an Olympic podium, it doesn't change the fact that Poland, with Zatorski heading the defense, has been one of the most consistently great teams in the world. He makes digs and plays by the bunches, winning by volume, not necessarily by flash.

Female indoor defensive players

Here are five of the top female indoor volleyball defensive players of all time:

- **Brenda Castillo:** It's a shame that Castillo hasn't had a better supporting cast around her because the Dominican Republic libero has routinely been named

Best Libero — in the 2012 Summer Olympics, the 2010 World Championships, the 2013–2014 CEV Champions League, and the 2015 World Cup — but she doesn't have a team that can win at the biggest events. That fact does nothing to diminish her stature as one of the best liberos in the business and one of the defensive greats of all time.

- **Monica De Gennaro:** You can't argue with the resume for this Italian libero: 2024 Olympic gold medal, 2022 World Championship gold medal, multiple Volleyball Nations League (VNL) titles and a European Championship gold. Legacies are made by winning the most iconic events, and De Gennaro has made a habit of doing just that.
- **Lin Li:** China has long been a volleyball power, and Li guided the federation into a modern golden era. The libero was an integral part of China's 2016 Olympic gold in Rio, a 2015 World Cup victory, and 2018 Nations League and World Championship bronze medal. Individually, she was named Best Libero at the 2016 FIVB World Grand Prix and the 2016 Olympic Games — the biggest stage of them all.
- **Yuko Sano:** One particular measure of just how elite a player is when they receive an award in a tournament their team didn't win. Such was the case for Sano at the 2012 Olympic Games, where Japan won bronze — and Sano was still awarded Best Libero. That's how much she stood out, not just then, but throughout her career, while she collected Best Libero nods at the 2008 World Grand Prix, 2011 FIVB World Cup, and multiple Asian Championships.
- **Fabiola de Souza:** Fabi was the defensive backbone of Brazil's strongest era, leading them to a pair of Olympic gold medals, in 2008 and 2012, while adding a World Championship silver in 2006 and 2010. She received her first Best Libero award in 2002, at the FIVB World Grand Prix, and continued collecting them at the 2008 Olympics, 2008 Final Four Cup, 2009 Montreux Volley Masters, 2011 FIVB World Grand Prix, and 2013 South American Championship.

Top Servers

Serving is at once the greatest offensive weapon, in that an ace can earn a point without a single other player touching the ball, and defensive because it can create havoc for the opposing offense. Chapter 8 covers serving, where we ponder whether you're on offense or defense at the service line (spoiler alert: the answer is yes!).

Male beach servers

Here are five of the top male beach volleyball servers of all time:

- **Phil Dalhausser:** Given that Dalhausser is perhaps the greatest offensive player to ever play beach volleyball (he's on our list in the section "Male beach offensive players" earlier in this appendix), you can easily understand why so few chose to serve him the ball. So, other than setting — and setting, and setting, and setting (he's also in the section "Male beach setters" earlier in this appendix) — this American had to figure out a way to get involved. He did that and then some by using one of the most formidable jump serves the game has ever seen — second, perhaps, only to Evandro Goncalves (also in this list). He also had a hand in blocking (he appears in the list in the section "Male beach blockers" earlier in this appendix).
- **Evandro Goncalves:** Although he's only 35 years old at the time of this writing, Goncalves (see Figure B-13) has already claimed the title of Greatest Server of All Time Tour and no one debates that choice. Armed with a jump serve that brings velocity the world has never seen, for eight straight years, he has been voted by his peers on the FIVB and Beach Pro Tour as the Server of the Year. By the time you're reading this book, he might have this award for nine years in a row, or even into double digits. Regardless of the number, Goncalves is the singular GOAT when it comes to serving in beach volleyball.

FIGURE B-13: Evandro Goncalves.

Volleyball World

- **Igor Kolodinsky:** How dominant was the 6-foot-6-inch Russian from the service line? He was voted Server of the Year by his peers on the FIVB and Beach Pro Tour in 2007 — the same year he debuted on tour as a rookie! That season, in which he won five medals, ignited a string of four straight years that he was voted Server of the Year, putting him on track to retire as one of the best servers of all-time, even in a career that spanned just four seasons.
- **Eric Koreng:** The casual fan may not recognize Koreng's name — but those he played against from 2005 to 2014 surely do. This German player's serve was so menacing that he was twice voted Server of the Year by his peers on the FIVB and Beach Pro Tour. In a single tournament in Stavanger, Norway, he knocked off two players also in this list — Igor Kolodinsky in the quarterfinals and Phil Dalhausser in the semifinals — en route to winning one of the most iconic tournaments of the 2010 season.
- **Taylor Sander:** Sander will certainly be remembered more for his brilliant indoor career than his excellent stint on the beach, but this American is one of the rare few who brought a bomb of an indoor serve and successfully converted it to the sand. Beginning with his rookie season in 2022, Sander has been named the AVP Server of the Year every year he has been a professional and counting.

Female beach servers

Here are five of the top female beach volleyball servers of all time:

- **Taliqua Clancy:** A long, lithe, and astonishingly explosive Australian, Clancy won an Olympic silver medal at the 2021 Tokyo Olympic Games with major thanks to a powerful jump serve and a fast, flat float that gave offensive players fits. Voted the Server of the Year in 2018 by her peers on the FIVB and Beach Pro Tour, Clancy is always dangerous from the end line.
- **Ana Paula Connelly:** The only player in the world, male or female, to win a major international gold medal with five different partners. How is that possible? Well, you don't need much team chemistry when you're simply acing your opponents off the court, which this Brazilian did so well that her peers on the FIVB and Beach Pro Tour voted her the Server of the Year in five straight seasons, from 2003 to 2007.
- **Duda Lisboa:** The 2024 Olympic gold medalist for Brazil, known as Duda, comes armed with a jump serve so powerful that often no one can do much about it. But she also has a nasty float that can move with the best of them, and she can use that contrast between jump and float to keep offensive players forever on their toes — and dreading whatever comes from the end

line. She also appears in the section "Female beach offensive players" earlier in this appendix.

- **Laura Ludwig:** It's a sure sign that you're special in any industry when you invent something that's so effective, the rest of the world takes note and attempts to copy you. Ludwig accomplished that feat with her devastating float serve, forever known as the *German float* and copied worldwide after her gold medal for Germany at the 2016 Olympic Games. You can read about the move called The Ludwig in the section "Female beach defensive players" earlier in this appendix.
- **April Ross:** You can attribute this American's successes over multiple decades to nearly a dozen of her skills, both tangible and intangible. (You can find her in the sections "Female beach offensive players" and "Female beach setters" earlier in this appendix.) But make no mistake: Her vicious top-spin jump serve should stand at the top of the list. Women's beach volleyball doesn't feature jump serving nearly as much as the men's, so when an individual such as Ross comes along, possessing a wicked jumper, it's best to take notice. We think she'll go down as the best jump server of all time, with a strong case as the best server, of any kind, ever.

Male indoor servers

Here are five of the top male indoor volleyball servers of all time:

- **Gilberto Amauri de Godoy Filho:** Not only was Giba, one of the best offensive players of all time (he appears in the section "Male indoor offensive players" earlier in this appendix), he's just one of the greatest of all time, as he added a lethal jump float that led to three Olympic medals for Brazil and multiple World Championship victories.
- **Wilfredo Leon:** We don't actually have a measure for this stat, but we think Leon put more fear into opposing defenses than anybody in men's volleyball, ever. (We also include him in the section "Male indoor offensive players" earlier in this appendix.) This fear also came when he was at the service line, ready to detonate (which he typically did). You'd be hard-pressed to find an ace leaderboard that does not include his name in any given event.
- **Maxim Mikhaylov:** This Russian jump float server and Sergey Tetyukhin (also in this list) won Olympic medals together in 2012 and 2016, and he added a silver of his own in 2020. Mikhaylov was a regular atop the leaderboards for aces and points scored, blending raw power with excellent placement and movement. He also appears in the section "Male indoor offensive players" earlier in this appendix.

- **Sergey Tetyukhin:** Won a medal for Russia in all five Olympics in which he competed — gold in 2000, bronze in 2004, silver in 2008, gold in 2012, and bronze in 2016. The consistency of his serve, a movement- and placement-based jump-float (see Chapter 8) gave opposing passers fits.
- **Ivan Zaytsev:** This Italian's arm swing should hang in the Louvre, so pure and smooth and pretty it is. That arm swing makes his jump serve so lethal, one of the most formidable the world has ever seen, and a huge reason that his teams have been so successful in his era.

Female indoor servers

Here are six of the top female indoor volleyball servers of all time (we just couldn't cut the list down to five):

- **Ekaterina Antropova:** The youngest player on this list, the 22-year-old (at the time of this writing) Russian-turned-Italian wasted no time in establishing herself as one of the most electrifying talents in all of volleyball. Standing 6 feet 7 inches, Antropova is a towering opposite with a withering serve, a major factor in her winning an Olympic gold for Italy in 2024, as well as the 2022–2023 CEV Cup, in which she was named MVP.
- **Tijana Bošković:** Simply put, unstoppable, regardless of where she is on the court. (We also include her in the section "Female indoor offensive players" earlier in this appendix.) The 6-foot-4-inch Serbian is one of the hardest hitters the women's game has ever seen — including from the end line, where her jump serve is a serious problem. She has led Serbia to a pair of World Championship gold medals, in which she was the MVP of both.
- **Sheilla Castro:** Possessed one of the fastest jump serves of her generation of players, and that was a major source of points during Brazil's pair of Olympic gold medals, in 2008 and 2012, in which Castro was a part.
- **Jordan Larson:** One of the American greats, Larson relied on a jump float to rack up aces. Her consistency and clutch play from the service line led the United States to an Olympic silver in 2012, a bronze in 2016, and, finally, a gold in 2021.
- **Zhu Ting:** Ting added to her lethal reputation as an outside hitter (you can find her in the sections "Female indoor offensive players" and "Female indoor blockers" earlier in this appendix) with an equally lethal serve, leading China to an Olympic gold in 2016 and a World Championship in 2015. She relied on a booming jump serve that provided an excellent change of pace in a women's game dominated by float and jump float servers. Perhaps just as important: She almost never missed, an enormous benefit to her team, and a constant source of anxiety for her opponents.

- **Kim Yeon-koung:** The 6-foot-3-inch Korean leaned on a mean jump float that came at opposing passers quick as a hiccup because she could almost hit the ball down while putting zero spin on it, making it a dancing devil of a serve. She'd finish a number of World Championships and Olympics atop the aces leaderboard and helped get South Korea a 2021 Olympic silver medal. She also appears in the section "Female indoor offensive players" earlier in this appendix.

Other Important and Influential Figures in the Volleyball World

It isn't just the players who have made a massive impact on this game. Coaches, members of the media, the businessmen and women who have taken gambles investing in volleyball — all of them have had outsize influence on growing the sport of volleyball which is, unquestionably, growing at a rapid pace. We're grateful for every individual here and what they have brought to the game.

Coaches

The coaches who have developed talent (and were, in most cases, talents in and of themselves) and continue to raise the level of volleyball:

- **Dain Blanton:** An Olympic gold medalist for the United States in 2000 with Eric Fonoimoana, Blanton would parlay his talents into winning four straight National Championships as the head beach volleyball coach at the University of Southern California (USC).
- **Anna Collier:** The original dynasty-builder in the sport of beach volleyball, Collier built the University of Southern California into an indomitable force, winning three straight National Championships (2015–2017) and 84.4 percent of her matches.
- **John Cook:** For 25 years, Cook coached the University of Nebraska's indoor team, winning 883 matches to just 176 losses, picking up four NCAA Championships along the way. Beyond the three American Volleyball Coaches Association (AVCA) Coach of the Year awards, Cook also architected the massively successful Volleyball Day, in which his Nebraska team played not in a gym, but in the university's football stadium, selling a record 92,003 tickets, drawing the biggest in-person crowd for a women's sporting event ever.

- **Marv Dunphy:** Regarded as one of the best coaches in volleyball, Dunphy won an Olympic gold medal with the U.S. men's indoor volleyball team in 1988 and claimed an NCAA Championship title in three different decades at Pepperdine: in 1978, 1985, and 1992.
- **Kathy Gregory:** A hugely influential figure, both on the beach and indoors, Gregory had an astounding 38-year run as the head coach of the women's indoor volleyball team at University of California (UC), Santa Barbara, in which she piled up 882 wins and 27 NCAA Tournament appearances, was named the Big West Coach of the Year seven times, and National Coach of the Year once by the AVCA.
- **Nikolay Karpol:** Talk about longevity — Karpol coached in the Russian women's volleyball club Uralochka for a staggering 51 years. He also led Russia to Olympic gold medals in 1980 and 1988, along with silvers in 1992, 2000, and 2004.
- **Hugh McCutcheon:** One of the greatest coaches in volleyball, McCutcheon led the U.S. men's indoor team to a gold medal at the 2008 Olympic Games and the U.S. women to a silver in the 2012 Games. Over his ten years as the head coach for the University of Minnesota, he finished with a 277–74 record, was twice named Big 10 Coach of the Year, and in 2015 was named Coach of the Year by the AVCA.
- **Holly McPeak:** A three-time Olympian on the beach — following an NCAA Championship-winning career indoors — McPeak won a bronze medal for the United States at the 2004 Olympic Games and has remained a hugely influential voice in the coaching world.
- **Nina Matthies:** One of the best players to touch the sand, Matthies helmed Pepperdine to 11 West Coast Conference (WCC) titles and 590 wins, making her the all-time winningest coach in the conference. On the beach, she also led Pepperdine to a National Championship, cementing her legacy as one of the most influential individuals in the sport.
- **Stein Metzger:** A 2004 Olympian and a tremendously successful college and professional player, Metzger has established himself as a powerhouse of a coach. The architect of a dynastic UCLA program that won back-to-back NCAA beach titles in 2018 and 2019, Metzger has similarly built Texas into a perennial contender, thrice winning AVCA Coach of the Year honors.
- **Brooke Niles:** The winningest female coach in NCAA Beach Volleyball history as the head coach at Florida State, and also the winningest coach of anyone, period. Her Seminoles are the only program in the country that has made every single NCAA Championship tournament as of 2026 — the same year she became the first beach volleyball coach to reach 300 wins.

- **Leticia Pessoa:** Pessoa has almost certainly worked with every great Brazilian player: Rego, Cerutti, Carol Salgado, Agatha Bednarczuk, Lisboa, and Rebecca Cavalcanti, among others, have called her coach.
- **Russ Rose:** Penn State University was both the proverbial immovable force and unstoppable object in women's indoor volleyball for more than a decade, and much of that dominance was thanks to head coach Rose, who led the Nittany Lions to seven National Championships and 1,330 wins — the most in Division I history.
- **John Speraw:** The longtime head coach of men's indoor volleyball at UCLA, Speraw also assisted on the U.S. men's indoor team that won a gold medal at the Olympics in 2008. He served as UCLA's head coach for more than a decade.
- **Marcio Sicoli:** One of the most decorated coaches of all time, Sicoli, the head coach for Pepperdine University's beach team at the time of writing, has won Olympic medals of every color for the United States on the beach — silver when assistant coaching for Adriana Behar and Shelda Bede in 2004, gold as the head coach for Walsh Jennings and May-Treanor in 2012, bronze with Walsh Jennings and Ross in 2016, and silver with Humaña-Paredes and Wilkerson in 2024. He inherited the Pepperdine program after Matthies (also in this list) retired, and he has won more than 100 matches with the Waves.
- **Mary Wise:** The all-time leader in NCAA wins for women's indoor volleyball, Wise's 1,068 victories at the University of Florida put her as one of the most successful coaches of all time.

Influential voices

The voices of the sport(s) of volleyball and beach volleyball, these men and women are the ones you've heard on TV, podcasts, and every other medium that dispenses the volleyball gospel. Here are some of the GOATs:

- **Kevin Barnett:** A two-time Olympian (in 2000 and 2004) for the United States in indoor volleyball, Barnett has transitioned into one of the central voices of volleyball, teaming up with Paul Sunderland to call the Olympic Games, and acting as one of the main commentators for the AVP.
- **Dain Blanton:** After winning an Olympic gold for the United States in 2000, Blanton started commentating multiple Olympic Games for NBC.
- **Lee Feinswog:** Perhaps the most comprehensive volleyball journalist the sport has seen. He bought, and then built, `Volleyballmag.com` into the daily hub of all things volleyball before selling and building yet another comprehensive outlet, a daily newsletter that he dubbed 900 Square Feet (`www.900squarefeet.com`). His coverage of the sport is unparalleled.

- **Chris Marlowe:** An Olympic gold medalist on the 1984 U.S. men's indoor team, Marlowe also played professionally indoors and is considered by many the best beach volleyball commentator of all time.
- **Chris McGee:** The most legendary emcee in the sport, nicknamed Geeter, this American became famous for his indelible introductions and hyping the crowd in the third set of big matches on the AVP Tour.
- **Holly McPeak:** After plenty of NCAA and Olympic victories on the beach, McPeak became one of the top commentators for both indoor and beach volleyball. We also identify her as a top coach in the previous section.
- **Paul Sunderland:** The voice of volleyball; wherever you find a significant volleyball match being played, you'll also find Sunderland, on the mic.

Professional volleyball organizers

Investing in volleyball takes no small amount of courage and temerity. Be it organizing events or running an entire tour, these are the men and women who have kept the sports humming along:

- **Leonard Armato:** Without Armato, the AVP wouldn't exist, and it's a legitimate wonder if the sport would have ever taken off without his influence. A high-powered agent, Armato helped found the AVP and propelled it into its golden era in the 1980s and 1990s. He regained control of the AVP again in the early 2000s and again turned volleyball into a thriving sport once more.
- **Tri Bourne:** One of the best American players of his generation, Bourne was a source of inspiration when he bounced back from *myositis,* an autoimmune disease, that sidelined him for two years. He won AVP MVP in 2022 and two Manhattan Beach Opens (in 2021 and 2022), competed in the Tokyo Olympic Games in 2021, and co-founded SANDCAST, a popular beach volleyball podcast (which he hosts with co-author Travis).
- **Kevin Cleary:** The first president of the AVP in 1983, American Cleary has competed in 48 consecutive beach volleyball Manhattan Beach Opens.
- **Mike and Patty Dodd:** Mike Dodd will go down as one of the best defensive players of all-time in beach volleyball, an Olympic silver medalist for the United States at the 1996 Atlanta Games who would win 75 tournaments over the span of his career. His wife, Patty, won an NCAA Championship at UCLA before winning 14 professional tournaments on the beach. Together, they founded MBsand, one of the top beach volleyball juniors clubs in the United States, and they continue to teach the next generation the game of beach volleyball.

- **Marvin Hall:** Known affectionately as Dancing Marv, Hall is the most well-known and beloved AVP ref, famous for his electric dances between sets and at side changes.
- **Nina Matthies:** Matthies founded the first professional women's beach volleyball tour through the Women's Professional Volleyball Association (WPVA) and helped found NCAA Beach Volleyball.
- **William G. Morgan:** As we talk about in Chapter 1, Morgan is the founder of volleyball. Without him, well, this sport — and this book — wouldn't exist.
- **John Speraw:** After serving as UCLA's head coach for over ten years, Speraw shifted into a new role as the CEO of USA Volleyball (USAV) in 2025. (We also mention him in the "Coaches" section earlier in this appendix.)
- **Donald Sun:** He owned and ran the AVP for most of the 2010s, keeping a healthy professional tour in the United States.

A few final shout-outs

Some individuals are difficult to categorize and impossible to quantify in terms of their influence and impact on the game. These are those individuals:

- **Dan Apol:** Apol left his mark in the officiating ranks before his sudden death in 2016. He worked the 2016 Paralympic Games and also the 2016 Summer Olympics in Rio de Janeiro. During his years as a high-level official, he worked at two Summer Olympics, one Paralympics, one Word ParaVolleyball World Championship, and two FIVB Beach World Championships.
- **Doug Beal:** Forever changed the trajectory of the United States National Team, leading it to a gold medal at the 1984 Olympic Games and launching the sport into a new stratosphere of popularity.
- **Adriana Behar:** A two-time Olympic medalist for Brazil who won silvers in 2000 and 2004, Behar also claimed an astounding six FIVB Tour Champion Awards.
- **Lorenzo Bernardi:** An Olympic silver medalist and two-time World Champion, Bernardi led Italy into a golden era from 1989–2006 and was so dominant that the FIVB named him Player of the Century in the 1990s.
- **Razzie Jonsson and Anders Kristiansson:** The architects of the budding Swedish dynasty in beach volleyball, these two introduced an entirely new way of playing beach volleyball, heavy on jump sets, option attacks, and pure electricity.

- **Pati Rolf:** After coaching stints at the University of Minnesota-Duluth, Marquette University, and East Carolina University, Rolf entered the officiating ranks and became one of the most influential referees in collegiate and international volleyball. She was the second referee in the women's gold match at the 2016 Rio Summer Olympics, the first referee for the 2016 NCAA women's National Championship, and the first female to be the first referee for the 2019 NCAA men's National Championship. She also served as Director of Officials for USAV.
- **The Sato family:** Have a look at these genetics: In the 1988 Olympic Games, Eric Sato won a gold medal with the U.S. men's team, while his sister, Liane, competed for the women and their brother, Gary, coached the men's team.
- **Dave Shoji:** We talk about Shoji and his sons, Erik and Kawika, in Chapter 11 but the patriarch of the family deserves his flowers, too, after winning 1,202 matches for the University of Hawaii and turning the islands into a volleyball-mad state.
- **Gene Selznick:** No one can say for certain whether Selznick was better on the beach or indoors, and he will be remembered as one of the greatest in his generation on either surface. The first U.S. player to be named to the FIVB All-World team, Selznick leaves an All-World legacy.

Index

Numerics

A

B

C

D

E

F

G

H

M

N

O

P

Q

R

S

T

U

V

W

Y

Z

About the Authors

Gabrielle Reece is a former collegiate indoor player for Florida State University and professional beach volleyball player, wellness entrepreneur, *New York Times* best-selling author, and host of *The Gabby Reece Show.* A pioneer in women's health and fitness, she was Nike's first female spokesperson and shoe designer and has built a career bridging elite performance with practical, sustainable wellness.

She cofounded Laird Superfood, a publicly traded company, and has developed multiple performance-driven fitness programs, including HIGHX. Alongside her husband, Laird Hamilton, she cocreated XPT (Extreme Performance Training), which has since evolved into Hamilton House — a modern wellness platform focused on mindset, movement, recovery, and community.

Today, Gabby is known for translating science-backed insights into actionable tools that help people build strength, resilience, and longevity in everyday life. She is a devoted mother of three and shares her life with her husband, big-wave surfer Laird.

Travis Mewhirter played professional beach volleyball for a little less than ten years, making his first main draw just three years after picking up a ball for the first time. In that span, he launched a podcast, *SANDCAST,* with Olympian Tri Bourne, which has since become the most-downloaded volleyball podcast in the world. A best-selling author, he has written four books on beach volleyball, including two Amazon best-sellers: *Kings of Summer*, alongside Olympic gold medalist Kent Steffes, and *We Were Kings.* He has also written a children's book, *Volleyball for Milkshakes*, and *The Playbook of Champions*, both with Tri Bourne.

During the summers, he serves as the lead beach volleyball color commentator for Volleyball TV. He is currently an assistant coach for the Florida State beach volleyball team. The few spare minutes he has outside of that, he spends mostly on the back patio with his wife, Delaney, and two kids, who typically want to . . . play volleyball.

Dedication

To Cecile Reynaud for being an extraordinary coach and an even more meaningful mentor during Gabby's time at Florida State.

To the Knudsen family — and especially Delaney, for obvious reasons — for allowing Travis to marry into their House of Volleyball.

Authors' Acknowledgments

In the end, we must go back to the beginning.

We wrote this book to pay it forward, teaching and inspiring others about the game that has changed both of our lives in so many ways. This wouldn't be possible if it weren't for the dozens, if not hundreds, of individuals who impacted us in indelible manners.

Gabby Reece would like to acknowledge Kenny Stevens ("Pups") from St. Thomas, who first gave me the opportunity to play on his team. His belief in me at such an early stage ignited a deep love and excitement for the game of volleyball that has stayed with me ever since. Thank you to Dean Soles for showing me what it truly means to be a great coach — not just in skill and strategy, but in leadership, care, and the ability to bring out the best in others.

To Dr. Cecile Reynaud, thank you for being an extraordinary coach and an even more meaningful mentor during my time at Florida State. Your guidance shaped not only my development as an athlete, but also as a person. I am deeply grateful to Gary Sato for helping guide me into the professional level and for pushing me to grow, refine my game, and compete at the highest standard. A big thanks, as well, to Barbara Bierman for encouraging me to move to California to play ball and for being my first beach partner, as well as Anna Collier and Holly McPeak for allowing me to work with them when I was new to the beach game.

Finally, to all of the women I had the privilege of competing with — thank you for your strength, your camaraderie, and for allowing me to be your teammate. You made the journey richer, more meaningful, and something I will always carry with me.

Travis Mewhirter's journey is a wild one, as unexpected as they come. A move from Baltimore to Navarre, Florida, in search of warmer weather and golf resulted in a lifelong detour into beach volleyball. Those who initially pushed me on that detour include the Bulldog Beach crew, and the many, many people who volunteered their time to coach a bumbling beach volleyball neophyte: Judd Smith, forever my volleyball dad; Meaghan and Scott Allen, and Joey Keener, the ones who initially identified latent talent in a 24-year-old rookie and took it upon themselves to develop it; Shaun Rannals, JD Hamilton, and Matt Blanke, the best, most patient partners I could have ever had in those early days.

Tri Bourne has likely altered my life in more ways than any single individual outside of my immediate family. Podcast partner, good friend, surfing partner, and the sensationally talented Hawaiian who strapped my career into a beach volleyball rocket ship and let that thing fly. Brooke Niles and Nick Lucena altered the course of that ship and helped it land in Tallahassee, giving me my first opportunity as a first-time coach at Florida State.

That, too, changed everything, and now my family and I have roots — true roots for the first time.

But this book, in particular, while it contains many original thoughts, is a several-hundred-page compilation of teachings, lessons, tips, and tidbits from dozens and dozens of individuals in the sport of volleyball. The process by which we wrote each chapter began with a headfirst dive into the world of volleyball YouTube. While we would come across hundreds of channels, the ones we kept coming back to, and therefore owe quite a debt of gratitude to, include the following: Coach Donny Hui at Elevate Yourself; The McKibbin Brothers, Maddison and Riley; Mark Burik, Brandon Joyner, and the Better at Beach crew; Joe and Gage Worsley from Out of System. Extra shout-out to Brian Cook for ensuring we didn't steer too far off the indoor path.

And so, so many more.

Publisher's Acknowledgments

Senior Acquisition Editor: Jennifer Yee

Project Manager and Development Editor: Chad R. Sievers

Copy Editor: Laura Miller

Senior Managing Editor: Kristie Pyles

Production Editor: Magesh Elangovan

Cover Image: © skynesher/Getty Images

Author Photo: Courtesy of Gabrielle Reece, Steve Gentry